D0899076

Harvard Studies in Romance Languages

Published under the Direction of
the Department of Romance Languages and Literatures

Volume XXXI

A SPANIARD IN THE PORTUGUESE INDIES

The Narrative of Martín Fernández
de Figueroa

James B. McKenna

Harvard University Press
Cambridge, Massachusetts
1967

For Beverly, Amy, and Sharon

Preface

Martín Fernández de Figueroa, a Castilian gentleman anxious
to see the world, set out from his native Salamanca in 1505 and
journeyed to Lisbon where he joined a Portuguese fleet bound for
the Indies. For the next six years he traveled extensively throughout
the expanding area of Portuguese activities in the East. He returned
home in 1511 and a year later published an account of his adventures.

I was first introduced to the original and only edition of
Figueroa's narrative in a seminar led by Professor Francis M.
Rogers at Harvard in 1962 and was immediately fascinated by it.
I had first gone to Spain in 1954, beginning what has proven to be
a continually deepening interest and enthusiasm for Spain and
Spanish culture. Several years later I had the good fortune to sail
to the Middle East in much the same fashion as Martín Fernández
de Figueroa, as member of a fleet marine force. Visits to such places
as Istanbul, Ephesus, Thessaloniki, and to Beirut as part of an
American expeditionary force quickened my interest in lands steeped
in history and legend. Reading Figueroa's account, I could easily
imagine myself in the place of a sixteenth-century Spanish marine
venturing forth to the fabled Indies.

Figueroa's narrative represents one of the earliest attempts to
bring to the attention of Spain the exciting world of the East which
the Portuguese were beginning to uncover. His book also reflects a
community of interest and harmony of action among Spaniards and
Portuguese. Figueroa and other Castilians enthusiastically served
with the Portuguese in the Indies in the interest of a higher unity,

that of Hispania and all Christendom. His narrative will command close attention today as one reviews the past history of Spain and Portugal and looks forward to the future course of these neighbors.

A man of the early sixteenth century, Figueroa reveals a dynamic combination of values old and new. In his narrative the vast expanse of the Eastern world, from the Cape of Good Hope through Socotra and Hormuz, to Goa and Ceylon, and on to the Spice Islands of Indonesia is but another battleground for the medieval struggle of Christian and Moor. Yet, as one reads of Santiago's miraculous intervention on behalf of his beloved Iberians, new values appear, among them the desire for knowledge to be gained through personal initiative and experience in a vigorous quest after the unknown.

This book seeks to present to the student of Iberian culture a critical edition and detailed study of the narrative of Martín Fernández de Figueroa. I shall begin by discussing the background against which his accomplishments may be assessed. A facsimile and critical edition of the narrative is accompanied by an English translation. An extensive commentary follows, designed to enhance understanding and enjoyment of the narrative. Finally, the work will be discussed in the light of its historical value and as an example of the literature of travel.

First and foremost, I want to thank Francis M. Rogers for his inspiration and assistance in the preparation of this volume. I would also like to thank Charles R. Boxer, F. J. Norton, Antonio Rodríguez-Moñino, Stephen Gilman, and Francisco Márquez Villanueva for their valuable suggestions. The Hispanic Society of America has kindly permitted me to include the excerpts from Leonard Bacon's translation of *The Lusiads* by Luís de Camões. Full responsibility for errors is of course mine.

J. B. McK.

March 1967
Stony Brook, New York

Contents

A SPANIARD
IN THE
PORTUGUESE INDIES

Surely there will not lack someone somewhere to write about him (Title XXXVII).

i. SETTING

The printed word played a vital role in the brilliant accomplishments of Europe's Age of Discovery. Books helped to furnish mariners with the technical information needed for the successful completion of their voyages, and by disseminating the news of their progress stimulated ever further exploration. As geographical horizons expanded with the voyages of discovery, intellectual assimilation of a wealth of new knowledge was facilitated by the printed book. A dynamic blend of political, religious, and economic factors underlay these voyages, and books contributed to the definition and refinement of these goals.[1]

Portugal and Castile were in the vanguard of Europe's quest for the Indies, and both nations were prompt to report on their progress. Perhaps the best known of the officially sanctioned newsletters is Columbus' letter of 1493.[2] The earliest printed account of Portuguese explorations appeared in Latin in 1485,

on the occasion of the royal profession of obedience to the new pope, Innocent VIII.[3] This obedience oration, proudly proclaiming the exploits of Portuguese navigators, was printed in Rome and widely disseminated throughout Europe. It established the pattern for a subsequent series of letters which were to parade Portuguese national achievement in the lands and waters beyond the Cape of Good Hope before an eager European reading public. Composed in Portuguese over the signature of King Manuel, these letters, adroit forerunners of today's official press release, were customarily translated into Latin by royal officials in Rome and from there circulated in many editions throughout the kingdoms of Europe, while the Portuguese versions were widely read in the Iberian peninsula.[4] They bear eloquent testimony to Portuguese pride in the nation's overseas achievements.

While the Manuel letters provided the raw information which so fascinated and excited Europe, other writers set out to evaluate the significance of the events and place them in historical perspective. Castile, especially, followed closely her neighbor's progress, since she too was seeking the Indies, albeit by a different route. This interest was reflected in a remarkable volume published in 1503. Attracted by Portuguese activities in the East and determined to assess the meaning of Columbus' voyages, the eminent theologian of Seville, Rodrigo Fernández de Santaella, brought out a book containing Castilian translations of the two best medieval accounts of the Orient, the Book of Marco Polo and the treatise of Poggio Bracciolini.[5] In preparing this book, Santaella relied heavily on Valentim Fernandes' famous Portuguese translations of the same authors, published in Lisbon in 1502. In fact, he acknowledges that in dealing with Marco Polo, "I thought to make a *Sevillano* of the Venetian" just as "Valentim Fernandes the German made him Portuguese." [6]

Santaella's aim was to present to his countrymen a sound historical and geographical orientation which would enable them to understand and differentiate between the Eastern operations of the Portuguese and the achievements of Christopher Columbus. In the accurate *Cosmographia breue introductoria,* with which he prefaced the narratives of Marco Polo and Poggio, Fernández de Santaella shows that he perceived a clear distinction between Castilian discoveries in the *gran mar occidental* and Portuguese endeavors in *partes australes e orientales.* The acceptance of this difference was to prove difficult for many others besides Columbus.

The history of the Portuguese search for the Indies is well known. Vasço da Gama's epic voyage was preceded by almost a century of carefully planned and executed exploration down the western coast of Africa, inspired and originally directed by Prince Henry from the renowned center at Sagres. Although Gama did not succeed in securing a trade agreement with the local ruler in Calicut, the cargo which he managed to bring back gave an exciting indication of the great wealth to be gained in the Indies. Thus began the annual departure of a Portuguese fleet for the Malabar coast of India. Pedro Álvares Cabral went out in 1500; his course carried him to Brazil before he turned east, and Pero Vaz de Caminha dispatched his famous letter to King Manuel announcing the discovery. João da Nova commanded the 1501 fleet, and Vasco da Gama returned a second time in 1502. Francisco de Albuquerque and his cousin Afonso shared command of the 1503 expedition with Antonio de Saldanha, and Lopo Soares de Albergária led the 1504 fleet.

Prior to the arrival of the Portuguese, Moslem merchants had enjoyed a monopoly of the carrying trade in the Indian Ocean. The highly desired spices and other merchandise were

carried in Islamic bottoms from the Spice Islands and Canton
to the great emporium of Malacca. From there the cargo was
shipped to Calicut and other ports such as Cochin and Cannanore on the Malabar coast, thence to Hormuz and Aden. From
Hormuz goods moved up the Persian Gulf, to be sold eventually
in the markets of the Middle East. From Aden the destination
was Alexandria, whence Venetian galleys transported the wares
to European markets. Along these trade routes, both carriers
and local rulers profited handsomely.

It is not surprising that the Moslems should vigorously
resist the Portuguese intrusion. They did so through open attacks and intrigues with local rulers. Some of the latter, however,
were to welcome the Portuguese as allies against neighboring
states and against the monopoly practices of the Moslem merchants. Nevertheless, it became increasingly clear that a Portuguese commitment limited to the annual fleet practice would
achieve but the most tenuous of footholds in India. Consequent-
ly, King Manuel decided to pursue a new policy. In 1505 he
dispatched Francisco de Almeida as his Viceroy with the mission of establishing a permanent naval force in India to protect
and develop Portuguese trading activities. Almeida was also
ordered to fortify the eastern coast of Africa, and he did so, at
Kilwa and Mombasa, before sailing on to India to commence
operations along the Malabar coast. A later section of the 1505
fleet, commanded by the Castilian Pedro de Añaya, was entrusted with establishing a captaincy and erecting a fort at Sofala
on the east African coast. Almeida's most decisive accomplish-
ment in India occurred off Diu early in 1509 when, vastly outnumbered, he defeated a fleet organized by the Sultan of Egypt
and equipped to a great extent at Venetian expense. With this
victory, known as the Battle of the Rumis, Almeida also avenged

the death of his son Lourenço, who had been killed in action against this same fleet the previous year.

When Afonso de Albuquerque returned to India in 1506 he carried with him royal authorization to assume command with the title of Governor upon the expiration of Almeida's commission in 1508; and, after much delay and dispute, the change of command was finally effected late in 1509. Albuquerque's policy was to expand and consolidate the naval dominion gained under Almeida by seizing and fortifying strategically located land bases, thus assuring Portuguese control of all shipping along the aforementioned trade routes. He chose as his targets Aden and Hormuz in the west, Goa at the northern end of the Malabar coast (to serve as headquarters), and Malacca (to serve as the eastern bastion). He had begun the subjugation of Hormuz prior to assuming the governorship; Goa fell to his fierce determination in 1510, and Malacca the following year. Only Aden eluded the control of this singular and controversial man.

Almeida and Albuquerque were enemies in India, both for reasons of policy and on purely personal grounds. Theirs was but the most salient of many such quarrels; the chronicles abound in descriptions of enmity and dispute among the Portuguese captains. It appears that desire for personal gain and personal glory often motivated them more than did dedication to the national mission. With royal control distant in time and space, confusion and contradictory orders often resulted in commanders operating at cross-purposes, although, as in the case of the Castilian captains in the New World, loyalty to the crown was not questioned.

It was into this complex and dynamic world of the Portuguese Operation Indies,[7] a world of bold military ventures

against Islam, but a world also of bitter rivalry and struggle among Portuguese captains, that an intrepid Castilian traveler ventured in the spring of 1505. A *gentilhombre* from Salamanca "anxious to see lands," Martín Fernández de Figueroa enlisted in the expedition bound for Sofala and was assigned to Captain Major Pedro de Añaya, a fellow Salamancan also in the Portuguese service.

For the next six years Figueroa served in various parts of the Portuguese Indies. He spent two years at Sofala,[8] helping to erect and defend the Portuguese fort there. He visited Mozambique, and he also spent a winter on Socotra, where he sympathetically observed the island's Christian inhabitants. In August of 1508 he left East African waters and sailed to India with Albuquerque and his fleet. While fighting under Almeida at Diu, Figueroa narrowly escaped death when the ship on which he sailed was sunk by Turkish bombardment. Rather than return to Portugal with Almeida, he stayed on in India with Albuquerque, and participated in the initial seizure of Goa in March 1510. He was also present and received several wounds when the Portuguese were driven out of Goa in May and forced to remain anchored in the Mandovi River until the end of the monsoon in August.

Finally, late in 1510, prior to the second and definitive conquest of Goa, Figueroa, who had by then more than satisfied his original three-year contract, sailed for home in the fleet of Duarte de Lemos, reached Lisbon in July 1511, and at the behest of his family returned to his native Salamanca. Aside from the above information, gleaned from his narrative, nothing else is known about Martín Fernández de Figueroa. What he did before going out to the Indies and what sort of life he led after his return remain unanswered questions.

Figueroa had diligently noted what he saw and heard in the Indies, and during the months following his return to Salamanca he no doubt spent many hours entertaining friends and relatives with accounts of his adventures. Apparently, however, he had little faith in his own literary talents, for he entrusted his manuscript to a professional writer, asking him to put it in form suitable for publication.

A considerable amount is known about Figueroa's editor, Juan Agüero de Trasmiera, who on occasion also called himself Juan Remón de Trasmiera. Much of this information he himself includes in his edition of Figueroa's manuscript. At one point he refers to Figueroa as "our neighbor and relative." While it is true that they both lived in Salamanca, I have been unable to determine whether they actually were relatives or whether Agüero has employed an editorial "our." Juan Agüero was born in Trasmiera, a mountainous region located to the southeast of Santander which derives its name from the Miera River. The Agüero bridge, close by the village of Agüero, spans the Miera as it runs toward the Bay of Biscay. Both bridge and village appear to date from Roman times. The Agüero family had originally been the most powerful and prominent in the district, but unsuccessful struggles with rival noble families throughout the fifteenth century had led to the loss of the family *solar* and decline of the Agüeros to the status of but one among many old noble families.[9]

Juan Agüero's literary production is quite varied. In his edition of Figueroa's manuscript he reveals having spent some time in Rome. This was evidently of sufficient duration for him to learn enough Italian to be able to translate into Castilian an Italian chapbook, a translation printed in Valencia around 1510, entitled: *Probadas flores. Romanas de famosos & doctos varones*

compuestas para salud & reparo delos cuerpos humanos . . .
trasladada de vulgar ytaliano en lengua castellana para vtilidad
de nuestra nacion por el bachiler. Juan aguero de trasmiera.[10]

As a *bachiller,* Juan Agüero knew enough Latin to write
the final Latin verses addressed to the reader in the 1511 Salamanca edition of the *Palmerín de Oliva.*[11] He also authored a
verse chapbook ridiculing the Jews, which is described as follows: "Este es el Pleyto de los Judios con el Perro de Alba, y de
la burla que les hizo; nuevamente trobado por el Br. Juan de
Trasmiera, residente en Salamanca, que hizo a ruego y pedi-
mento de un Señor."[12]

Under the name of Juan Remón de Trasmiera, Figueroa's
editor composed an interesting heraldic study. A short versified
history of the noble families of Salamanca, with descriptions of
their coats of arms and genealogy, it was published in Salamanca around 1512: *TRIUNFO RAIMUNDINO, en el cual*
muchas antiguedades de la ciudad de Salamanca se traen, y en
los dos bandos de la (iglesia) de Sanct Benito y Sancto Tome se
escribe de los caballeros, claros varones, mayorazgos, armas, in-
sinias y blasones dellas.[13] In the course of this book I shall have
occasion to note that the many heraldic references to be found
in Agüero's edition of Figueroa's narrative have been taken
directly from the *Triunfo Raimundino.*

Little else is known about Juan Agüero or Juan Remón de
Trasmiera. Pérez Pastor lists Juan Remón de Trasmiera as a
collaborator in a type of astrology manual entitled *Repertorio de*
los tiempos, published in Toledo in 1546.[14] It is also claimed
that Juan Remón y Trasmiera was *corregidor* of the town of
Alcaráz, in Albacete, from 1547 to 1550.[15] The bulk of the information known about him thus centers around Salamanca during
the first fifteen years of the sixteenth century.

No doubt after conversations with Figueroa and a perusal of the traveler's manuscript, Juan Agüero found himself quite willing to accede to his request. Agüero was evidently very interested in Iberian overseas activities. In his proem to Figueroa's narrative he shows that he was familiar with Fernández de Santaella's *Cosmographia* and its valuable information on Portuguese and Castilian discoveries. He was also able to harmonize Figueroa's account with a King Manuel newsletter written in Portuguese. In the proem Agüero states that he was most anxious to help his friend Figueroa, first of all in order to learn for himself, and then in order to pass along to his fellow Spaniards authentic news of what Portugal, and particularly Castilians in the Portuguese service, were accomplishing in the far-off Indies.

The printing of Juan Agüero's summary edition of Fernández de Figueroa's manuscript was completed on September 1, 1512, in the "very noble and loyal" city of Salamanca, in the shop of Micer Lorenzo de León de Dei.[16] It bears the following title: *COnquista delas indias de Persia & Arabia que fizo la armada del rey don Manuel de Portugal & delas muchas tierras: diuersas gentes: extrañas riquezas & grandes batallas que alla ouo.*

An exemplar of the *Conquista* was purchased around July 1514 in Medina del Campo for fifteen maravedis and entered the library of Hernando Colón. The Register of the original Colón library has the following description: "Conquista de las yndias de portugal de arabia y persia en espanol compuesta por martyn fernandez de figueroa . . . Salamanca. 1. Septiembre ano. 1512. costo en Medina del Campo. 15. maravedis por Julio de. 1514. . ."[17]

The *Conquista* was not present in the *Biblioteca Colombina*

when the multivolumed inventory was prepared,[18] nor is it mentioned in several interesting lists compiled between 1603 and 1620. During these years four valuable books appeared in Portugal and Spain, each containing a list of works written about the Portuguese Indies; the *Conquista* is missing from all of them.[19]

The collaboration of Juan Agüero and Martín Fernández de Figueroa in the publication of the *Conquista*—at the end of whose proem is the name Johannes Augur Transmierense—as well as the circulation of Figueroa's original manuscript gave rise to considerable confusion among bibliographers which has only recently been clarified.

In 1624 the royal chronicler Tomás Tamayo de Vargas prepared a manuscript catalogue of books which had been produced in Spanish, and attributes the following work to Fernández de Figueroa: "MARTIN FERNANDEZ DE FIGVEROA, de Salamanca, Summo. La historia del viaje, i armada queel Rei D. Manuel de Portugal mando facer paralos reinos de Persia, i Arabia enquefuepor Capitan maior Pedro de Anaia."[20]

In 1629 the bibliographer Antonio de León Pinelo, who had knowledge of both the manuscript and the printed book, lists two works, a book printed in 1512 and ascribed to Juan Augur, that is, the *Conquista,* and a work written by Martín Fernández de Figueroa: "IVAN AVGVR TRANSMIERIENS. De las Islas de Persia i Arabia, sus guerras, i lo que en ellas vio, el año de 1508. imp. 1512. 4." Directly under that listing is the reference to Figueroa: "MARTIN FERNANDEZ DE FIGVEROA. Historia del viage de la Armada de Pedro de Anaya a la Persia i Arabia."[21]

Nicolás Antonio in his important 1672 bibliography also records two distinct works. The first entry refers to a volume

written by Augur and printed in Salamanca in 1512; Antonio
remarks that Tomás Tamayo de Vargas had seen the book:
"IOANNES AVGVR, quem Transmierensem vocatum propter
natalem locum *Trasmiera* in montanis Burgensibus existimo,
author inscribitur operi, cuius lemma, Tratado *de la Conquista
de las Islas de Persia y Arabia, de las muchas tierras, diversas
gentes y estrañas y grandes batallas que viò.* Salmanticae apud
Laurentium de Leon de Rey 1512. in 4. Vidit D. Thomas Tama-
jus." In referring to Figueroa, Antonio takes Pinelo as his
authority and states specifically that the work is in manuscript:
"MARTINVS FERNANDEZ DE FIGVEROA, scripsit, An-
tonio Leonio mihi authore in *Bibliotheca Indica Orientali* tit. IX.
forte Lusitanicâ linguâ, Historia del viage de la armada de Pedro
de Anaya a la Persia y Arabia por mandado del Rey D. Manuel.
M.S." [22] Hennings' study in 1766 lists only the Augur volume:
"AUGUR (Io.) de la conquista de las islas de Persia y Arabia,
de las muchas tierras, div. gentes y estrannas y grandes batallas
que vio, *Salmant. ap. Laur. de Leon de Rey* 512. 4 *Antonio* ex
Th. Tamajo tantum cogn." [23]

In 1800 Panzer lists the *Conquista* and attributes it to Augur
but, following Hennings, makes no mention of a work by
Figueroa;[24] Brunet follows Panzer in 1860.[25] Gallardo's 1863
bibliography fails to list either Augur or Figueroa but does contain a reference to Juan de Trasmiera's *Pleyto de los Judios.*[26]

In the first edition of his great *Manual*, Palau y Dulcet does
not list any work by Juan Augur. Palau does, however, make a
very important contribution, for he goes back to the original
Colón Register and records that catalogue's reference to Martín
Fernández de Figueroa: "FERNANDEZ de Figueroa (Martín)
Conquista de las Indias de Portugal, de Arabia y Persia. *Salamanca, 1 de Setiembre,* 1512, 4 (Fernando Colón)." [27] Palau repeats this description in his second edition and corrects his earlier

oversight by listing a volume attributed to Juan Augur: "AUGUR o de Trasmiera (Juan) Tratado de la Conquista de las Islas de Persia y Arabia, de las muchas tierras, diversas gentes y estrañas y grandes batallas que vió . . ." [28]

In effect, Palau's second edition lists the same work, the printed *Conquista,* twice. F. J. Norton was the first scholar to perceive a connection between the two references. It was his suggestion which led F. M. Rogers to realize that the *Conquista,* one of the treasures of the Fernando Palha Collection of the Harvard College Library, is in fact a volume written by Martín Fernández de Figueroa and edited by Juan Agüero de Trasmiera.[29]

The purpose of this edition, the first since 1512,[30] is to offer the reader maximum clarity while retaining lexical and syntactical features of Figueroa's narrative. The orthography of the original is wholly inconsistent, as is the use of punctuation. With the exception of place and person names, identified and discussed in my Commentary, modern orthography and punctuation have been adopted in this edition. In some places a word or words are missing, probably due to a typesetter's oversight; in this edition the appropriate addition is indicated by brackets. Other typographical errors have been corrected with an explanatory footnote.

There are some holes in pages toward the end of the text. In several instances someone has patched them and written in his version of what was missing; these additions are indicated by braces. Where the earlier addition is considered incorrect, my solution is indicated in the text in braces, with the previous addition in a footnote. Standard editorial procedure has been followed in designating recto and verso of each folio. Unnumbered folios have been indicated by brackets, such as [avi]^r.

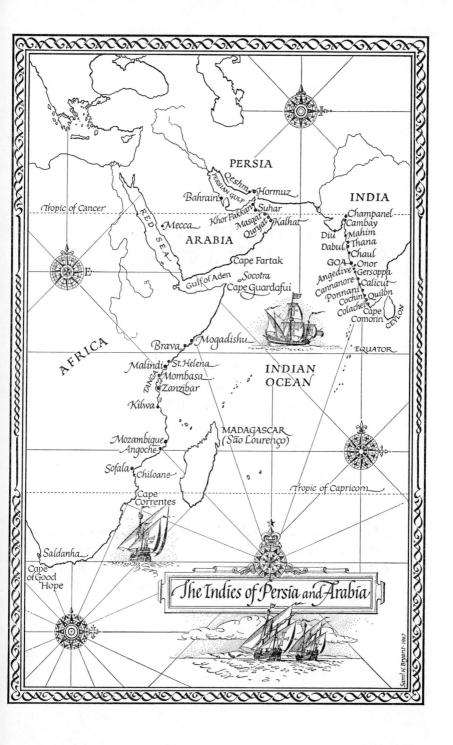

The Indies of Persia and Arabia

ii. THE CONQUISTA: CRITICAL EDITION

Conquista de las Indias de Persia e
Arabia que hizo la armada del rey
don Manuel de Portugal e de las muchas
tierras, diversas gentes, extrañas
riquezas e grandes batallas que allá hobo.

Cum privilegio.

[[a]ᵛ] *Suma e breve, útil aviso e historia del viaje e armada*
que el rey don Manuel de Portugal a gran costa suya mandó
hacer para los reinos e Indias de Persia e Arabia en que fue
por capitán mayor el muy nombrado caballero Pedro de Añaya.

ii. THE CONQUISTA: TRANSLATION

The Conquest of the Indies of Persia and Arabia✠ Effected by the Fleet of King Manuel of Portugal:✠ About the Many Lands, Diverse Peoples, Strange Riches, and Great Battles which Took Place There.

Cum privilegio.

Summary and brief, useful historical account of the voyage and fleet that King Manuel of Portugal at great expense✠ ordered made to the kingdoms and Indies of Persia and Arabia, on which the very renowned knight Pedro de Añaya✠ went as captain major.

✠ This device indicates the particular points that are discussed in my commentary, Chapter III.

En el nombre de Dios e de su gloriosa madre, guía de los viandantes e peregrinos, sin mancilla siempre virgen, señora e adbogada nuestra, principiaremos a contar muchas tierras de las Indias de Persia e Arabia: diversidad de gentes, sectas, costumbres, frutos, árboles, edificios, mares, ríos e otras cosas maravillosas de ver e más de oir, como animales e peces, aves fieras e sierpes que en aquellas partes habitan, cuanto larga tengamos licencia. Lo cual muy copiosa e verdaderamente trajo escripto Martín Fernández de Figueroa, gentilhombre, natural e pariente nuestro que en compañía del honrado caballero e virtuoso capitán Pedro de Añaya anduvo. Las vio e conquistó, según de las empresas que los vencidos le dejaron dan testimonio. El cual, como caseramente mucho aprovechó e a la larga tuviese recompilado, me rogó porque los lectores no se enojasen del cumplido proceso de su camino lo sumase e abreviase como me pareciese, al uso moderno. Que tove por mucha dicha, lo uno por me informar de él llenamente de lo que yo siempre deseé saber, e lo otro por el tan claro varón Pedro de Añaya. Pues que en vida no lo conocieron, en muerte [aii^r] no carezca de la buena fama que mereció. Que en verdad, habida la noticia de los portugueses a las manos, bien aventurada fue la estirpe que lo procreó, la generación que de él viniere e la que de su tronco salió. E por tener más que entender en ello escribí esta breve suma sacada, como dicho tengo, de su libro e información verisimil e concordada con la cosmografía de Pogio florentino e Marcopaulo veneciano; e otrosí con una letra del alto, rico e poderoso rey don Manuel

In the name of God and His Glorious Mother, guide of travelers and pilgrims, perpetually Immaculate Virgin, and Our Lady and Advocate, we shall begin to give as extensive an account as we are able of many lands of the Indies of Persia and Arabia: of diversity of peoples, sects, customs, fruits, trees, buildings, seas, rivers, and other things marvelous to behold and more so to hear about, such as animals, fishes, wild birds, and serpents which inhabit those parts. All this our neighbor and relative Martín Fernández de Figueroa, a gentleman who accompanied the honorable knight and virtuous captain Pedro de Añaya copiously and truthfully wrote down and brought back. He saw and conquered them, according to the testimony of the deeds he worked against the vanquished.* Having wisely and modestly compiled this at some length, he asked me to summarize and abbreviate it as I saw fit, after the modern fashion, so that the reader might not tire of the lengthy unfolding of his account. I was very pleased, first of all, in that I would inform myself fully from him on matters about which I had always desired to learn, and also for the sake of so distinguished a man as Pedro de Añaya. Although not afforded recognition while he lived, now that he is dead he must not be denied the good fame that he has earned. For in truth, having at hand the news about the Portuguese, we know that fortunate is the race which produced him, as are the generations yet unborn as well as those already issued from it. In order to understand these events better, I have written this brief summary, taken, as I have said, from Figueroa's book and his reliable information, and harmonized with the cosmography of Poggio the Florentine and Marco Polo the Venetian,⁜ and likewise with a letter⁜

---

* según de las empresas que los vencidos le dejaron dan testimonio. The Spanish is not altogether clear here.

que en lengua portuguesa hobe a las manos de las ciudades e batallas que su armada, combatiendo e crudamente peleando, señaladas e inmortales hizo. E para que mis amigos hayan placer e se deleiten en leer cosas nuevas, extrañas e algo diferentes a las de España, de lo cual mucho bien se sigue: conocimiento de cosas claras acá no participadas, allá domésticas e sabidas. Por lo cual en los poetas e cosmógrafos asaz escripturas están sin puerto de luz por ignorancia de las tierras, propriedades de cosas, trato de gentes e navegación de mares, que ahora más sin escrúpulo se entenderán. Será útil este tratado para saber peregrinar, sufrir trabajos, salvarse de peligros, conquirir honras e ganar en esta miserable vida las mundanas mercedes e estados sobre que todos (e más en España) nos fundamos. Para nuestra fe otrosí no dañoso, ante necesario, por el cual conoceremos diversas cosas que de sus maravillas, por sus perficiones loaremos a Dios que las crió e reprehenderemos las malas costumbres, tomando ejemplo en las santas o buenas obras que tan idiota gente sin predicación evangélica aún ha querido aceptar. Verse han diversas suertes de gentes, maneras de matrimonios, buenas, torpes o bestiales vidas que en las Indias viven, atavíos, vestidos, armas, casas, manjares, tratos e muertes, exequias, e en poca gente diversidad e multitud de sectas: desde Lisbona hasta cuatro mil e más [[aii]^v] leguas que en el dicho viaje fueron señoreadas ya descubiertas. Podrían decir lo del sabio marqués: los casos de admiración no los cuentes, ca no saben todas gentes como son. Pero como esto sea notoria verdad, más quiero ser reprehendido por hablarla que con temor de reprehensión darla a

I had at hand. Written in Portuguese by the mighty, rich, and powerful King Manuel, it deals with the cities and battles that his fleet in fierce combat and struggles rendered immortal. I have written this so that my friends might find pleasure and delight in reading about new things strange and somewhat different from Hispania.✳ Much good comes from this: the knowledge of important things unheard of here but everyday occurrences out there, for which reason many writings of the poets and cosmographers are steeped in darkness, out of ignorance of the various lands, the nature of things, trade among peoples, and the navigation of seas. Now without further ado these things will be understood. This treatise will be useful in learning how to make a pilgrimage, endure hardships, save oneself from perils, conquer honors, and gain in this miserable life the worldly favors and estates in which we all (and more so in Hispania) place such stock. Likewise, not only will it not be harmful, but necessary for our faith, for in it we shall come to know diverse things in whose marvels and perfection we shall praise the God who created them. We shall reprimand evil customs, taking example from the good and holy works that such ignorant people have accepted even without having had the gospel preached to them. You will encounter different kinds of peoples, marriage customs, good, twisted, and bestial ways of life out there in the Indies, fineries, garments, weapons, houses, foods, types of trade, deaths, exequies, and among few peoples a great diversity and multitude of sects. All these things are to be found in the area, extending more than four thousand leagues from Lisbon, that was subjugated after being discovered. Someone might recall the wise *Marqués'* advice:✳ "Do not talk about wondrous events, for not everyone knows what they are like." But, since the truth of this is notorious, I would prefer to face reprimand for speaking out about it than through fear

olvido o callarla. E porque desearán saber los que ignoraren la
forma como las dichas Indias se descubrieron, ante todas cosas
contar o narrarse ha lo tan sabroso, útil e necesario. E sabido esto,
procederse ha por el tratado como adelante se contiene, aunque
presurosamente notado de espacio, bien visto e concordado, do
si falta hobiere en la descripción del notador, seso, juicio, saber
e virtud supla del prudente lector.

Johannes Augur Transmierense, bachiller.

[*aiii*^r] **Título I.** *Introductorio. De como por la gracia de Dios
e industria de Vasco de la Gama fueron descubiertas e con-
quistadas por los cristianos en el primer viaje las Indias de
Persia e Arabia, año de 1497.*

La común sentencia de los portugueses sabios e castellanos
que en el primero viaje se acertaron acerca la invención e conquista de las Indias que ahora de Portugal llamamos, do mucha
riqueza de especiería se trae a España, e lo que he visto de ello
escripto, sabido de un piloto que en el dicho viaje se halló e de
algunos estudiantes e honradas personas (que con la riqueza
que allí su trabajo e industria alcanzó tratan en esta ciudad en
otra especie de sabiduría, conmutando su haber en cosa do
más ligeramente puedan sacar su caudal) es que como el rey
don Johan de Portugal fuese inclinado a saber cosas nuevas, lo
cual descubriendo e ganando tierras se podría aquirir, regido
por algunos sabios astrólogos, expertos pilotos e marineros
doctos e enseñados en el movimiento de los cielos e en la grandeza e condición de las tierras e aguas marinas, muchas naos e
caravelas envió por sus mares, diciendo que no aventurando en

of reprimand cause it to be forgotten or silenced. And, as those who are uninformed will wish to know how the said Indies were discovered, before anything else let us narrate that which is so enjoyable, useful, and necessary. Having learned this, we may proceed with the treatise as contained below. Though hastily written, it is seemly and verified. Should there be any short-comings in the writer's description, let the prudent reader contribute his intelligence, judgment, knowledge, and virtue.

Juan Agüero de Trasmiera, Bachelor.

Title I. *Introductory. About how through the grace of God and perseverance of Vasco da Gama the Christians discovered and conquered the Indies of Persia and Arabia on the first voyage, in the year 1497.*

The common belief among informed Portuguese and Castilians concerning the invention and conquest of the Indies✻ we nowadays call Portuguese, whence great wealth of spices comes to Hispania, and what I have seen written about this and learned from a navigator who was on the said voyage and from students and honorable persons (who with the wealth their industry and sacrifice earned them out there cultivate in this city another kind of knowledge, investing their wealth in things from which they may more easily take a profit) is that King João of Portugal✻ yearned for that knowledge of new things which the discovery and acquisition of new lands could provide. Guided by wise astrologers, expert navigators, and mariners tried and tested in the movement of the heavens and the expanse and conditions of bodies of land and water, he dispatched many ships and caravels over his seas,✻ saying: "If

su hacienda, mal ganaría en la ajena. Así que llegaban al cabo de Buena Esperanza, que de Lisbona dista dos mil leguas, el cual nunca habían osado pasar por la braveza e altura de las ondas, que toda fuerza de naos e industria de marineros era vista exceder, e por la diversidad de aves e suertes de peces que llaman voladores. En lo cual todos concordan e dicen que vuelan e caen asaz veces en los navíos entre los ganosos pasajeros e desvergonzados, hambrientos marineros, en quien o emplean la gula o amatan la hambre, tan temerosos [[aiii]ᵛ] de quedar allí como [in]ciertos de volver a sus tierras. Hay en el mes de julio e agosto e en el más caluroso tiempo grandes fríos, heladas, nieves, granizos e muchas tempestades de aguas e vientos. Así que con recelo no entrasen en la cuajada mar o no muriesen* porfiando en el viaje, todos se volvían hasta que un escudero no muy rico, hidalgo portugués que se llamaba Vasco de la Gama (e después fue almirante), no temiendo la muerte e queriendo aventurar la vida do comoquier que le sucediese cobraría honra, dijo al rey don Johan que él pasaría el cabo de Buena Esperanza o perdería la vida en cumplimiento de su deseo. A quien el rey dio naos muy bastecidas de armas e mantenimientos convenientes, todas rubricadas e señaladas de sus armas e señales quinas que en el campo de Orique, venciendo cinco reyes moros el primero rey de Portugal ganó. El cual Gama caminó hasta el dicho cabo de Buena Esperanza (que ante fue dicho *Finis Tormentorum*), donde cuando su gente, viendo los días chicos, los tiempos ásperos, los mantenimientos algo merecedores de renovarse, tentaron de incitar a vuelta al don Vasco de la Gama (que es ahora almirante). E él dijo

* muriese

I do not run risks in my own domains, precious little will I
gain elsewhere." Thus they reached the Cape of Good Hope,✷
two thousand leagues from Lisbon, which they never dared
pass because of the fierceness and height of the waves that
seemed to exceed all endurance of ships and ability of mariners,
and on account of the diverse kinds of birds and those fish
called flying fish. Everyone agrees on this, saying that they do
fly and often times fall aboard ship among the hungry passengers and desperately famished mariners. Men either sate their
gluttony or assuage their hunger with these fish, so afraid are
they of remaining there and uncertain of getting back to their
homeland. In the months of July and August and during the hot-
test season there is severe cold, frost, snow, sleet, and many storms
of rains and winds. So that from fear of being engulfed by the
frozen sea and dying from insisting on such a voyage, they all
turned back.✷ Finally, a not very wealthy Portuguese squire, a
nobleman named Vasco da Gama (who later became an
admiral),✷ unafraid of death and determined to venture his life
for a cause wherein whatever happened he would gain honor,
said to King João✷ that he would round the Cape of Good
Hope or lose his life in fulfilling his desire. The King provided
him with ships well supplied with arms and appropriate foodstuffs. All were marked with his coat of arms, depicting the
quinas which the first king of Portugal won by his victory over
the five Moorish kings on the battlefield of Ourique. This Gama
proceded as far as the Cape of Good Hope (which used to be
called *Finis Tormentorum*).✷ There his men, finding the days
grown shorter, the weather hostile, and the provisions somewhat
in need of replenishing, besought Vasco da Gama (who is now
an admiral) to turn back. He said he could not head back to

que él no había de volver de allí con la vida a Portugal sin traspasar el cabo; que cuando entró en la nao luego había dicho entraba en el ataúd, no con propósito de volver atrás sin ver lo que adelante le podría suceder. E porque rehuían ásperamente, les dijo: al que de él allí murmurase lo colgaría de las entenas o lo lanzaría en la mar. Ellos, cercados de dos muertes, una atrás e otra delante, perseverando en el mayor temor, hicieron los pilotos el norte sul e tornaban para Portugal. Lo cual sintió el almirante e con grandes amenazas les hizo seguir el determinado camino. E en veinte* días con grandes afruentas del mar caminaron quinientas o seiscientas leguas e se hallaron en el mar más caliente e templado. E fueron a una tierra que se llama Melinde donde tomaron puerto e fueron pacíficamente recibidos.

Título II. *Como el almirante Gama fue honrado del rey de* [aiv^r] *Melinde e descubrieron hasta la India, que dista ochocientas leguas.*

Llegados los cristianos a Melinde, su rey, que era moro, los recibió con mucho amor e trató muy cortésmente al almirante e a su gente, dando un intérprete piloto moro e gente para pasar a la India, ochocientas leguas distante de Melinde. En la cual India hallaron a un Gaspar ahora llamado, que de Sevilla había pasado a Alexandría; judío, con su mujer e hijos se fue por tierra hasta Jerusalén, de donde a la India había pasado por el estrecho de Meca. Del cual fueron conocidas las naos de España en las señales de que iban autorizadas e arriba

* veite

Portugal alive without getting round the Cape. For when he came aboard ship, right then he said he was entering his coffin, determined never to turn back without seeing what might happen to him up ahead. And because they opposed him bitterly, he told them that any man who murmured against him he would hang from the rigging or throw overboard. Seeing death ahead of them as well as behind and persisting in their extreme fear, the navigators switched north for south on their compasses and put about for Portugal. The Admiral sensed this and, issuing the gravest of threats, made them follow the appointed course. In twenty days of severe buffeting from the sea they traveled some five or six hundred leagues and found themselves in a warmer and calmer sea. They then went to a land called Malindi* where they made port and were peacefully welcomed.

Title II. *How Admiral Gama was honored by the King of Malindi, and how they discovered India, eight hundred leagues away.*

When the Christians reached Malindi, its king, who was a Moor, received them with great affection and treated the Admiral and his men very courteously. He provided a Moor to act as navigator and interpreter* and men for the passage to India, eight hundred leagues from Malindi. In this India they came across one Gaspar,* as he is now called, who from Seville had passed to Alexandria; a Jew, with his wife and children he went overland to Jerusalem, whence he had passed over to India by way of the Strait of Mecca.* He recognized the ships

dije. E allegándose a ellas, fue preguntado por un faraute de don Vasco de la Gama: qué tierra era aquella, si era la India, o pobre o rica, e si había en ella el aljófar, oro o especiería o algunas cosas de trato. Al cual el judío respondió que aquella tierra no era la por que preguntaba e que era muy pobre e despreciada. Lo cual él hacía por no descubrir tantos bienes a gente cristiana española. Pero como no hay traición que no sea ante sentida que cometida si hobiese lugar la pena ante de la culpa, el buen almirante (de generación noble por antigüedad) conoció ser cosa contraria no solo a razón pero a toda conjetura de verisimilitud. E preguntó al piloto moro que el rey de Melinde con él enviara si aquella respuesta era así, tanto por tentar si concordaba en el mal como si acertaba en el bien. El cual lealmente respondió como era falsa la respuesta e cierta la mucha riqueza, haberes e especiería de la India, de donde Alexandría se proveía e toda la redondez de las tierras, así cristianas como infieles. Lo cual oído por el almirante e regradecido mucho (como era razón los leales servicios remunerarse), lo tovo en más estima. E envió a decir a Gaspar que viniese a comer e holgar con él a su nao, asegurando por prender lo que de otra forma no pudiera haber. E venido, le mandó atar crudamente pies e manos e ásperamen- [[aiv]ᵛ] te azotar porque la verdad que con halagos había encubierto con mortales azotes e crueles presiones su lengua confesase, como aquel pertinaz que mejor la sabía en el caso. Pero el endurecido, pensando escaparse con la vida (que es sombra de muchos trabajos), teniendo lo pasado por bien empleado, que sí era en él e en los semejantes, nunca quiso confesar lo que asaz veces con las pasiones que le daban había su lengua querido manifestar visto. El almirante lo mandaba colgar, de forma que viendo que al muerto poco provecho le traía el tener en secreto las riquezas de los otros, con unas pa-

of Hispania by their official coat of arms (which I have described above). As he approached them, he was asked by one of Vasco da Gama's interpreters what land that was, if it was India, rich or poor, and if there were pearls, gold, spices, or any other items of trade there. The Jew replied that that land was not the one they sought, for it was poor and worthless. He did this in order not to reveal such good things to Christians from Hispania. But since there is no betrayal that will not be discovered beforehand if the punishment precedes the crime, the good Admiral (scion of a venerably noble race) realized that this answer was contrary not only to reason but to all semblance of truth. And he asked the Moorish navigator the King of Malindi had given him if that reply was correct, wanting to see whether he concurred with that evil deception or followed the path of truth. The Moor loyally responded that false was the answer and certain the great riches, treasures, and spices of India, whence Alexandria and all the lands around were supplied, Christian as well as infidel. When the Admiral heard this, he rewarded him generously (as it was right to remunerate loyal services) and held him in higher esteem. He sent word for Gaspar to come and dine and have a pleasant time with him aboard ship, wishing to be certain of seizing what otherwise might have slipped away. When Gaspar arrived, he ordered him bound tightly hand and foot and whipped fiercely, so that with mortal lashes and cruel torments his tongue might confess the truth he had concealed so flatteringly, and which that pertinacious individual knew so well in this regard. But he was obstinate, and, thinking he would escape with his life (which is a shadow of many tribulations),* he considered what he suffered to be worthwhile (as it certainly was with him and his ilk). He refused to confess what many times, under the

labras claras aunque forzosas e temerosas descubrió las riquezas grandes de aquella India, de todas aquellas tierras, mares, vías e gentes a la larga. Lo cual sabido del almirante, entró en la tierra, hizo sus ricas provisiones e tratos con los señores de ella, e así volvió muy próspero con su compañía, aunque harta muerta, a Portugal.

Título III. *Como llegó a Portugal con muchas riquezas don Vasco de Gama; era muerto el rey don Johan e volvió por el rey don Manuel a Calicut.*

Cuando el almirante llegó a Portugal ya con poca gente de la que llevó en compañía, halló ser muerto el rey don Johan de Portugal, que había quedado señoreando e holgando en su tierra. E él vio que con tan doblados trabajos la vida había asaz veces, de ventura buscada, visto peligrosa. E el rey don Manuel de Portugal que le sucedió le hizo muchas dádivas e mercedes e lo hizo almirante, que hasta estonces no lo era. Diole catorce naos ricas e grandes en que trajese especiería, el cual muy más cumplidamente el segundo viaje que el primero solicitó. E dejando gente en Calicut, volvió a Portugal próspero, con tan buen ejemplo cual quedará en augmento de más honras a sus descendientes. A la gente que en Calicut quedó los indios mataron, por cual razón el rey de Portugal les hizo guerra, según delante se narrará. Lo cual habido por presupuesto, prin-

punishment they were giving him, his tongue must have
wanted to admit. The Admiral ordered him hanged, whereupon he saw that little would it profit a dead man to keep secret
the riches of others; so with clear, though forced and fearful
words he revealed at length the great riches of that India and
all those lands, seas, routes, and peoples. Knowing this, the
Admiral went ashore and traded with the rulers of the land for
valuable provisions. He and his company returned to Portugal⌗
very prosperous, although sore many had died.

Title III. *How Vasco da Gama reached Portugal with many
riches; King João had died, and he went back to Calicut for
King Manuel.*

When the Admiral reached Portugal with but few of the
men he had left with, he found that King João of Portugal
had died, he who had been ruling and flourishing in his land.
And he saw that as a result of many strenuous exertions in search
of fortune he had often seen his life endangered.* King Manuel
of Portugal who succeeded him, rewarded Gama with many
gifts and favors and made him an admiral (which until that
moment he had not been). He assigned him twenty-four large
and handsome ships to bring back spices, which Gama solicited
much more thoroughly on this second voyage than the first.
Leaving men in Calicut, he returned to Portugal, where his
exemplary prosperity will bestow ever-increasing honors on his
descendants. The Indians killed the men who remained in
Calicut,⌗ for which reason the King of Portugal waged war

---

* E el vio. . . The Spanish does not indicate clearly whether Gama
  or the King saw his life endangered.

cipiarse ha a contar el viaje e armada que el buen [[av]ʳ] caballero Pedro de Añaya hizo, de quien no es razón que lo que los
extranjeros publican sus naturales callen.

Título IV. *Como se partió de Portugal el buen caballero Pedro
de Añaya, capitán mayor de seis naos.*

Siete años después del descubrimiento primero, año de 1505,
el rey don Manuel de Portugal mandó gridar por su corte: todo
hombre de armas que quisiese recibir su sueldo para ir a las
Indias de Persia e Arabia le daría cada mes dos cruzados e dos
quintales de pimienta cado año e de comer hasta la vuelta en
su reino. E a los que fuesen a Sofala, tierra encubierta e enferma,
darían veinte mil maravedís e dos quintales de pimienta e para
sus provisiones mil e doscientos e cincuenta maravedís e parte en
los que prendiesen infieles e enemigos de nuestra fe. De lo cual
mucha alegría hobieron los que allá querían ir e los ricos cobdi-
ciosos que con su vuelta esperaban prosperar. En el cual viaje
envió por su capitán mayor de seis naos grandes la vía de Sofala a
Pedro de Añaya, su muy amado caballero, que había de quedar
en aquella tierra por capitán. El rey dio luego sueldo de cuatro
meses a los que con él iban, con el cual asentó Martín Fernández
de Figueroa, deseoso de ver tierras, e otros muchos esforzados e
valientes castellanos que aseguraban las espaldas a sus cristianos*
e hacían cara a los enemigos. E estando de partida, cegó la
vista a Tristán de Acuña, capitán mayor que iba para las Indias.
Lo cual visto por el rey, hizo capitán en su lugar a don Francisco de Almeida, bisrey que fue en la India. E le dio veinte

---

* cristianons

against them, as will be narrated below. With this foundation of knowledge, let us begin to tell of the voyage and fleet led by Pedro de Añaya, about whom there is no reason for his countrymen to be silent when foreigners proclaim his deeds.

Title IV. *How the good knight Pedro de Añaya set forth from Portugal as Captain Major of six ships.*

Seven years after the first discovery, in the year 1505, King Manuel of Portugal ordered proclaimed throughout his realm: "All men-at-arms✻ desirous of being paid for going out to the Indies of Persia and Arabia will receive in salary two cruzados a month, two hundredweights of pepper each year, and board until their return to the realm." To those who would go to Sofala,✻ an unknown and unhealthy land, they would give twenty thousand maravedis, two hundredweights of pepper, twelve hundred and fifty maravedis for provisions, and a share in the infidels and enemies of our Faith they might capture. This greatly pleased those who were of a mind to go, as well as the covetous rich persons who expected to profit from their return. On this voyage he sent as captain major of six ships bound for Sofala his dearly beloved knight Pedro de Añaya, who was to remain there as captain. Martín Fernández de Figueroa, anxious to see lands, signed on with him, as did many other determined and valiant Castilians who thus protected their fellow Christians' rear and met their enemies face to face. As they were about to depart, Tristão da Cunha,✻ who was to have been captain major in the Indies, lost his sight. In view of this, the King appointed as captain in his place Dom

naos gruesas e menudas, el cual luego partió con su flota. E en el puerto de Portugal una de las naos, vizcaina, se enagó e el rey le proveyó de otra, que tardó en aderezarse dos meses. Don Francisco partió de Lisbona a veinte e cinco de marzo, año del señor de mil e quinientos e cinco, e Pedro de Añaya a diez e ocho de mayo, los cuales discurrieron por las bravas ondas del mar como adelante se contiene.

Título V. *Como navegaron Pedro de Añaya e sus gentes por recios e tempestuosos mares e tomaron el puerto de* [[av]ᵛ] *Bezeguiche, e de las condiciones de sus pobladores.*

Saliendo del puerto a diez e ocho de mayo de 1505, navegaron e corrieron con asaz tormentas del mar, bonanzas de los vientos e mudanzas de vía* trescientas leguas, que distan las islas Canarias, por do pasando no hicieron detenencia hasta entrar más en su deseo. Caminaron doscientas leguas más adelante e tomaron puerto en Bezeguiche por se proveer de viandas e refresco que bien necesario tenían. La gente de aquella tierra es negra, crespa, la habitación caliente demasiadamente, así que los negros crespos de ella andan desnudos. Tienen en gran estima cuentas azules, verdes o amarillas o de latón, manillas e semejantes joyeles para las piernas, lo cual usan en asaz partes los moros. Traen flechas e arcos e azagayas todos por armas ofensivas e defensivas. E viendo a la dicha gente cristiana que en tierra salió, se asentaban en la arena a hacer oración e echaban la arena por sobre la cabeza e hombros atrás. A la noche la gente volvió a las naos e otro día en la alba se partió, dejada Bezeguiche a la mano siniestra. En el cual viaje hallaban peces

* vida

Francisco de Almeida (who became viceroy in India)✼ and gave him twenty ships, large and small, and he straightaway set out with his fleet. In the Portuguese harbor one of the ships, of Biscayan make, floundered,✼ so the King provided him with another, which was two months in fitting out. Dom Francisco departed Lisbon on the twenty-fifth of March 1505, Pedro de Añaya on the eighteenth of May, and they beat their way through the fierce ocean waves as is to be related below.

Title V. *How Pedro de Añaya and his men sailed through rigorous and tempestuous seas to the port of Bezeguiche,*✼ *and about its inhabitants.*

Leaving port on the eighteenth of May 1505, they made their way through many storms, favoring winds, and changes of course to the Canary Islands,✼ three hundred leagues away. Rather than stop, they chose to bypass them and sail two hundred leagues farther on to the port of Bezeguiche, where they put in for food and fresh supplies, which they sorely needed. The people of that land are black and have curly hair. The place is excessively hot, wherefore these curlyheaded Negroes go about naked. They place great value on blue, green, and yellow beads and tin bracelets and similar ornaments for their legs. These things are worn in many Moorish countries. They all carry bows and arrows and spears as offensive and defensive weapons. Seeing the Christians coming ashore, they sat down in the sand and began saying prayers, all the while throwing sand back over their head and shoulders. The men returned to the ships at nightfall and at daybreak set sail,

llamados tubarones que comen los hombres que pueden haber en la agua, e los voladores que tienen alas de murciégalos e otros diversos pescados sabrosos de comer. E anduvieron sin ver tierra, navegando ochenta días hasta llegar a una isla que estaba al través del cabo de Buena Esperanza, donde los vientos e tempestades cosas nuevas e temerosos pasos les mostraron. El cual mar casi anda cuajado de ballenas e lobos marinos. En el cual lugar se pierde el norte de vista, que distará mil leguas de Portugal, e estonces se rigen por el sul o polo antártico. Pasaron el dicho mar en espacio de quince días e fueron a la mano siniestra e la tierra donde aportaron fue el cabo de las Corrientes, acerca la cual anduvieron ocho días sin poder fender una legua por la mar. Volvieron a la mar por cuatro días e llegaron a una bahía do se proveyeron de asaz pescado e caminaron para Sofala su viaje.

[[avi]ʳ] **Título VI.** *Como aportaron Pedro de Añaya e su gente a Quiloam e de la manera de sus moradores, e como hallaron doce cristianos que se habían perdido en la mar.*

Andando peregrinando por tan extrañas tierras, el buen caballero Pedro de Añaya e los suyos llegaron a una [ciudad] llamada de sus pobladores Quiloam, que dista de Sofala doce leguas. Su gente es moros, cáferes ricos, los cuales no se circuncidan como hacen los moros o los judíos. A la cual gente envió el capitán un batel o galeón con gente armada, de la cual fue por capitán e caudillo Francisco de Añaya su hijo, digno de ser loado por quien es, en cuyo ánimo bien se mostró siempre la limpieza de sus armíneos e la fortaleza de las férreas barras en

leaving Bezeguiche behind on their left.* On this voyage they encountered fish known as sharks, that devour any man they catch in the water, and flying fish with wings like a bats', and other tasty fish. They navigated for eighty days without once seeing land until they reached an island off the Cape of Good Hope, where winds and storms showed them unheard of things and frightening occurrences. This sea is practically brimming over with whales and sea wolves. There, some one thousand leagues from Portugal, one loses sight of the North Star and begins to guide on the South or Antarctic Pole. They passed through this sea in fifteen days and then sailed to the left. The land they reached was Cape Correntes,* round which they beat for eight days without making as much as one league on account of the currents. They stood out to sea for four days and finally reached a bay where they took on a good supply of fish before continuing their journey toward Sofala.

Title VI. *How Pedro de Añaya and his men put in at Chiloane** and about its inhabitants, and about how they found twelve shipwrecked Christians.**

Wending their way through such strange lands, the good knight Pedro de Añaya and his men reached a city its inhabitants call Chiloane, twelve leagues from Sofala. These people are rich Kaffirs, Moors who do not circumcise themselves as do Jews and other Moors. To meet these people the Captain dispatched armed men in a longboat or galleon under the command of his son, Francisco de Añaya.* This captain is worthy of praise in his own right, for he always lived up to his coat of arms:* to the purity of his ermines and the strength of those

que el castillo cruzado nuevas hazañas convirtieron. E como llegó a tierra, halló doce cristianos de Portugal que en el cabo de las Corrientes con un capitán de los de don Francisco de Almeida se habían* perdido, la nao hecha piezas: en tierra tocando, con el cruel viento se rompió. E escaparon de aquello† ciento e trece personas, e el capitán e otros siete hombres la cobdicia ahogó. Con los cuales holgó mucho Francisco de Añaya, conociendo que eran cristianos e suyos. Los llevó para el capitán Pedro de Añaya su padre a las naos, que fueron bien recibidos. Iban desnudos, negros e encanijados, que parecían embalsamados, despojados por los cáferes de todos sus atavíos, de gente armada cercados e escarnecidos. No comían sino yerbas porque no lo‡ habían, e cangrejos; e por amor de Dios les daban allí algún puño de mijo, el cual crudo comían como pájaros. E ante que les diesen limosna, contaban que los hacían bailar una hora hasta que cansados mortales en el suelo caían, en que los cáferes se deleitaban; e como estaban ya esperando a Pedro de Añaya que ellos bien sabían sería presto en Sofala. Los cuales fueron cubiertos de algún atavío que en las naos les dieron e bien tratados e recreados por mandado del capitán mayor. E otro día levantaron sus áncoras e fueron a tomar puerto en Sofala.

[[*avi*]ᵛ] **Título VII.** *Como llegaron a Sofala e de las cosas que ahí vieron.*

Verisímile es e de creer el gran placer que la gente hobo cuando tierra tanto deseada vio, por quien tantos trabajos por las desamoradas aguas sufrieron, donde llegaron a diez e nueve

     * había   † aquellos   ‡ lo no

diagonal bands of iron under the castle that he earned by his own deeds. Upon landing, they found twelve Christians from Portugal who had been shipwrecked at Cape Correntes with one of Dom Francisco's captains; the ship had been driven aground by the cruel wind and dashed to pieces. One hundred and thirteen had survived, and greed caused the drowning of the captain and seven others. Francisco de Añaya was very pleased to learn that they were Christians and comrades. He took them back to his father, Captain Pedro de Añaya, on the ships, where they were given a hearty welcome. They were naked and so burned and emaciated that they looked as if they had been embalmed. They had been stripped of all their clothing by the Kaffirs and surrounded and taunted by armed men. They had nothing to eat except grass and crabs. And when out of love of God they did give them a handful of millet, they ate it raw, like birds. They told how, before giving them alms, the Kaffirs would make them dance around for an hour until they fell to the ground mortally exhausted, at which the Kaffirs would take great delight. They told how they had been waiting for Pedro de Añaya, for they well knew he would soon reach Sofala. The Captain Major saw to it that they received clothing and proper care and treatment aboard the ships. Next day they weighed anchor and proceeded to the port of Sofala.

Title VII. *How they reached Sofala, and about what they saw there.*

You can certainly believe that the men were happy to see that longed-for land on whose account they had suffered such tribulations at the mercy of a hateful sea. They arrived on

de septiembre. E el buen caballero Pedro de Añaya hizo o mandó a los pilotos tentasen si la agua del río podría sufrir las naos para entrar con ellas hasta Sofala. E por la poca agua que hallaron dijeron que no, pero que las chicas podrían entrar. Lo cual visto del buen capitán, mandó que saliese la gente de las naos mayores e se entrase en las menores, que prestamente, como mandamiento deseado, fue cumplido, e al tercer día eran llegados. Do grandes palmares e frutos de diversos mantenimientos hallaban. En los cuales palmares no dátiles había, porque no era su fruto, pero cocos así nombrados, o nueces de India, las cuales dice Pogio Florentino que son símiles al higo. Pero como quien las ha visto, en esto le osaré contradecir. La cual fruta es sabrosa, cada nuez como una cabeza de hombre e otras menores. Quítanle la casca, que es gruesa cuanto un dedo, de la cual como sea febras dicen hacerse cuerdas e maromas, que es ya seco como esparto. Llámanse cocos de India porque tienen ojos e narices e parece que están cocando. Yo la vi e pareció cabeza de muerto e así todas las señales tiene e cosas que en ella se hallarán. Dentro en la casca tiene fruto blanco, grueso como la casca; su sabor es de almendra, lleno de agua muy sabrosa, e en todo el año dan las palmas el dicho fruto. De los Sofaleses se llama la dicha neuz *nazi,* del cual se hace vino e vinagre, aceite e miel, madera e teja e aún atavíos de miserables personas. Había otrosí higueras de maravilloso fruto cuyos higos se vuelven en la boca manteca, cuyas hojas son tan grandes como adargas, e otras cosas notables de ver que adelante se contarán.

Título VIII. *Como Pedro de Añaya mandó apercibir su gente para se ver con el rey de Sofala e concertar sobre lo que era venido.*

the nineteenth of September,❊ and the good knight Pedro de
Añaya had the navigators take soundings to determine whether
the ships could continue up the river to Sofala. Finding shallow
water, they said no, but the smaller craft could; whereupon the
good Captain ordered the men out of the large ships and into
the smaller ones, which, as a welcome order, was immediately
carried out, and three days later they entered Sofala. There
they found large palm trees and other varieties of fruit trees.
These palm trees do not bear dates, for this is not their fruit.
Instead, they bear so-called *coco* or India nuts❊ that Poggio the
Florentine❊ says are similar to figs. But as one who has seen
them, I shall dare to contradict him. It is a savory fruit, each
nut the size of a man's head, and they come in smaller sizes.
They take off the shell, which is as thick as one's finger; since
this is fibrous, they say one can make cord and rope from it,
because it is dry like esparto grass. They are called India *cocos*
because they have eyes and a nose and look as though they are
making faces. I saw one, and it looked just like a skull, for it
had exactly the same characteristics. Inside the shell is a white
fruit of the same thickness as the shell. It has an almond taste
and is filled with a delicious juice. The palm trees bear this
fruit all year round. The Sofalese call this nut *nazi*. From it
can be made wine, vinegar, oil, honey, planks, thatches, and
even garments for destitute people. Likewise there were fig
trees with leaves as big as shields, whose marvelous figs turn
to butter in your mouth, and other noteworthy things to see,
as will be told below.

Title VIII. *How Pedro de Añaya had his men prepare for him
to meet with the King of Sofala*❊ *and reach an agreement concerning his mission there.*

[[avii]^r] Como la gente estaba ya ganosa de salir en tierra, el buen capitán Pedro de Añaya holgaba de ello, para lo cual era venido. Hizo apercibir e armar su gente de las armas que asaz llevaban e envió un faraute al rey de Sofala, como el que era capitán mayor del rey de Portugal en aquella banda le quería ver e hablar, si su alteza quería. De que el rey holgó mucho, diciendo que sí e luego, si a él pluguiese. Pedro de Añaya, que era hombre tan bien proveído como esforzado, placiéndole la respuesta (como más valga señorear por amor que por temor), mandó su apercibida gente* entrar en los bateles, quedando alguna gente en las naos por guarda, de las cuales muchos tiros de alegría hicieron. Dicen que salían todos por orden con sus banderas e estandartes en los bateles. E salieron en tierra con Pedro de Añaya hasta diez hombres, no consintiendo salir los que en los bateles estaban. La causa que daba era porque si el rey de Sofala no viniese en la concordia que él hablase e gente tuviese contra ellos secreta, que más presto se podrían recoger en los bateles diez que mil, e que en las naos se podrían aprovechar de la artillería o salir apercibidos de riesgo a tierra contra sus enemigos; lo cual se hizo como ordenó. La gente de los negros que a verlos salió era cosa maravillosa e del rey de Sofala fue bien recibido. El cual dijo a Pedro de Añaya que se asentase cabo él sobre un tapete de seda, que allá todos se asientan en el suelo. E Pedro de Añaya mandó a su faraute hablar su embajada largamente, lo cual hizo. Entre la cual habla el rey de Portugal le rogaba le diese campo para edificar una casa en que pusiese sus mercancías. En lo cual todo el rey de Sofala vino e diole un palmar que estaba lleno de casas en que

---

* egnte

The good Captain Pedro de Añaya was delighted to find his men so anxious to go ashore, for this was why he was there. He had them make ready and arm themselves from their ample supply of weapons, and he sent an interpreter to the King of Sofala, saying: "He who is the King of Portugal's Captain Major for this coast wishes to meet and speak with you, if it please Your Highness." The King was delighted and answered: "Certainly, and immediately if you would like." Pedro de Añaya, prudent as well as brave, was pleased by this reply, knowing that it is far better to rule through love than fear. He ordered his well prepared men into the longboats, leaving some behind to guard the ships, whence many rounds were fired in celebration. They say that everyone boarded the longboats in proper order, displaying their banners and standards. Pedro de Añaya went ashore with only ten men and would not allow the rest to leave the longboats. The reason he gave was that, should the King of Sofala not observe the agreement as he had said and have men in hiding to send against him, then ten men could get back to the longboats more easily than a thousand. From the ships they could then take advantage of their artillery or come ashore against the enemy, alert to the dangers. This was done just as he ordered. The number of Negroes who came out to gaze at them was amazing. The King of Sofala welcomed Pedro de Añaya and bade him sit near him on a silken carpet, for there everyone sits on the ground. Pedro de Añaya ordered his interpreter to deliver his message in full, which he did. In it the King of Portugal requested land upon which to build a house to store his merchandise. The King of Sofala agreed to everything and provided a palm grove filled with houses where Pedro de Añaya's men

su gente pudiese reposar. Los cristianos las cercaron de cavas, sacaron mucho de lo que en las naos tenían e aposentáronse en tierra como su capitán mayor les mandó.

Título IX. *De la tierra, gente e mercancías de Sofala e* [[*avii*]ᵛ] *su rico valor.*

La distancia que de Portugal a Sofala hay son dos mil e quinientas leguas, su tierra caliente, de mucho arroz e mijo. Trigo no lo hay. Los carneros de aquella tierra son grandes, no tenientes cuernos ni lana; el pelo es como de perro blanco. Dice Figueroa que en aquel río hay caballos marinos que salen a pacer en tierra e se vuelven a la mar, las cola e ancas como potros, que en ninguna cosa difieren excepto en el efecto del fin para que su nombre suena. Hay cañas de azúcar. La gente de Sofala es toda negra hasta el estrecho de Meca, que dista tres mil leguas. Los moradores de Sofala son cáferes que adoran al sol e las estrellas. Andan vestidos con paños de algodón pintados e otros cubiertas solamente las partes vergonzosas. No hay lino. Las mujeres traen descubiertas las cabezas, manillas de latón en las piernas. Traen los labios* foradados, seis o siete agujeros, lo cual tienen por hermosa e apuesta cosa. Hay sandalo blanco, oro, ambar e otras riquezas. Una gallina vale un mitical, que son quinientos maravedís, el cual aprecian allá como acá medio real. E cient leguas dentro en la tierra, en un reino de cáferes que se llama Benamotapa se halla el oro con que tratan en aquellas partes muy copiosamente.

* labros

could rest. The Christians encircled this with trenches, brought ashore a good deal of what they carried aboard ship, and installed themselves as the Captain Major directed.

Title IX. *About the land, people, and products of Sofala⁜ and their high value.*

The distance from Portugal to Sofala is two thousand five hundred leagues. It is a hot land which produces much rice and millet. There is no wheat. The sheep of that land are large with neither horns nor wool; their hair is like a white dog's. Figueroa says that in that river there are sea horses which come ashore to graze and then return to the sea. They have tails and croups like colts and differ from horses only in name. Sugar cane grows there. From Sofala to the Strait of Mecca, three thousand leagues away, everyone is black. The inhabitants of Sofala are Kaffirs, who adore the sun and the stars. They wear colored cotton garments, and others cover only their shameful parts. There is no linen. The women wear nothing on their heads, and tin bracelets on their legs. They pierce their lips in six or seven places, which they consider very beautiful and elegant. There are white sandalwood, gold, amber, and other riches. A chicken is worth one mitical, which is equivalent to five hundred maravedis, which would be worth half a real here. And one hundred leagues inland, in a Kaffir kingdom called Monomotapa,⁜ lies the gold in which they trade very copiously in those parts.

Título X. *Como cercaron con madera los cristianos su aposento
e como empezaron adolecer, de que pesó mucho a Pedro de
Añaya.*

Como el rey de Sofala les hobo dado do pudiesen edificar
la lonja del rey de Portugal, habitar su gente e tener sus mercancías e en el campo casas algunas despobladas, las cuales las
gentes del buen caballero Pedro de Añaya cercaron de cavas e
barreras de madera lo mejor que supieron a gran priesa e
saliéronse allí a posar. Lo cual velaban noche e día, puesta la
arti- [[aviii]ʳ] llería en orden, como hombres que se recelan
de guerra e se aparejan para hacerla. Principiaron los más de
ellos a enfermar de calenturas e morir cualquier día dos o tres
personas, con que temblaban sus ánimos e se mudaban sus pensamientos. Quisieran ante ir con la vida por trabajos que esperar
la muerte en tierra de sus enemigos. En lo cual no consintió el
esforzado capitán mayor, que su vida o muerte daba el seguro
que para sí tenía a los suyos. E dijo que nunca Dios tal permi-
tiese, que hasta haber efecto de su venida diese vuelta su persona.
En esta tierra es una maravillosa cosa que la madera se hunde
en la agua e la piedra nada. Lo cual, como haya muchos testigos
de vista, no ternéis por dificultad creer. El capitán envió por
provisiones el río arriba cincuenta leguas, do vieron en unas
sierras carbúnculos como perros, que en la frente una piedra
traían que de noche mucha luz daba como muy encendido
fuego. Donde andaban a caza de ratones como si liebres o cosa
más deseada fueran. E si el ratón en alguna casa se metía,
llegaban los cazadores a derrocar la casa. Sus armas de caza son
arcos e flechas. El pan hácenlo de mijo e cuézenlo en ollas e no
en hornos, según más largamente muchos que en aquellas partes
se han hallado de vista podrán contar.

Title X. *How the Christians surrounded their encampment with a wooden barrier, and how they began to fall sick, which sorely grieved Pedro de Añaya.*

Since the King of Sofala had provided a parcel of land where they could build the King of Portugal's warehouse, quarter their men, and store their merchandise, as well as some empty houses in the field that the men of the good knight Pedro de Añaya encircled with trenches and wooden barriers as well and rapidly as they could, they came ashore to live there. They guarded it night and day, keeping the artillery ready, in the manner of men who anticipate war and make ready to fight it. Most of them began to fall sick with fever, and every day or so two or three would die. At this their souls trembled, and they began to waver in their convictions. They wanted to go and risk their lives* in harsh ordeals rather than just wait for death in the land of the enemy. The determined Captain Major refused to consent to such a thing, for his life or death was their bond. He said God forbid that he should ever go back without accomplishing his mission. In this land it is an amazing thing: wood sinks in water, but stones float,* which, since there are so many eyewitnesses, you will not find difficult to believe. The Captain sent fifty leagues up river after provisions, where they saw in the hills carbuncles in the shape of dogs. In their foreheads were stones that at night gave off as much light as a blazing fire. There they hunt mice as though they were hares or some other desirable thing. If the mouse happens to enter a house, the hunters come along and tear the house down. Their hunting weapons are bows and arrows. Bread they make from millet, cooking it in kettles rather than ovens. Many who have been in those parts personally can tell you about all these things in greater detail.

Título XI. *Como llegaron dos naos de don Francisco a Sofala e contaron de la toma de Mozambique,* Quiloam e Mombasa.*

En este conmedio dos naos de don Francisco, portuguesas, llegaron con mercancías a trocar por oro, e sabido de Pedro de Añaya, recibieron mucho placer, así los unos como los otros. E bien recibidos del capitán mayor, preguntó cómo se ganaron aquellos lugares de Mozambique, Quiloam e Mombasa, que ya se había sabido en Sofala do estonces eran. E el capitán de las naos respondió como don Francisco vino a tomar puerto en Mozambique, que es buen puerto, e fue de allí sobre Quiloam, ciudad [[aviii]^v] principal. E víspera de Santiago apóstol la tomó e desbarató, jueves, veinte e cinco de julio de 1505. Do mandó edificar una fortaleza e hizo e levantó por rey de la misma ciudad un mercader moro muy rico, como el rey moro que ante había sido fuese en huída, llamado Habraen, el segundo Mahometorconi. Quedó allí por capitán Pedro de Herrera, cuyo generoso origen de Ferrara en España antiguamente vino e traspasó acá sus calderas barradas e serpentales cabezas, insignia misteriosa que por este capitán no mereció menos que por sus mayores. E el bisrey don Francisco fue sobre la ciudad de Mombasa miércoles, trece de agosto. Allá llegando, ordenaron de la combatir e el viernes, día de nuestra señora, adelante el capitán mayor, con toda su gente salió en tierra. E puesta a fuego e a sangre la ciudad e gente de ella, que crudamente se defendía, robada toda su riqueza, don Francisco se partió para la India.

* Mocambique

Title XI. *How two of Dom Francisco's ships arrived at Sofala
and told of the taking of Mozambique, Kilwa, and Mombasa.*

At this juncture, two of Dom Francisco's Portuguese
ships sailed in to exchange merchandise for gold, and when
Pedro de Añaya learned of this, he was very pleased, as were
they. Once the Captain Major had welcomed them, he asked
how they had taken Mozambique, Kilwa, and Mombasa, which
there in Sofala they already knew had occurred. The captain
of the ships replied that Dom Francisco had put in at Mozambique,✴ which has a good port, and that from there he had set
out against Kilwa,✴ a principal city. On the eve of the Feast
Day of Saint James the Apostle he routed the defenders and took
it, Thursday, the twenty-fifth of July 1505. He had a fort built,
and he acclaimed a wealthy Moorish merchant king of the city,
for the former king, named Abraham,✴ had run off. The second
king's name was Mohammed Ankoni. Pero Ferreira✴ was
assigned there as captain. His generous forebears had long ago
come from Ferrara to Hispania, bringing hither their bars, caul-
drons, and serpentine heads, a mysterious insignia which this
captain honored as much as any of his predecessors. The Viceroy
Dom Francisco then moved against the city of Mombasa,✴
where he arrived on Wednesday, the thirteenth of August. They
made ready for the attack, and on Friday, the Feast Day of
Our Lady, the Captain Major led his entire force ashore. The
city and its people, who put up a fierce defense, were put to
the torch and the sword. Carrying off all the city's wealth, Dom
Francisco set sail for India.

Título XII. *Como, idas las dos naos de don Francisco e enfermando la gente de Pedro de Añaya, el rey de Sofala le cometió traición.*

Mucho fue el placer que en oir la vitoria de don Francisco hobo el buen caballero Pedro de Añaya. E las naos de él despedidas, quedó con su gente, que enfermó tan gravemente que no se podían tener sino en tres pies y no había quien velase su fortaleza e aposentos. E porque esto no se sintiese del rey de Sofala, enviaba dos o tres negritos Pedro de Añaya para que velasen. E muchas veces se levantaba el mismo capitán a tañer una campanilla que en medio de la fortaleza estaba, lo cual él hacía por disimular la falta que la sanidad en su gente hacía e la enfermedad que los suprimía. Pero como nada sea oculto que no sea revelado, fue sabido o presumido del rey de Sofala, el cual envió en su tierra por cáferes para tomar la fortaleza a Pedro de Añaya e matar toda su gente, a un lugar de su habitación que se [b^r] decía Nangabe. De lo cual todo un moro grande amigo de Pedro de Añaya había avisado, que se nombraba Cidiacoti, el cual era malquisto de los moros porque a los cristianos amaba mucho; decían que era cristiano e por ello le habían querido matar. El rey de Sofala e los cáferes llegaron a los cristianos dando voces e alaridos, echando tierra e levantando arena con los pies, tirando flechas. Lo cual sentido de Pedro de Añaya, mandó llamar e armar su gente a mucha priesa. E algunos salían en camisa aunque flacos, que a penas dos podían armar una ballesta, según cuenta Figueroa que ahí estaba. E los bombarderos cristianos pusieron fuego a las bombardas e artillería; así con los tiros gran gente mató de cáferes; e se retraían atrás cuanto podían. Quién podría contar la excelencia, grande ánimo e orden de Pedro de Añaya, fiero león a sus

Title XII. *How, following the departure of Dom Francisco's two ships, Pedro de Añaya's men continued to fall sick, whereupon the King of Sofala betrayed him.*

The good knight Pedro de Añaya took great pleasure in hearing about Dom Francisco's victories. Bidding farewell to the ships, he continued on there with his men, who became so seriously ill that they were unable to stand but on three feet, and there was no one to guard the fort or encampment. In order to keep this from the King of Sofala, Pedro de Añaya would send two or three little Negro boys to stand guard. On many occasions the Captain himself would go up and ring a bell that was in the middle of the fort. He did so to hide the effects caused by the lack of health in his men and the sickness that was wearing them down. But since nothing can be kept secret for long, the King of Sofala learned about or assumed these conditions. He sent inland to a place in his kingdom called Nangabe※ for Kaffirs to come and seize the fort from Pedro de Añaya and kill all his men. A Moor who was a great friend of Pedro de Añaya informed him of all this. His name was Cidi Akoti,※ and he was hated by the Moors because he liked the Christians so much. They said he was a Christian and for this reason had sought to kill him. The King of Sofala and the Kaffirs came against the Christians,※ screaming and shouting, kicking up clouds of dust and sand, and firing their arrows. On perceiving this, Pedro de Añaya quickly summoned his men to arms. Some came out in shirttails, although they were so weak that two with difficulty managed to wind up a crossbow, according to Figueroa who was there. The Christian gunners fired their mortars and artillery, and their shots killed a great many of the Kaffirs, who then retreated as far as they could. Oh, to be

enemigos, armado e a punto, que decía como viese venir infinidad de saetas e flechas, dardos e azagayas de los cáferes: "¡A ellos, compañeros e hermanos míos, generosos cristianos de España! Dad en ellos, que la guerra de los cáferes más parece juego de cañas que gente de lid. Aquí podéis salvar la vida, acrecentar la honra e hacer mucho servicio a Dios, exaltar* la santa fe católica e honra de la valiente e magnánima España nuestra patria." No se pasaba, pues, su tiempo en razones, que más era tiempo estonces de acorrer con vendas para las heridas que de consejos para ganar honras. Con su tajante espada fieramente despedazaba la enemiga gente, que en arroyos de sangre se convertía e sus cuerpos en polvos: que ésta es su costumbre, de quemar los cuerpos muertos. E algún fuego que pusieron en los aposentos por de fuera los cristianos amataron con agua e paños mojados. E así duró el cerco tres días, e desque no pudieron vencer, antes su gente era así muerta, herida e maltratada, huyeron e se desviaron de los aposentos de Pedro de Añaya e su compañía, e [[b]ᵛ] el rey se volvió donde había salido. Esta gente anda desnuda; llámanse unos a otros con silbatos de cuerno. Sus armas son arcos, flechas e porras de madera.

Título XIII. *Como el rey de Sofala envió a hacer paces con Pedro de Añaya e su respuesta.*

Bien quisiera el rey de Sofala si pudiera hacer luego paces con Pedro de Añaya, al cual envió dos moros. E oída su emba-

* exalcar

able to tell of the excellence, the grand spirit and composure of Pedro de Añaya, a fierce lion to his enemies, armed and ready, who, in the face of an infinite hail of Kaffir slings, arrows, darts, and spears, said: "Charge!* Have at them, my friends and generous Christian brethren of Hispania! For the warfare of the Kaffirs is more like a tournament than one of true warriors. Here you can save your lives, increase your honor, render great service to God, and exalt the Holy Catholic Faith and the honor of that valiant and magnanimous Hispania our fatherland." He did not, however, waste his time in discourses, because right then it was more a time to hasten with bandages for the wounded than to give advice on how to gain honors. With his fierce sword he sliced to pieces the enemy host, turning them into rivers of blood and their bodies into dust (for this is their custom, to burn the dead bodies). The few fires set to the outside of the buildings the Christians killed with water and wet cloths. Thus the siege lasted three days, and, since they could not conquer, but on the contrary their men were being killed, wounded, and beaten, the attackers fled from the encampment of Pedro de Añaya and his company, and the King went back to where he had set out from. These people go about naked. They call one another by blowing horns; their weapons are bows and arrows and wooden clubs.

Title XIII. *How the King of Sofala sent men to make peace with Pedro de Añaya, and his answer.*

The King of Sofala would very much have liked to have been able to make peace with Pedro de Añaya, to whom he

jada, el capitán mayor le respondió que lo que después de hecho no había de aprovechar por de más era gastar tiempo en lo concertar. E* porque sabía que ellos no habían de la guardar, no quería hacer paces, mas que dejase al rey de Sofala su señor, que en viniendo más gente cristiana del rey de Portugal, por quien él allí era venido, él lo iría a buscar e le cortaría la cabeza porque a él fuese castigo e a los venideros ejemplo. Con lo cual recontado por los moros, el rey se aseguró, pensando que Pedro de Añaya no había de hacer nada hasta que más gente le viniese. E esto habíalo él hecho por lo tomar más descuidado e a su voluntad, como el rey hizo con él.

Título XIV. *Como, los moros despoblando los lugares con miedo, el buen caballero Pedro de Añaya fue sobre el rey de Sofala con cincuenta hombres de su compañía.*

Los cáferes con gran temor que a las defensivas armas tenían despoblaron los lugares cerca de la fortaleza, e Pedro de Añaya fue avisado como el rey de Sofala estaba muy solo con sus criados en el palacio. Mandó aparejar muy bien cincuenta hombres de los que más recios o esforzados se sentían, dejando su fortaleza a buen recabdo con gente, a la cual mandó que toda aquella noche que él salía no durmiesen. E entró en un bergantín e parte de su gente en un batel, a los cuales mandó so pena de muerte ninguno de otro, todos de uno ni uno de todos se desman- [bii^r] dase, que así hicieron. Río arriba callada e se-

* e e

sent two Moors. After listening to their proposal, the Captain Major replied that it was foolish to waste time negotiating something that would have no meaning. Because he knew they would not abide by any peace, he did not want to make one. Instead, he would allow the King of Sofala to continue to rule, for when the King of Portugal, who had stationed him there, sent out more Christians, he would then go looking for him and would cut off his head as punishment for him and an example for future generations. When this was reported by the Moors, the King was reassured, thinking that Pedro de Añaya would do nothing until more men arrived. But the latter had said these things* in order to take the King unawares and when it pleased him, just as the King had done to him.

Title XIV. *How, as the terrified Moors abandoned their positions, the good knight Pedro de Añaya attacked the King of Sofala with fifty men from his company.*

The Kaffirs, sorely afraid of the defensive weapons, abandoned their positions near the fort, and Pedro de Añaya was informed that the King of Sofala was all alone with his servants in the palace. He ordered fifty of those who felt healthiest and strongest to equip themselves very well. He assigned men to guard the fort carefully and ordered them not to sleep while he was away during the night. Then he boarded a brigantine and put part of his men in a longboat, giving strictest orders that under pain of death they must all stay together and no one wander off, and they did as directed. Up river, secretly and quietly, after midnight, they went ashore and set fire to some

cretamente después* de la media noche salieron en tierra, poniendo fuego a las casas que en el camino había e haciendo el daño posible hasta el palacio del rey de Sofala. Donde mataron muchos moros que a la puerta bien descuidados dormían, dando con la puerta en el suelo, que para todo llevaban aparejo. E entró Pedro de Añaya con seis caballeros delante e la otra gente quedó fuera matando moros. E el rey se levantó alborotado de la cámara e andaba de cámara en cámara tanto con temor como con priesa por la súbita muerte que ante sí tenía. Al cual andando buscando de celda en celda Pedro de Añaya encontró detrás la puerta de la cocina. E el rey con gran furia le dio por el pescuezo a Pedro de Añaya con una azagaya que tenía e no le llevó sino el cuero de la carne. Pero como Pedro de Añaya se sintió herido, llamó los suyos que trajesen luz, siquiera para buscar quien así lo tratara. E venidos con una entorcha, vieron al rey de Sofala moro estar en pie, e dieron muchas heridas hasta que lo dejaron sin reino e sin vida. Cortándole la cabeza, puesta en el hierro de lanza, se volvieron a la fortaleza, do estovo en memoria de su señalada vitoria, de haber robado toda la tierra e ciudad do el† rey de Sofala tenía sus palacios.

Título XV. *Como Pedro de Añaya capitán mayor enfermó e murió e como en su lugar‡ eligieron otro de su compañía.*

Como todas las grandes alegrías sean mensajeras de cercana tristeza, porque el hombre la mudable fortuna no deja estar siempre triste ni alegre, veinte días después que así gozoso el buen caballero Pedro de Añaya volvió a su fortaleza, como fuese

* despus   † del   ‡ loganr

houses, causing as much damage as possible along the road to
the King of Sofala's palace. There they killed many Moors who
were sleeping at the entrance completely unawares. They
knocked the door down, for they carried equipment for every
eventuality. Pedro de Añaya, followed by six knights, led the
way inside while the rest of the men remained outside killing
Moors. The King jumped up from his bedchamber all excited
and went running from chamber to chamber, terror-stricken by
the sudden death he could feel hard upon him. Going from
room to room in search of him, Pedro de Añaya met up with
him behind the door leading to the kitchen. The King with
great fury hit Pedro de Añaya in the neck with a spear but
only managed to break the skin. Nevertheless, Pedro de Añaya,
knowing he had been wounded, called for his men to bring a
light, if only to find out who had struck him. Arriving with a
torch, they saw the Moorish King of Sofala standing there.
They struck him blow upon blow, taking from him his kingdom and his life. Cutting off his head✤ and placing it on a
lance, they carried it back to the fort, where it remained in
memory of their signal victory: that of having pillaged all the
land and city where the King of Sofala had his palaces.

Title XV. *How Captain Major Pedro de Añaya fell sick and
died,✤ and how in his place they elected another of the company.*

All great joys are but harbingers of imminent sorrow,
for fickle fortune never permits a man to be either always sad
or always happy. Thus, twenty days after the good knight Pedro
de Añaya had so joyfully returned to his fort, since he was

mortal e el rey de Portugal su señor no tuvo poder para le dar seguro de la vida, enfermó de calenturas. De la cual dolencia plugó a nuestro Señor Jesucristo, redemptor nuestro, llevarlo para sí como a católico cristiano, que como tal feneció [[bii]ᵛ] a su gloria, para la cual todos deseando ir en este peligroso* e trabajoso mar de vida navegamos. Que no menos puso mancilla en su gente de lloros e sentimiento que gloria en su fama de valiente e esforzado caballero cristiano, persiguidor de moros enemigos de nuestra fe. E dichas sus misas e exequias lo más honradamente que allá pudo ser, fue sepultado, e en su lugar elegido por la gente cristiana Manuel Fernández, que con ellos por mayordomo venía; e de ahí adelante fue tenido por su capitán mayor.

Título XVI.† *Como la gente de Pedro de Añaya que con Manuel Fernández quedó ordenó hacer la fortaleza de piedra en el mes de abril.*

Muertos los dos principales de las huestes, Pedro de Añaya capitán mayor e el rey de Sofala, los cristianos juntamente con el capitán Manuel Fernández quisieran alzar por rey de Sofala al hijo mayor e hacer paces con él e con los moros cáferes. Al cual enviaron sus mensajeros sobre ello, e él respondió que nunca Dios quisiese que él fuese amigo de los enemigos e homicidas crueles de su padre, en quien se habían encarnizado; e que haría gran traición a quien lo engendró e gran injuria a los

---

* pelgroso
† Text erroneously reads "XV." All succeeding title numbers have been adjusted to reflect this correction.

mortal and his lord the King of Portugal had not the power to
guarantee him life, he fell sick with fever. By reason of this
sickness it pleased Our Lord and Redeemer Jesus Christ to
call him unto Himself. He died a Catholic Christian, gaining
that glory to which we all, charting our course through this
perilous and stormy sea of life, aspire. Although his death
burdened his men with tears and sorrow, in equal measure did
it leave them the glory of his fame as a valiant and dedicated
Christian knight, a relentless foe of the Moorish enemies of our
Faith. After saying their Masses and exequies as honorably
as could be done out there, they buried him. In his place the
Christians elected Manuel Fernandes, who had come out with
them as factor, and from then on he was considered their
captain major.

Title XVI. *How the men of Pedro de Añaya under Manuel Fernandes arranged to build the fort of stone, in the month of
April.*

With the leaders of the rival hosts—Captain Major Pedro de
Añaya and the King of Sofala—dead, the Christians and Captain
Manuel Fernandes sought to acclaim as king of Sofala the
eldest son and make peace with him and the Kaffir Moors. To
this end they sent their messengers to him, and he replied: God
forbid✤ that he should ever be a friend of the enemies and
cruel murderers of the father they had treated so brutally. It
would be grave treason to the man who engendered him and

huesos e cabeza cortada de su padre. Que el reino era suyo e
que si de mano de ellos lo había de recibir, no lo quería; e lo
que no hiciera en vida de su padre menos lo quería hacer en
muerte, pues ninguno más que él, que era primogénito, la
honra de su padre había de sublimar. Que no sin causa los hijos
mayores doblado mantenimiento e atavío suelen o estaba ordenado recibir e de su padre la bendición, para poderla dar a
sus menores hermanos; e aún de derecho de cristianos las escripturas e munimientos de honras e hacienda en poder del primogénito quedar debían. Que él guerra, sangre e enemistad quería
con ellos como si su padre viviera, e no paz. Lo cual sabido por
[biiiʳ] los cristianos, hicieron rey a otro hijo menor del rey
de Sofala, que lo aceptó e les dio esclavos para hacer la
fortaleza de piedra que principiaron. El cual rey se llamaba
Soltán Sulema e estaba en un lugar que se decía Buani, que no
quiso habitar do su padre, por mostrar la tristeza que la muerte
paterna suele causar al hijo.

Título XVII.* *Como por mandado del bisrey fue entregada la
fortaleza a Nuño Vaz Pereira.*

   Ya que la fortaleza se edificaba e crecía de piedra, vino allí
Nuño Vaz Pereira con mandamiento del bisrey e le fue por
Manuel Fernández (el cual se partió para la India) e por los de
su compañía la fortaleza e capitanía mayor de aquella costa
entregada. De ahí a cuatro meses vino a ver la gente cristiana
por la fama que de ella oyera e por ser blancos un gran señor
que había nombre Muconde, que era cáfer, señor de grandes
tierras, e traía un hijo consigo e mucha gente armada. Los

   * VI

deep insult to his bones and severed head. The kingdom belonged to him, and if he had to receive it from their hands, he did not want it. What he would not do while his father lived, he certainly would not do now that he was dead. For no one but he, as first-born, must exalt his father's honor. Not without reason is the eldest son supposed to receive the double portion and his father's blessing, so that he may pass it along to his younger brothers. Even according to Christian law and stipulations the estate should belong to the first-born. War, blood, and enmity was what he wanted from them, just as if his father were alive, and not peace. When the Christians heard this, they named as king a younger son, and he accepted and gave them slaves to build the stone fort which they started. This King's name was Sultan Sulema,✳ and he took up residence in a place called Buene:✳ he did not want to live where his father had resided, in order to demonstrate the sorrow which a father's death is wont to cause his son.

Title XVII. *How by order of the Viceroy the fort was handed over to Nuno Vaz Pereira.*✳

While the stone fort was being built, Nuno Vaz Pereira arrived carrying orders from the Viceroy, and Manuel Fernandes (who left for India) and his company handed over to him the fort and captaincy major for that coast. Four months later there came to visit the Christians because of their fame and because they were white a great lord named Mokondi.✳ A Kaffir who ruled over many lands, he brought with him a son and many armed men. The Christians, well prepared, gave

cristianos apercibidos los recibieron bien e habláronse Nuño Vaz
Pereira e él por intercesión de seis intérpretes: que iba la palabra
en seis lenguas vuelta ante que la entendiesen. E quedaron muy
amigos para adelante; e a su hijo, por contentar al Muconde,
dio el capitán dádivas, que ellos tuvieron en mucha estima,
porque por su tierra habían de pasar los tratantes con oro a
Sofala. E fuese a su reino muy contento e obligado a los
cristianos.

Título XVIII. *Como la fortaleza de Sofala de la cristiana gente
fue entregada por Nuño Vaz Pereira a Vasco Gómez de Abreo.*

Edificada la fortaleza de piedra a la mayor priesa que
pudieron, como en la prosperidad nunca falta compañía ni
quien acepte lo seguro, vino a Sofala un capitán llamado Vasco
Gómez de Abreo con cuatro naos de armada. E notificó a Nuño
Vaz su poder que del rey don Manuel traía, de que por los otros
capitanes [[biii]ᵛ] de su compañía fue informado. E fuele
entregada la fortaleza e capitanía de Sofala un domingo después
de oir misa en fin de septiembre, según lo cuenta Figueroa que
ahí estaba. El cual buenos caballeros e capitanes en sus naos e
compañía traía. E mandó apregonar: so pena de muerte toda la
gente que con Pedro de Añaya había ido saliese dentro de tres
días de la fortaleza e que nadie les comprase los esclavos de
Sofala. Esto fue tenido a mucho mal, aunque la partida tenían
por buena. Pero de ningún hombre de malos pensamientos e
enemigo de virtud e de los que la gloria primero merecieron
puede hacer obra virtuosa. E así salieron de Sofala e embarcaron
con Diego de Melo, capitán, e Nuño Vaz Pereira para la India.

them a good welcome. He and Nuno Vaz spoke through the intercession of six interpreters, for their words passed through six languages before being understood. Thenceforth they remained good friends. In order to please Mokondi, for through his lands had to pass the merchants bringing gold to Sofala, the Captain gave gifts to the son, which they greatly appreciated. He went off to his kingdom very satisfied and much obliged to the Christians.

Title XVIII. *How the Christians' fort at Sofala was handed over to Vasco Gomes de Abreu* *by Nuno Vaz Pereira.*

Since in prosperity one never lacks for company, nor for someone to accept what has already been secured, no sooner had they finished their hastily built stone fort than a captain named Vasco Gomes de Abreu sailed into Sofala with a fleet of four ships. He had Nuno Vaz notified and informed of his warrant from King Manuel by the other captains of his company. The fort and captaincy of Sofala were handed over after Mass one Sunday toward the end of September,* according to Figueroa who was there. He brought many good knights and captains in his ships. He proclaimed that under pain of death all who had come out with Pedro de Añaya were to leave the fort within three days, and no one was to purchase their Sofalese slaves. This they considered an evil deed, although they were glad enough to leave. But no man can do virtuous deeds when he is an enemy of virtue and of the men who first earned the glory. And so they left Sofala and embarked with Captain Diogo de Melo* and Nuno Vaz Pereira for India.

Título XIX. *Como Nuño Vaz Pereira e los que con él embarcaron llegaron a Mozambique, ciento e veinte* leguas de Sofala.*

Después que embarcaron en las naos de Diego de Melo, hobieron recio e contrario viaje por las corrientes de la mar e tardaron de Sofala a Mozambique cuarenta e cinco días, en ciento e veinte leguas de camino o viaje, do invernaron aquel año. Los habitadores de Mozambique son moros cáferes, mercaderes ricos, su lengua más clara que algarabía. No tienen trigo sino arroz e mijo, de que hacen pan; gallinas, cabras, vacas e carneros asaz. Aquí fueron bien recibidos del alcaide que ahí estaba, cristiano. E aquel año edificaron allí una fortaleza de piedra los capitanes e alcaide como la que dejaron en Sofala.

Título XX. *Como vino un bergantín con nueva que Vasco Gómez que quedó en Sofala era perdido por la mar con cuatro naos.*

No quiso Dios que Vasco Gómez que tan furioso entró en Sofala gozase del sudor e trabajo de los que hizo salir de ella. E según contó al alcaide de Mozambique un bergantín que en el puerto entró sin regocijo de tiros de pólvora como se suele hacer, Vasco Gó- [biv^r] mez era perdido en la mar. El cual había partido de Sofala víspera de navidad con cuatro naos e con la más de la gente que en Sofala quedara. E venía a Mozambique e de allí a Sant Lorenzo, que es una isla, a descubrir clavo. E como en una isla, de Engox, se quedaron diez e siete cristianos

* cxc.

Title XIX. *How Nuno Vaz Pereira and his traveling companions reached Mozambique, one hundred and twenty leagues from Sofala.*

After embarking in Diogo de Melo's ships, they had an arduous and adverse voyage on account of the currents, and it took them forty-five days to travel the distance of one hundred and twenty leagues from Sofala to Mozambique, where they wintered that year.* The inhabitants of Mozambique are Kaffir Moors, rich merchants, their language* clearer than Arabic. They have no wheat, but rice and millet, from which they make bread, as well as chickens, goats, cattle, and many sheep. They received a good welcome from the mayor there, a Christian, and that year the captains and the mayor built a stone fort like the one they left behind at Sofala.

Title XX. *How a brigantine came in with the news that Vasco Gomes who had taken over at Sofala had been lost at sea with four ships.*

God did not want Vasco Gomes, who had so furiously entered Sofala, to enjoy the fruits of the sweat and toil of those he had forced to leave. For, according to the account given the mayor of Mozambique by a brigantine that entered port without firing the customary salutes, Vasco Gomes was lost at sea.* He had set out from Sofala on Christmas Eve, with four ships and most of the people who had remained at Sofala. He was bound for Mozambique and from there to São Lourenço,* which is an island, in search of cloves. On the island of An-

de la compañía de Vasco Gómez, que había allí salido por mantenimientos. E de la forma que había sido anegado, en lo cual hobieron bien entendido no haber placido a Dios la manera que tovo en la entrada de aquella tierra.

Título XXI. *Como Tristán de Acuña aportó en Mozambique con siete naos de especiería.*

Tristán de Acuña, que había de venir por bisrey si no cegara, sanó de su vista. Después de navidad llegó a Mozambique con siete naos que ya traía cargadas de especiería, donde él con su gente fue bien recibido. E el capitán Tristán de Acuña contó nuevas de su viaje como adelante largamente oiréis.

Título XXII. *Del razonamiento que hizo de las nuevas cosas e maravillosas que al bisrey e a él avinieran.*

Después de bien recibido, Tristán de Acuña les hizo un cortés razonamiento e principió a contar las nuevas que muy deseosos estaban oir. En las cuales decía Cananor haber estado cercado por los enemigos e él con su gente llegó e se descercara. E lo que más hacía al propósito era que don Francisco había tomado a Quiloam e a Mombasa; saliendo del puerto de Mombasa que tardaron ocho días. E fueron a Melinde e a Santa Helena, do tomaron agua fresca, e es cinco leguas de Melinde. E de allí yendo para la India, atravesaron el golfo de Meca, en que hay setecientas leguas. E llegaron a una tierra que se decía Angediva, en India, isla pequeña, do hizo su gente un castillo

goche[*] there were seventeen Christians from Vasco Gomes' company; they had gone ashore there for provisions. From the manner of his drowning they understood full well that he had not pleased the Lord with his way of taking over that land.

Title XXI. *How Tristão da Cunha arrived at Mozambique*[*] *with seven spice ships.*

Tristão da Cunha, who was to have come out as viceroy had he not lost his sight, later regained it. He came to Mozambique after Christmas with seven spice-laden ships. After Captain Tristão da Cunha and his men had been welcomed, he gave an account of his voyage, as you shall now hear at length.

Title XXII.[*] *About the report he gave of the amazing and remarkable things that had befallen him and the Viceroy.*

After being welcomed, Tristão da Cunha addressed them courteously and began to recount the events they were all very anxious to hear about. Among other things, he reported that Cannanore had been besieged[*] by the enemy and that when he and his men arrived, the siege was lifted. More apropos, however, was his news that Dom Francisco had seized Kilwa and Mombasa,[*] and that it had taken them eight days to get out of the Mombasa harbor. They went to Malindi and Saint Helena,[*] five leagues beyond Malindi, for fresh water. Heading toward India, they crossed the Gulf of Mecca, a distance of seven hundred leagues. They reached a place called Angedive,[*] a small island in India. There his men built a castle and a

e una galera, en que tardaron un mes; en el cual quedó Manuel Pazaña capitán. E luego el bisrey se partió e aportó ante el río de Onor, que es del rey [[biv]ᵛ] de Garsapa, vasallo del rey de Narsinga. E su gente puso fuego a veinte casas e más, e queriéndose recoger a las naos, comenzaron a tirar flecheros, los cuales hirieron [a] algunos de los cristianos e a don Francisco en un pie. E sabido por el rey de Garsapa, vino con don Francisco en toda concordia e amistad. El rey de Narsinga es de los mayores señores que hay en la India e tiene sesenta reyes vasallos grandes. Que en su hostal hay más de mil e quinientos caballos; cualquier rocín vale sesenta ducados e si es bueno trescientos o cuatrocientos. E don Francisco partió de allí para Cananor, donde llegó a veinte e dos de otubre. Luego otro día se vio con el rey de Cananor e confirmaron sus paces. Do mandó so color de casa llana hacer un castillo el bisrey, e quedó Lorenzo de Brito por capitán [con] un navío, nao grande e una galera. E el bisrey se partió para el puerto de Cochín, do vino nueva como en Coulán mataran los judíos a Antonio de Sá e cuanta gente con él estaba. De que don Francisco hobo gran pesar, e envió luego sobre ellos a don Lorenzo su hijo con siete naos. E llegaron al puerto, que es veinte e cuatro leguas de Cochín e quemaron veinte e siete naos de moros con grande riqueza de especiería, e así volvió vitorioso a su padre don Francisco. En el cual tiempo el rey de Calicut hizo armada de ochenta naos gruesas, ciento e veinte más pequeñas e cient bateles que ellos llaman *paraos*. E a los doce días de marzo de 1506, ante Cananor se encontraron las armadas del rey de Portugal e del rey de Calicut, en que venían diez mil moros juramentados. E llámase el rey Zamorín. En el

galley, which took them a month, and Manuel Paçanha[*] was stationed there as captain. The Viceroy then moved on and anchored outside the river at Onor,[*] which belongs to the King of Gersoppa, a vassal of the King of Narsinga.[*] His men set fire to more than twenty buildings, and, as they were making their way back to the ships, bowmen began firing at them. They wounded several Christians and hit Dom Francisco in the foot. As soon as the King of Gersoppa heard of this, he betook himself to Dom Francisco, and they concluded a fully amicable agreement. The King of Narsinga is one of the most powerful lords in India. He has sixty great kings as vassals. In his stable there are more than fifteen hundred horses.[*] Any nag is worth sixty ducats and a good horse three or four hundred. Dom Francisco left that place for Cannanore,[*] which he reached on the twenty-second of October. Next day he met with the King of Cannanore, and they confirmed their peace treaty. Under the guise of an ordinary building the Viceroy had a castle built. Lourenço de Brito[*] was placed there as captain with one large ship, a smaller one, and a galley. The Viceroy set out for the port of Cochin, where he received word that in Quilon the Jews had murdered Antonio de Sá and all the men with him.[*] Deeply grieved, Dom Francisco immediately sent his son Dom Lourenço[*] after them with seven ships. They reached this port, twenty-four leagues from Cochin, and burned twenty-seven Moorish ships[*] and their rich spice cargoes, and thus Dom Lourenço returned victoriously to his father. It was then that the King of Calicut assembled an armada[*] of eighty heavy ships, one hundred and twenty smaller ones, and one hundred longboats which they call *paraos.*[*] On the twelfth of March 1506, the fleets of the King of Portugal and the King of Calicut clashed off Cannanore. The King, called Zamorin, came with

cual encuentro don Lorenzo mostró mucho ser industrioso e esforzado, que aferró cinco naos e las sorbió la mar, de las de los moros. E desbarataron e vencieron todas las otras, que huyeron. E con esta grande vitoria se volvió don Lorenzo para el bisrey su padre que estaba en Cochín. De quien fue con grandes fiestas recibido, e del rey de Cochín, que es enemigo de el de Calicut e amigo de don Manuel, rey de Portugal, rico e poderoso príncipe. Del cual [[bv]ʳ] encuentro quedó muy hostigado el rey de Calicut e envió a demandar paces, las cuales el bisrey no quiso hacer por aplacer al rey de Cochín su amigo. E pasado el invierno, a ocho días del mes de agosto, adelante don Lorenzo, hijo del bisrey, partió con siete naos a descubrir las islas del través de Cochín. E con tempestades recias e contrarios vientos fue aportar a Ceilán, isla de la canela, muy preciada de rubís, safiros e otras preciosas piedras. E tratóse paz con el rey de Ceilán e quedó el dicho rey por vasallo del rey de Portugal. E vino por un puerto del rey de Coulán, el cual quemó, e desbarató muchas naos e casas principales, matando e descabezando muchas gentes, así moros como gentiles. Partióse para Cochín, adonde llegó doce días de noviembre. E después en marzo vinieron sobre Cananor ciento e ochenta mil moros de todo el Malabar de la India. E uno de los combates que hobieron fue día de Santiago, entre los moros e Lorenzo de Brito (con gente de dos naos gruesas que el bisrey le envió). Fueron los cristianos vencedores e mataron cuatrocientos indios. E hecha paz, contaron un grande miraglo: que andaba entre los cristianos señor Santiago anciano, con la barba larga e una porra de madera en

ten thousand Moors sworn to die in battle against Christians. In this encounter Dom Lourenço amply demonstrated his industry and courage.* He grappled with five Moorish ships and sent them to the bottom. They routed and defeated the rest, which ran away. With this fine victory Dom Lourenço headed back for Cochin and his father the viceroy, by whom he was greeted with huge celebrations,* and also by the King of Cochin, who is an enemy of the King of Calicut and friend of Dom Manuel the King of Portugal, a rich and powerful prince. The King of Calicut had been soundly thrashed in this encounter, and he sent word requesting peace, but the Viceroy refused, in order to please the King of Cochin, his friend. When winter had passed, on the eighth day of August, Dom Lourenço the son of the Viceroy led out seven ships to explore the islands off Cochin.* Fierce tempests and contrary winds carried him to port at Ceylon,* a cinnamon island highly esteemed for its rubies, sapphires, and other precious stones. He signed a peace treaty with the King of Ceylon, and the said king became a vassal of the King of Portugal. He came upon a port belonging to the King of Quilon, and he burned it and razed many ships and important buildings, killing and beheading many, Moors as well as pagans. He set out for Cochin, arriving on the twelfth day of November. Later, in March, one hundred and eighty thousand Moors from the entire Malabar coast of India descended upon Cannanore.* One of the battles between the Moors and Lourenço de Brito, supported by men from two heavy ships the Viceroy had sent him, took place on the Feast Day of Saint James. The Christians were victorious and killed four hundred Indians. After peace had been made, they told of a great miracle:* Saint James the Greater had been present among the Christians, with a long beard and a wooden club

la mano. Al cual los cristianos no veían e los moros más de él que de otro se quejaban, por quien preguntaban e no hallaban nuevas en Cananor. E se había vuelto Tristán de Acuña a Cochín, que había venido ayudar al de Brito, e llegaron. Fueron todos con el bisrey a quemar unas naos que estaban en Panán, puerto principal de Calicut. E quemaron veinte naos de moros que estaban para ir a Meca. Tomaron diez e siete bombardas gruesas sin morir, aunque herida, gente cristiana. E el bisrey se volvió a Cananor; su hijo don Lorenzo fue a correr la costa, e Tristán de Acuña se había partido primero día de deciembre, como habéis oído.

Título XXIII. *Como Tristán de Acuña se partió.*

[[bv]ᵛ] A cabo de doce días que hobo tomado algún refresco e holgado con la gente española, proveído de mantenimientos, despedido otrosí muy cortésmente, Tristán de Acuña se partió para el reino de Portugal. E determinaron de se ir de allí a su ventura próspera o adversa Diego de Melo e Martín Coello, capitanes, para la India o en busca de Alfonso de Alburquerque, que mucho loaban, e estaba en el estrecho de Meca con seis naos e seiscientos hombres en ellas para vedar el paso de la India a Babilonia. E tomaron una tierra que se nombra Quiloa, la que el bisrey hobiera ante ganado. En la cual isla hay Songo, que es una villa cercada, a dos leguas de Quiloam Songosongo, a seis leguas Manfia, tierra viciosa e fresca. A quince leguas contra el norte de la isla están Tomagunda, tierra de granadas, e Calebejar, que es reino; quince leguas de la isla hacia el norte una gran ciudad que se dice Zenguibar, isla muy fértil e abun-

in his hand. The Christians had not seen him, but the Moors complained about him more than anyone else. They inquired about him in Cannanore but could find out nothing. Tristão da Cunha, after helping Brito, returned with him to Cochin. From there they all went with the Viceroy to burn some ships at Ponnani,❋ an important port belonging to Calicut. They burned twenty Moorish ships that were about to leave for Mecca. They took seventeen heavy mortars, with no Christians killed, though some were wounded. The Viceroy returned to Cannanore; his son Dom Lourenço set out to make raids along the coast; and Tristão da Cunha departed on the first of December, as you have heard.

Title XXIII. *How Tristão da Cunha departed.*

At the end of twelve days, during which he had found rest, refreshment, and provisions among his Hispanic brethren, Tristão da Cunha received a fond farewell and set out for the kingdom of Portugal. Captains Diogo de Melo and Martim Coelho❋ decided to go and seek their fortune, be it prosperous or adverse, either in India or with Afonso de Albuquerque, whom they praised highly. He was at the Strait of Mecca with six ships and six hundred men, blocking the passage from India to Babylon.❋ They went to a land called Kilwa, which the Viceroy had originally seized. On this island is Songo,❋ an enclosed city; two leagues from Kilwa lies Songo Songo;❋ six leagues away is Mafia,❋ a fresh and verdant land. Fifteen leagues to the north of the island lie Tomagunda,❋ a land of pomegranates, and Kwale,❋ which is a kingdom. Fifteen leagues from the island toward the north is a great city called

dosa, de buen puerto e mantenimientos, donde hay los mejores limones e naranjas que haya en cualquiera parte. Acerca de ella hay otra isla muy viciosa e en todas estas hay paz. En derecho de las dos islas está una tierra firme llamada Otando desde la cual empieza el reino de Mombasa. Del puerto de Quiloa se partieron después que siete o ocho días holgaron con Pedro de Herrera, capitán de la fortaleza. E fuéronse para Melinde, do la gente de aquella tierra hace estrecha vida. Llámanse buzarates, muy retraídos e ajenos de conversación. Muchos de ellos no comen cosa mortal, quiero decir, que reciba muerte e que tenga sangre. Llámanse por otro nombre brámenes. En aquella isla bien recibidos fueron los cristianos. E de ahí a doce días aportó una nao a Melinde de Alonso de Alburquerque, en la cual venía por capitán Francisco de Tabora. E desembarcando, fue a hacer sabidores los cristianos de las cosas que a Alon- [[bvi]^r] so de Alburquerque acaecieron en la toma de una ciudad que se llamaba Barava, e en otra isla de Sacatora como había tomado el castillo de Fortaque a los moros, e que quedaba en el cabo de Guardafuni.

Título XXIV. *En que se recuentan las vitorias de Alfonso de Alburquerque, capitán del estrecho de Meca.*

Dijo Diego de Tabora como bien sabían haber ido Alonso de Alburquerque por capitán mayor de seis naos para el estrecho de Meca. E les hacía saber haber llegado a una ciudad que está en tierra firme, Brava nombrada. E la entraron por fuerza de armas, matando muchos moros e robando grandes riquezas, las cuales sus dueños no quisieron salvar pensándolo defender, ni sus mujeres que allí quedaron muy ricas e apuestas con siete e

Zanzibar,✳ a very fertile and luxurious isle which has a good port and good supplies and produces the best lemons and oranges to be had anywhere. Nearby is another very verdant island,✳ and in all these lands there is peace. Opposite the two islands is a mainland called Tanga,✳ where the kingdom of Mombasa begins. They left Kilwa after resting for seven or eight days with Pero Ferreira, the captain of the fort. They went to Malindi, where the people lead a frugal life. Called Gujarati,✳ they are very withdrawn and sparing of conversation. Many of them will eat no living thing; by that I mean anything that must be killed and has blood. By another name they are known as Brahmans. On that island the Christians received a good welcome. Twelve days later one of Afonso de Albuquerque's ships, captained by Francisco de Tabora,✳ put in at Malindi. After landing, he proceeded to inform the Christians about what had happened to Afonso de Albuquerque in the seizure of a city called Brava, and on the island of Socotra✳ how he had seized the Fartak castle from the Moors, and how he was at Cape Guardafui.

Title XXIV. *In which are related the victories of Afonso de Albuquerque, Captain of the Strait of Mecca.*

Diogo de Tabora said that, as they well knew, Afonso de Albuquerque had set out for the Strait of Mecca as captain major of six ships. He then informed them of his arrival at a city on the mainland called Brava.✳ The Portuguese entered it by force of arms, killed many Moors, and carried off great riches which their owners had not thought to save, thinking they could defend the city. Nor could they save their women,

ocho manillas a cada brazo e otras tantas a las piernas, muy gruesas e preciosas. Lo cual fue ocasión de mucha crueldad porque la gente, ciega de la avaricia más que alumbrada de misericordia, por no se detener poco espacio les cortaban los brazos e piernas e orejas en que traían joyeles sin memoria de piedad. Esto no lo hiciera la gente de bien, sólo por ser mujeres arcas de generación e ser de blandas e delicadas carnes e molles condición. ¡Quién no se moviera a piedad contemplando la hermosura que en ellas era! ¡A quién no se le cayera la espada de la mano ante que ensangrentarla en mujer! Dignos son los crueles vitoriosos en la tal crueldad de ser reprehendidos, pero bien se cree que los que tal obraron no serían de los mejores ni medianos. Andaban todas llorando por las calles bañadas en sangre, e otras con los niños en los brazos huyendo sin hallar guarida. Algunas [[bvi]ᵛ] e hartas de ellas defendían e amparaban los virtuosos que ahí se hallaron. La cual ciudad fue mandada abrasar e así se hizo. E fueron sobre otra ciudad que se dice Magadaxo, que estaba acerca. En la cual, puesto que los enemigos temerosos fuesen, la ferocidad de los vientos e contrariedades hizo a los cristianos no esperar o combatirla; e así el tiempo contrario estorbó su bueno e deseado propósito. De donde partidos, llegaron a Sacatora, cuya gente es tenida entre sí por cristiana. Ayunan las cuaresmas e avientos sin comer carne ni pescado. Tienen iglesias e altares, cruces en ellas, e la mayor parte de las fiestas principales e así de los apóstolos,* e se nombran por sus nombres. Hacen limosnas; oyen todos los días matines, vísperas e completas. Tienen en tanta veneración la cruz que el [que] consigo la trae no teme daño de enemigo ni de justicia,

* apóstolos

very rich and handsome with seven and eight bracelets on
each arm, and just as many, thick and valuable, on their legs.
This occasioned severe cruelty,❊ for the men, blinded by
avarice rather than enlightened by mercy, so as not to lose a
moment's time, cut off the arms, the legs, and the ears which
bore that jewelry, without a trace of pity. Good men would
never do such a thing, if only because women are "vessels of
generation" and of tender, delicate flesh and gentle condition.
What man would not have been moved to pity contemplating
their beauty! What man would not have cast down his sword
before bloodying it on a woman! Worthy of reprimand are
such cruel victors and their cruel deeds, but you may be sure
that the ones who did such foul things were not the ordinary
nor the best of the men. The women all ran crying through the
streets, covered with blood. Some went fleeing with children in
their arms but could find no haven. Quite a few of them were
defended and sheltered by the virtuous men who were there.
The city was finally ordered burned, which was done, whereupon they set out for another city, Mogadishu,❊ which was
nearby. There, although the enemy was sore afraid, the ferocity
of contrary winds kept the Christians from waiting and attacking, and thus hostile weather frustrated their good and
worthy goal. They left that place and went to Socotra,❊ whose
inhabitants consider themselves Christians. They fast during
Lent and Advent, eating neither meat nor fish. They have
churches and altars with crosses on them. They observe most
of the principal feast days, as well as those of the Apostles,
whose names they take. They give alms. Every day they hear
Matins, Vespers, and Compline. They hold the Cross in such

según la carta que del rey de Portugal en su lengua hobe a mis manos largamente recuenta (aunque en ella da la honra a Tristán de Acuña). Esta tierra está bien cercada de agua. Ancoraron acerca el castillo, e como conocieron que eran portugueses sacaron bombardas e pusiéronse en gran defensión, no queriendo paces ni aún dejar proveerse de agua de Sacatora. E allí mataron los cristianos un capitán Sacatorí. La batalla fue muy cruda e en ella se mostró costante e esforzado un capitán cuyo nombre era Leonel Coutiño, e mucho a los del castillo apresuraba con fieros golpes que de su mano hacía; e los moros desamparando el muro e él poniendo escalas, así que los cristianos que primero entraron abrieron la puerta del castillo e entró la gente cristiana e tomaron la fortaleza. Do ningún moro escapó, porque ante quisieron morir que rendirse ni quedar con la vida perdiendo su patrimonio. E luego los vencedores aseguraron la tierra. Aquella gente era de Fortaque, tierra de Arabia, aunque vencida, muriendo esforzada. E pasado el invierno, [[bvii]ʳ] fueron los españoles sobre la ciudad de Hormuz con el capitán Alonso de Alburquerque, de generación castellano. La conquistaron e ganaron. Los moros se levantaron contra los cristianos e fueron otra vuelta a Sacatora e de allí al cabo de Guardafuni, esperando las naos infieles. E de ahí Alonso de Alburquerque envió a Diego de Tabora a tierra de Melinde por mantenimientos. A cuyo ruego los dichos capitanes Diego de Melo e Nuño Vaz e los que con ellos andaban afilando sus espadas en las moriscas gentes se fueron al cabo de Guardafuni para el próspero capitán mayor.

veneration that he who wears it goes about without fear of harm from the enemy or the authorities. So states at length the King Manuel letter written in Portuguese that I had at hand (although it gives the honor to Tristão da Cunha).⁕ This land is completely surrounded by water. They anchored opposite the castle, and as soon as it was realized that they were Portuguese, mortars were hauled out and a stout defense made ready. They did not want peace or even to let the Portuguese take on Socotran water. There the Christians killed a Socotran captain. The battle was very rough, and a captain named Leonel Coutinho⁕ proved himself unflinchingly courageous. With the fierce blows he dealt them, he sorely pressed the castle defenders. As he drove the Moors back from the walls, he put up scaling ladders. Thus, the first Christians who succeeded in entering opened the castle gates, and the Christians entered and captured the fort. No Moor survived, because, rather than surrender and live without their patrimony, they chose to die. Then the conquerors consolidated the land. Although these people, who come from Fartak⁕ in the land of Arabia, were defeated, they died courageously. When winter passed,⁕ the men of Hispania attacked the city of Hormuz under the orders of Captain Afonso de Albuquerque (who is of Castilian ancestry).⁕ They conquered and took possession of it. The Moors rose up against the Christians, so they went to Socotra again and from there to Cape Guardafui to lie in wait for infidel ships. From there Afonso de Albuquerque dispatched Diogo de Tabora to the land of Malindi for supplies. At the latter's request, the said captains Diogo de Melo and Nuno Vaz and their companions (who were busy honing their swords against the Moorish breed) set out for Cape Guardafui and the prosperous Captain Major.

Título XXV. *Del viaje que los capitanes hicieron para Alfonso de Alburquerque.*

Caminando su viaje, los dichos capitanes llegaron a Magadaxo, de que ya hablamos, e vieron una nao de moros, que a tierra enderezaban. E cuando a ella llegaron, la gente fuera vieron que estaba, e pusieron fuego con cuanta riqueza dentro tenía a sus mercancías. Sin parar, hicieron viaje para Alfonso de Alburquerque, de quien fueron honorablemente recibidos. El cabo de Guardafuni llámase cabo porque allí la costa del mar fenece. E hay allí otro cabo que se dice Fortaque, entre los cuales entra el mar que llaman estrecho de Meca. Llámase Arabia *Felix* por una población que allí *Felix* se nombra. Es tierra doliente, el aire cálido. Sus habitadores son alárabes, criadores de ganados. La agua dulce está lejos, que traen a vender en cueros. De allí se fueron a Sacatora a tener el invierno.

Título XXVI. *De las cosas que Figueroa cuenta de la isla Sacatora, en que estovo cuatro meses.*

Estuvieron los capitanes, con los cuales estaba Martín Fernández de Figueroa, todo el invierno (que allá es desde el mes de abril hasta mediado agosto) en la isla de Sacatora. En la cual hay [[bvii]ᵛ] hombres bien dispuestos. Estas iglesias no tienen santos ni santas, excepto cruces como de la orden de la Trinidad. E su clérigo se llama *cacis*. Tañen a misa con tablas. En la iglesia los varones entran por* una puerta e las mujeres por otra, sin quebrantar el tal uso. Las cruces untan con man-

* po

Title XXV. *About the voyage the captains made en route to Afonso de Albuquerque.*

During their voyage, the above-mentioned captains came upon Mogadishu, of which we have already spoken. They sighted a Moorish ship and drove it ashore. When they reached it, they saw that everyone was gone, so they set it afire along with its entire rich cargo. Without stopping, they journeyed to Afonso de Albuquerque, by whom they were honorably welcomed.✠ Cape Guardafui is called a cape because there the seacoast comes to an end. There is another cape there, called Fartak, and between these two enters the sea they call the Strait of Mecca. Arabia *Felix*✠ is so called because of a large settlement there named *Felix*. It is a wretched land; the airs are torrid. Its inhabitants are Arabs, cattle-raisers. Fresh water is far away and is brought there in leather gourds to be sold. From there they went to Socotra to spend the winter.

Title XXVI. *About the things Figueroa tells concerning the island of Socotra, where he spent four months.*

The captains, and Martín Fernández de Figueroa with them, spent the entire winter (which out there runs from the month of April through the middle of August) on the island of Socotra. On this island one finds good-natured men.✠ These churches do not have statues of men or women saints, only crosses like that of the Trinitarian Order.✠ Their priest is called *cacis*. They sound for Mass with wooden tablets. The men enter church by one door and the women by another, and

teca en las solemnidades. Las mujeres aman mucho a la gente cristiana española. Saben algunos arábigo; tienen lengua propria. Los hombres andan desnudos excepto las partes vergonzosas. Las mujeres traen camisas moriscas, los cabellos largos, esparcidos por las espaldas. Las mujeres son comunes, que es una abominable costumbre. Así que el marido vos convidará que durmáis con su mujer e el padre e la madre con sus hijas. Es gente libidinosa. En aquella tierra muy pocas veces llueve excepto rocío. No nace en ella trigo, arroz, mijo, ni cebada. Hay mucho ganado e palmares. Do cuesta un cántaro de vino mil e seiscientos maravedís, una aguja veinte maravedís, e así otras muchas cosas necesarias.

Título XXVII. *De como se conquistó Hormuz e las condiciones de sus gentes.*

Un caballero de la compañía del capitán mayor Alonso de Alburquerque contó fidelísimamente a los capitanes de la otra costa la conquista de Hormuz, que Figueroa escribió en un libro de las cosas que allá había, con lo cual concordaba la letra del rey don Manuel portuguesa. E dijo como después que la fortaleza tomaron a los fortaquines, que a manera de suizos o soldados pelean, la cual dejado habían proveída de gente, yendo a buscar mantenimientos, fueron guiados por la mar a la parte de Arabia e fueron a Calayate, ciudad rica de puerto, de que el capitán mayor holgó, por se hallar en tierra de [[bviii]ʳ] buenos mantenimientos. Do tomaron puerto, aunque dificultoso, por estar apoderado de hermosas naos e la tierra de más bellos

this practice never varies. On solemn occasions they anoint the
cross with lard. The women dearly love the Christians of
Hispania. Some of these people know Arabic, but they have
their own language. The men go about naked except for their
shameful parts. The women wear Moorish tunics; they wear
their hair long and comb it down their backs. Women are held
in common, which is an abominable custom. Thus the husband
will invite you to sleep with his wife, and fathers and mothers
with their daughters. They are a libidinous people. In that land
it rarely rains except for the dew. No wheat grows there, nor
rice, millet, nor barley. There are lots of cattle and palm
groves. A pitcher of wine there costs sixteen hundred maravedis,
a needle twenty maravedis, and similar prices must be paid for
many other necessary things.

Title XXVII. *About the capture of Hormuz and the ways of
its inhabitants.*

A knight from Captain Major Afonso de Albuquerque's
company scrupulously related to the captains of the other coast❋
the conquest of Hormuz; and what Figueroa wrote in his book
about the things that took place there coincided with King
Manuel's Portuguese letter. He told how, after they had seized
the fort from the Fartaks, who fight like Swiss mercenaries,❋
they left it strongly garrisoned and set out in search of provisions.❋ Sailing along the Arabian coast, they came to Kalhat,❋
a rich port city, and the Captain Major was delighted to have
come upon a land of good supplies. They entered the harbor,
although with difficulty, for it was occupied by many handsome ships and ringed by elegant buildings along the shore.

edificios. Donde gran ruído con la artillería hicieron por los
atemorizar, e tomaron mantenimientos de que los moros proveyeron; e no les hizo daño el capitán porque les había dado
seguro e en señal un anillo suyo. Calayate, que fue después
cuando Hormuz se levantó destruída, era más poblada fuera
que dentro. Alonso de Alburquerque se partió otro día e llegaron
a un puerto nombrado Curiate, que es otrosí del rey de Hormuz.
Es una población en la ribera muy rica, bien guarnecida de
bombardas. A la cual el capitán mayor rogó les dejasen tomar
mantenimientos, de que los moros no se hicieron caso. E otro
día Alonso de Alburquerque apercibió su gente e capitanes de
reguarda e dioles batalla. Destruyólos, e los moros huyendo, los
cristianos matando, fueron las naos bien proveídas de riquezas e
mantenimientos que en tierra hallaron, conviene saber: abundancia de trigo, harina, arroz, dátiles, pescado, manteca e miel.
Donde reposaron tres días. En todo el dicho recuentro o lid no
mataron de la gente de los cristianos excepto un negro del
capitán mayor que se había desmandado. La cual vitoria habida,
entraron sus naos, quemaron e abrasaron la mezquita, tierra
e navíos, que nada quedó. E fueron por la mar adelante a
Mascate, que es del rey de Hormuz, mayor que Curiate, cuyo
puerto era muy bueno e bien apercibido a defenderse. Pero
como los moros con seguro se vieron con el capitán mayor, el
cual asaz temor e espanto les puso, hicieron lo que les mandó
e quedaron por vasallos del rey de Portugal. Donde los cristianos
hobieron muy frescas e ricas provisiones, pero ante pelearon con
ellos bravamente e fue la batalla cruel porque los moros que-
brantaron la paz que prometieron, [[bviii]ᵛ] la ciudad puesta
a sacomano, el regidor de ella muerto e un capitán cristiano
herido, la ciudad, naos e riquezas de ella abrasadas e
vueltas ceniza. Con la cual vitoria se recogieron a las naos,

They gave a thunderous artillery display to frighten the inhabitants. They took the supplies the Moors provided, and the Captain did not harm them, because he had given them a guarantee
and one of his rings as token thereof. Kalhat, later destroyed
when Hormuz revolted, was more populated outside the city
than within. Afonso de Albuquerque departed next day, and
they went to a port named Quryat,✳ which also belongs to the
King of Hormuz. It is a very wealthy town located at the
water's edge, well stocked with mortars. The Captain Major
requested provisions, but the Moors paid no attention. So next
day Afonso de Albuquerque organized his men and the captains of the rear guard and commenced the attack. He destroyed
the enemy, and, with Moors fleeing and Christians killing, the
ships were well stocked with the riches and supplies they found
ashore, namely an abundance of wheat, flour, rice, dates, fish,
lard, and honey. They rested there for three days. In all this
said encounter or battle no Christian was killed, only one of
the Captain Major's Negroes who had strayed off. After this
victory, they boarded their ships. They had burned and razed
the mosque, the land, and the ships; nothing remained. They
sailed forth to Masqat,✳ which belongs to the King of Hormuz.
Larger than Kalhat, it had a good port and stout defenses.
However, the Moors met with the Captain Major (who truly
awed and terrified them) under a flag of truce, whereupon they
did as he directed and became vassals of the King of Portugal.
There the Christians secured very fresh and rich provisions,
but first they had to fight a fierce and cruel battle, for the Moors
broke their promise of peace. The city was sacked, the ruler
killed, and one Christian captain wounded. The city, its ships and
riches were burned and reduced to ashes. With this victory they
returned to the ships; the battle had taken place on a Sunday

domingo, de mañana, tres horas de batalla. E de allí embarcaron e fueron Alfonso de Alburquerque e su gente costa a costa a un lugar que se decía Sohar, do estaba fortaleza, capitán e gente de guarnición por el rey de Hormuz. E vistas las naos de los cristianos, con el temor que hobieron el capitán e su gente, los moros e Sohar se hicieron vasallos del rey don Manuel de Portugal; e hicieron grandes fiestas, quedando la bandera de las quinas en la fortaleza, diciendo moros e cristianos: "¡Portugal e España!"

Título XXVIII. *Como llegaron a Orfacán los cristianos e qué les sucedió.*

Alegres con las pasadas hazañas, ensangrentados los cristianos en aquella canina e perra gente que no osaba esperar, partidos de Sohar para Orfacán, que es muy más rica e poderosa, aportaron sin contradición (por las guerras comarcanas ya todos los moros absentes de ella), a la cual pusieron fuego. Yendo en el alcance a los moros, sacados los ganados e agua que robaron, e desque se proveyeron, e abrasada toda, caminaron al reino de Hormuz do aportaron.

Título XXIX. *De la ciudad de Hormuz, como viven sus pobladores e su grandeza.*

Hormuz es una nombrada e populosa ciudad de grandes gentes e trato, la cual tiene su asiento en la boca del mar de Persia en la costa de Arabia. E es isla estéril de mantenimientos,

morning and lasted three hours. From there Afonso de Albuquerque and his men moved along the coast to a town called
Suhar,✽ where there was a fort garrisoned by a captain and men
of the King of Hormuz. As soon as they saw the Christian ships,
the captain and his men were terrified, so Suhar and its Moors
became vassals of King Manuel of Portugal. Great celebrations
were held, and the Portuguese banner was raised over the fort,
with Moors and Christians shouting: "Portugal and Spain!"

Title XXVIII. *About what happened when the Christians
reached Khor Fakkan.*✽

Thrilled by their recent feats and steeped in the blood of
those mangy curs who had not dared to stay and face them,
the Christians left Suhar for Khor Fakkan, which is much
more rich and powerful, where they landed unopposed (on account of local wars the Moors were all away). Setting fire to
the city, they went out in search of the Moors, then carried off
cattle and water. As soon as they had taken provisions and
burned everything, they made their way to the kingdom of
Hormuz and entered the harbor.

Title XXIX. *About the city of Hormuz: how its inhabitants
live and its magnificence.*

Hormuz is a renowned and populous city, a great trading
center for many peoples. It is situated at the mouth of the
Persian Sea off the Arabian coast.✽ It is a barren island, for

que agua dulce tiene poca; porque es sierra de sal e piedra sufre. Provéese de agua de otra cercana isla que Quéxumen se dice; la tierra firme de que se provee es Persia, do hay uvas, [c^r] melones e higos e otras cosas. Es cabeza de reino que tiene muchas ciudades, villas e lugares. Edificóse en tal lugar porque más fuerte fuese. E tiene dos puertos, de levante e poniente, muy buenos. Es cercada, sus edificios de piedra, altos. A la parte de la mar tiene un castillo do el rey se aposenta, en la otra parte sierras. En medio de ella está la mezquita, muy grande e hermosa, si más puede ser. Hay en la ciudad mercancías ricas de sedas, aljófar e piedras preciosas. El aljófar traen de la isla Baharén e allí lo pescan. Acerca de ahí hay un rey que se llama de Lara, que es reino suyo.

Título XXX. *Como fue conquistada Hormuz por Alonso de Alburquerque e la gente que llevaba cristiana.*

Llegados los capitanes cristianos al reino e ciudad de Hormuz, vieron estar en el puerto trescientas velas muy poderosas de moros que en aquella tierra trataban. E ellos iban con seis naves, su bandera puesta en la gavia, que ancoraron junto con las más gruesas naves. E mandó Alonso de Alburquerque al capitán de la nao del rey de Cambaya, que ya temeroso estaba, que con dos moros fuese a llevar una embajada a Cojatar, que era moro e gobernador, que el rey era mozo. La cual era que lo venía a sujetar al rey de Portugal su señor e que él era su capitán mayor. A lo cual respondió Cojatar que él era

there is little fresh water; it suffers because it is a series of hills composed of salt and stone. The water supply comes from another nearby island called Qeshm.※ The mainland from which it gets supplies is Persia, where there are grapes, melons, figs, and other things. It is the seat of a kingdom which possesses many cities, towns, and villages. It was built on that spot to be as fortified as possible. There are two very good harbors, one to the east and one to the west. It is an enclosed city, and the buildings are tall and made of stone. Facing the sea it has a castle where the king resides; in the other direction are hills. In the center of the city stands the mosque, huge and beautiful as can be. The city has rich stores of silk, pearls, and precious stones. The pearls come from the island of Bahrain,※ where they fish for them. Nearby there is a king called Larak,※ ruler of a kingdom of the same name.

Title XXX. *How Hormuz was conquered by Afonso de Albuquerque and his Christian company.*

When the Christian captains reached the kingdom and city of Hormuz, they saw in the harbor three hundred very powerful ships belonging to the Moors who traded in that land. They anchored their six ships, banners waving in the topsails, right next to the largest ships. Afonso de Albuquerque made the captain of the King of Cambay's ship,※ who was already terrified, go with two Moors and carry a message to Coje Atar,※ the Moor who governed, because the king was only a boy. The message said that he had come to place them under the rule of the King of Portugal his lord, and that he was his captain major. To which Coje Atar replied that he was the captain

su capitán mayor. A lo cual respondió Cojatar* que él le pro-
metía hacer toda honesta paz e concierto. No obstante eso, los
moros e sus naos e gentes con asaz armas vinieron a cercar a
Alonso de Alburquerque. E a los cristianos el remedio fue poner
fuego a la artillería española e tirar bombardas. E luego la mar
sorbió una grande nao de moros de un hijo del rey de Cambaya,
que a Cojatar favorecía, e infinidad de moros que fueron
muertos, al menos sin cuenta. E los que de ellos quedaron
huyeron con Cojatar, encallando sus naos, e otros a nado o como
posible les fue, que pare- [[c]ᵛ] cía la mar ir toda cubierta de
ellos rodando. Los navíos de moros fueron combatidos e en
breve señoreados de los cristianos. Bien se podría estonces llamar
el mar bermejo, que tal iba él con la sangre de los moros
muertos. Pero la causa porque así se dice es porque las arenas
son coloradas, que la agua es como la de los otros mares.
Fenecieron estonces más de tres mil moros e por espacio de tres
días se anduvieron así muertos holgando sobre la agua en las
mareas, que era placer de los ver danzar a son. Pero aún después
no los dejaban menear a su sabor, que con garfios agudos de
hierro los sacaban para ver si llevaban joyas ricas. Algunos
cristianos fueron heridos e con la vitoria e buena andanza
presto fueron ricos e sanos, que nunca por mejor empleadas
dieron llagas que aquellas. E el capitán mayor volvió a correr
la ribera muy osado como aquel a quien bien suele decir. E
quemó más de ciento e cincuenta naos, que era hermosa cosa
de ver, e los arrabales de la ciudad. Lo cual viendo los moros,
desampararon muchos a Hormuz, que un moro gran astrólogo
había dicho a Cojatar que en tal hora los cristianos allí habían

---

* There is a printer's error in the repetition of words here. Coje Atar
  may well have responded that he was his own captain major;
  Albuquerque did make a peace offer to the city.

major. Afonso de Albuquerque promised them an honest and
harmonious peace, but nevertheless the Moors set out with a
great number of men, ships, and arms to surround Afonso de
Albuquerque. The solution for the Christians was to fire the
artillery and mortars of Hispania. Right away the sea swallowed
up a large Moorish ship belonging to the King of Cambay's
son, who was supporting Coje Atar. An infinite number of
Moors were killed,※ so many that one lost count. Those
who survived drove their ships aground and ran away with
Coje Atar. Others tried swimming or whatever means possible:
the sea seemed to be covered with thrashing Moors. The Moorish warships were attacked and quickly captured by the Christians. One could certainly call it the Red Sea※ then, it was so
red with the blood of dead Moors. But the reason for this name
is that the sands are colored, for the water it just like that of
other seas. On that occasion more than three thousand Moors
perished. For three days they floated in and out with the tides,
and it was a pleasure to watch them dance about. But they were
not even to be permitted to bob about on their own: with sharp
hooks they were hauled out to see whether they were wearing
any valuable jewelry. Some Christians were wounded, but
victory and good fortune soon made them rich and healthy, for
they knew that no wounds had been as worthwhile as those.
The Captain Major continued his daring raids along the coast
in a manner befitting him.* He burned more than one hundred
and fifty ships, a beautiful sight, and set fire to the outskirts of
the city. Seeing this, many Moors abandoned Hormuz, for a
great Moorish astrologer※ had told Coje Atar that the Christians
were arriving at such a time that they would be able to do

---

* como aquel a quien bien suele decir. The Spanish is not altogether clear here.

llegado que habían de cumplir su voluntad; de como huían no fue sabidor Alonso de Alburquerque. E Cojatar envió a pedir misericordia e hacerse vasallo del rey de Portugal e dio grandes riquezas al capitán mayor. Lo cual fue concertado como el capitán quiso, sujetándolo cuanto ordenó; e la letra de paz fue escripta en papel con letras de oro, la lengua de Persia, e otra en arábigo cavada en tablas de oro, cada una metida en caja de plomo. El rey de Hormuz por quien* Cojatar gobernaba se decía Cefadín Abenadar.

Título XXXI. *De la solemnidad que con la bandera de Portugal se hizo.*

Bien aventurada se pudo decir la bandera de Portugal e el conde don Enrique de Costantinopla, padre de don Alonso Enríquez, primero rey de él, de quien son e han sido descendientes reyes e vitoriosos prín- [cii^r] cipes de Portugal. Quiero que sepáis el parentesco que los reyes de Portugal tienen con muchos caballeros de Salamanca cuyas señales son las de Aragón cruzadas del conde don Remón. Que descienden de dos hermanos e así de un padre: porque don Enrique de Costantinopla e don Remón de Tolosa (que reedificó a Salamanca, de quien vienen los Remones de bastones o varillas, padre del emperador don Alonso) e el papa Calisto, gran pontífice en la iglesia de Dios, fueron hermanos; e el conde don Remón de San Gil (tuerto de un ojo, de quien descienden los Remones de Ledesma e de don Pedro Remón su hijo) e el conde don Remón de Tolosa e don Enrique fueron cuñados e primos, casados con

* quen

whatever they wished. Afonso de Albuquerque did not know they were fleeing. Coje Atar sent word begging for mercy and asking to become a vassal of the King of Portugal; he gave great riches to the Captain Major. A peace was arranged whereby he submitted to all the Captain Major's commands. The words of the pact were written on paper in gold letters in the Persian tongue, and a copy in Arabic was carved in tablets of gold, each placed inside a lead chest. The King of Hormuz for whom Coje Atar governed was called Saif ud Din Ibn ud Dar.

Title XXXI. *About the solemn homage rendered the banner of Portugal.*

Blessed indeed were the banner of Portugal and Count Henrique of Constantinople, the father of Dom Afonso Henriques, Portugal's first king, from whom the kings and victorious princes of Portugal have descended. I want you to know the relationship between the kings of Portugal and many knights of Salamanca꙳ whose coats of arms are those of Aragon crossed with those of Count Remón. For they descend from two brothers and thus from one father: Dom Henrique of Constantinople and Don Remón of Toulouse (who rebuilt Salamanca; from whom descend the Remones of the bars or staffs, the father of the Emperor Don Alfonso), and Pope Calixtus, that great Pontiff of God's Church, were brothers; and Count Remón of Saint Gilles (blind in one eye; from whom descend the Remones of Ledesma and Don Pedro Remón his son) and the Count Remón of Toulouse and Dom Henrique were

tres hijas del rey don Alonso. Volviendo* al propósito, fueron concertadas las paces, muy festejada la bandera del rey don Manuel: que por mandado del capitán mayor salieron a caballo e de atavío por las calles de la ciudad Cojatar e los principales de ella. E tanta era la gente que mucho los cristianos se maravillaban de su vitoria, e descabalgaron a las puertas de los palacios reales, a quien el rey salió a recibir. E Jorge Barreto que la bandera llevaba se la entregó, diciendo si recibía aquella bandera como de su rey e señor. E tres veces preguntando, respondió que sí, e fue puesta en la principal torre del castillo, donde estovo la señal cristiana poderosamente triunfando.

Título XXXII. *Como hobo después muchas revueltas e lides entre Alonso de Alburquerque e Cojatar.*

Muchas discordias hobo, asegurado Hormuz, entre los capitanes españoles, que causaron cuatro cristianos pasarse a Cojatar e que él pensase hacer traición a Alonso de Alburquerque. E porque las guerras fueron muchas, grandes e diversas, [[cii]ᵛ] no me deterné en ello, pero quiero que sepáis que en las diferencias de este año† la principal ciudad de Quéxumen e grandes‡ lugares§ de Hormuz [fueron puestos] a fuego e a sangre. Cojatar e su gente fueron siempre muy maltratados, tomando otra vez con cuatro navíos a Calayate los cristianos, que corrieron e persiguieron tan cruda e ensangrentadamente la tierra de Hormuz que Cojatar e el rey Cefadín enviaron a don Francisco bisrey de las Indias por seguro, el cual mostraron a Alonso de

---

* volviedo   † destano   ‡ grando   § logaren

brothers-in-law and cousins, married to three daughters of King Alfonso. Getting back to the story, peace was arranged and the Portuguese banner of King Manuel honored. By order of the Captain Major, Coje Atar and the leading dignitaries of the city came forth on horseback in their finest robes. There were so many people that the Christians marveled at having gained the victory. They dismounted at the gates of the royal palaces, and the King came out to receive them. Jorge Barreto,※ the flag-bearer, handed it to him, asking if he accepted that banner as from his King and lord. He asked the question three times, and each time the King answered yes. The Christian banner was raised over the main tower of the castle, and there it remained in powerful triumph.

Title XXXII. *How there later ensued many disputes and quarrels between Afonso de Albuquerque and Coje Atar.*

Following the seizure of Hormuz, there were many disagreements among the captains of Hispania,※ which led four Christians※ to go over to Coje Atar and encouraged him to plot to betray Afonso de Albuquerque. Because the battles were many, large, and diverse,※ I shall not dwell on them, but I do want you to know that during this year's disputes the principal city of Qeshm and important towns around Hormuz were burned and put to the sword. Coje Atar and his men were constantly defeated. The Christians took Kalhat a second time※ with four ships. They pursued and attacked the lands of Hormuz in such a fierce and bloodthirsty manner that Coje Atar and King Saif ud Din sent word to Dom Francisco, the

Alburquerque, que ya en el puerto estaba para los combatir. E como vio las paces e que el rey Cefadín e Cojatar eran vasallos del rey de Portugal, cesó su guerra que esperaba* hacer con grande e esforzado ánimo, que contra infieles e moros siempre tovo. E aún después, porque Cojatar no le quiso dar los cuatro cristianos que a él se pasaron, le desbarató e destruyó a Nahán, que era cerca la isla de Lara, que dista cuatro leguas de Hormuz. Donde hacia la parte de Quéxumen fue desbaratado un galeón de Diego de Melo e él muerto, que como iba todo armado, no pareció encima de la agua. De que los cristianos hobieron mucho pesar, pero él murió por la fe de Cristo e como buen caballero, e en el cielo e en la tierra terná perpetua gloria. De ahí se partió Alonso de Alburquerque para la India e hallaron él e su gente al bisrey de grande armada en Cananor, con los cuales hobieron unos e otros gran placer e alegría; e contáronse las cosas que les acaecieran largamente, como era razón.

Título XXXIII. *Como contaron los del bisrey la muerte de don Lorenzo de Almeida e lo que les había*† *acaecido.*

Los de la compañía de don Francisco empezaron a contar a sus huéspedes la muerte de don Lorenzo de Almeida, hijo del bisrey, vertiendo lágrimas de sus ojos, que fue de la manera que oiréis. Después que Tristán de Acuña fue ido a Portugal con las naos de especiería, don Lorenzo de Almeida, católico cristiano e buen caballero, [ciii^r] como su muerte da testimonio, se partió de Cananor a correr la costa hasta Caúl. Llegó a un puerto

* esperanba   † habían

Viceroy of the Indies, requesting a written assurance.✳ They
showed this to Afonso de Albuquerque just as he was entering
the harbor to attack them. When he saw the peace document
and that King Saif ud Din and Coje Atar were vassals of the
King of Portugal, he ceased the campaign he had hoped to
wage with the magnificent and determined spirit he always
showed against infidels and Moors. Even then, since Coje Atar
would not surrender the four Christians who had gone over to
him, he razed and destroyed Naband,✳ located near the island
of Larak, which is four leagues from Hormuz. Near Qeshm,
Diogo de Melo's galleon was sunk, and he was killed, for, being
fully armed, he could not stay afloat. This sorely grieved the
Christians, but he died a good knight for the Faith of Christ,
and in heaven and on earth perpetual glory shall be his. From
there Afonso de Albuquerque set out for India, where he and
his men found the Viceroy at Cannanore with a huge fleet.
They were all pleased and happy to see each other✳ and related
at length the things which had befallen them, as was fitting.

Title XXXIII. *How the Viceroy's men told of Dom Lourenço's
death and what else had befallen them.*

With tears flowing from their eyes, the men of Dom
Francisco's company began to tell their guests about the
death of the Viceroy's son Dom Lourenço, and you shall
hear how it happened. After Tristão da Cunha had left for
Portugal with the spice ships, Dom Lourenço de Almeida, a
Catholic Christian and good knight as his death testifies,
embarked from Cannanore on a series of raids along the coast

que se llama o nombra Dabul, lleno de muchas naos, aunque no apercibidas. E los moros con temor que habían de los cristianos acometieron paces, sin las cuales, como no hacían ciertas e se aparejaban de guerra, los cristianos dieron en ellos e desbaratáronlos, quemando diez naos que despojaron e habían dado en seco. Los cristianos con Pero Barrueco e Diego Pérez capitanes salieron en tierra, tomaron el baluarte e toda la artillería de Dabul, volviéndose a las naos sin peligro. E partieron de allí para Caúl sin llevar ningún herido ni muerto. En la cual ciudad de Caúl aportaron, que es el puerto muy bueno e dista por veinte leguas de Dabul. E fueron pacíficamente recibidos porque sus habitadores tenían paz con los cristianos, que se proveyeron de agua e de palomas, que muchas hay allí, e caminaron su viaje para Angediva do don Francisco de Almeida bisrey estaba. Del cual bien recibidos, fueron enviados otro viaje con veinte cinco naos de Cochín que el bisrey encomendó a su hijo don Lorenzo defendiese e guardase porque el rey de Cochín era del rey de Portugal, que iban a cargar de trigo a Caúl. Donde en llegando, estovo don Lorenzo todo el mes de febrero hasta doce de marzo. E queriéndose partir para Cochín,* vieron venir por la costa de la mar cinco naos de manera de las de España, con gavias, e siete galeras que parecían ser de las de Alonso de Alburquerque a *prima facie*. Con todo, se recogieron los cristianos a sus naos porque tenían nuevas que en la ciudad de Dio estaban naves de rumes o de turcos allá así dichos. E llegando al puerto, fueron muchos los tiros de artillería e grande la lid que hobieron; e hirieron veinte e cinco hombres con flechas en la compañía del capitán mayor, de los cuales solo uno murió. E otro día por la mañana grande fue el combate que otrosí hobo, porque aferraron

* Caúl

as far as Chaul.✱ He reached a port named Dabul;✱ it was
filled with many ships which were not yet ready for battle. The
Moors, because of their fear of the Christians, sued for peace,
but, since they would not confirm it and began to arm themselves for battle, the Christians attacked and routed them. They
burned ten ships they had stripped and driven aground. The
Christians surged ashore behind captains Pero Barreto✱ and
Diogo Pires,✱ seized the bulwarks and all of Dabul's artillery,
and returned safely to the ships. They went off in the direction of
Chaul, having suffered neither dead nor wounded. They made
port at the city of Chaul, a good port twenty leagues from
Dabul. They were peacefully received because the inhabitants
are at peace with the Christians. Taking on water and pigeons,
of which there are many thereabouts, they made their way to
Angedive. There they were welcomed by Viceroy Dom Francisco de Almeida and sent out on another voyage with twenty-
five Cochin ships which the Viceroy entrusted to his son Dom
Lourenço to defend and protect, since the King of Cochin was
friendly to the King of Portugal. They were bound for Chaul
for a cargo of wheat. Dom Lourenço was at Chaul the entire
month of February, until the twelfth of March. Then, as
they were preparing to leave for Cochin, they sighted five ships
like those of Hispania, with topsails, approaching along the
coast, and seven galleys that prima facie appeared to be Afonso
de Albuquerque's. Nonetheless, the Christians drew back to
their ships because they had word that in the city of Diu was
a fleet of Turks,✱ or Rumis as they are called out there. Coming
into the harbor, these ships started to attack them, firing many
rounds of artillery. Their arrows wounded twenty-five of the
Captain Major's company, of whom only one died. Next

las naos de los [[ciii]ᵛ] cristianos a las de los rumes e las
desbarataron cuasi todas e metieron muchos de ellos sangrientos
en la mar, que era maravilla cuan colorada estaba. E fue muerto
estonces Mamalí, el mayor armador del rey de Calicut. Duró
aquella batalla hasta hora de vísperas; solas dos naos de los
rumes quedaron. Las cuales estando puestas en la agonía de la
muerte, vieron de las naos del rey de Cambaya grande armada
venir por la mar, cuyo capitán era Malicayaz, señor de una
ciudad que es dicha de Dio, en ayuda de los rumes con cuarenta e nueve navíos de remos, e llegáronse al puerto. Lo cual
visto por los cristianos, ordenaron de se salir del puerto por
poder más a su salvo pelear. E la nao en que iba la capitanía
de don Lorenzo e él quedó trasera e fue tan desdichado que fue
a caer en unas estozas do nunca pudo salir, yendo muy delanteras las de su compañía. Allí los rumes sin ninguna piedad*
con sus naos e gentes ocurrieron e forzada la defensión de los
cristianos, la metieron debajo de la agua, donde murió de dos
bombardadas don Lorenzo de Almeida, delante los suyos como
excelente capitán, buen cristiano por la fe de Cristo e señalado
caballero de Portugal, que en su linaje será a los parientes eterna
corona. De allí Malicayaz llevó vivos diez e ocho cristianos, los
cuales envió a Campanel, que es una villa muy fuerte e viciosa
donde está cuasi siempre el rey de Cambaya. El cual es criado
e suele ser con ponzoña: cuando niños [se la dan] en poca
cuantidad e así se la acrecientan creciendo. E si algún grande de
su reino le ha enojado, hácele vestir una camisa suya, e sudando
con ella muere. O mándales comer betel mascado en su boca e
luego hinchado de la ponzoñosa saliva muere. E el rey de
Cambaya holgó mucho de ver aquellos cristianos, que nun-

* piadad

morning equally fierce combat took place, as the Christian ships grappled with the Rumis' and routed almost all of them. They sent many bloody Moors sprawling into the water — it was amazing how reddish it was — and killed Mamaly, the King of Calicut's chief armorer. That encounter lasted until the hour of vespers; only two Rumi ships were left, and with these about to be finished off, they sighted a great fleet belonging to the King of Cambay approaching. Commanded by Melik Yas,※ ruler of a city called Diu, forty-nine oared galleys came into the harbor to aid the Rumis. In view of this, the Christians resolved to leave the harbor,※ in order to be able to fight more freely. Dom Lourenço's flagship was the last to leave, and he had the misfortune to have it get snarled among some fishermen's stakes, from which it never could break loose, especially when the other ships of the company had already sailed on ahead. Ruthlessly converging on them with their ships and men, the Rumis breached the Christian defenses and sent the ship to the bottom. Dom Lourenço de Almeida was killed by two mortar shots.※ In the forefront of his countrymen, this excellent captain gave his life as a good Christian for the Faith of Christ. A distinguished knight of Portugal, he shall ever stand as a shining light to all of his lineage. Melik Yas seized eighteen Christian survivors and sent them to Champanel,※ a fortified and luxurious city where the King of Cambay almost always resides. This King is raised on poison as a matter of course. They give it to him in small doses as a child and increase it as he grows older. Thus, should some high person of the kingdom anger him, the King makes him put on one of his shirts. As soon as the man sweats, he dies. Or else he has them eat betel that he has been chewing, and right away they swell up from

[civ^r] ca los había visto. E de allí los llevaron a la ciudad de Dio, donde era señor Malicayaz. E los rumes se fueron para allá, que hay buen puerto e de allí se querían ir a fortalecer en Calicut. Los cristianos cuando acordaron de poner remedio en la nao de don Lorenzo que atrás quedara, viéndola so el agua e muerta la gente, no pudieron remediar, que ya para ello estaban en sus bateles aparejados. E así muy tristes se partieron a Cochín do el bisrey estaba. E con las nuevas ninguno osó ir excepto Francisco de Añaya, capitán en una caravela de vela latina, porque entendió ser don Francisco tan cuerdo que no se ofendería de aquello en que ellos no habían sido culpantes. Oída la triste relación, con el mayor esfuerzo de corazón que pudo, disimuló, diciendo que gran gloria le quedaba por la muerte de su hijo, en haber muerto como bueno e católico cristiano e leal caballero, e que Dios lo dio e Dios lo tomó, que se hiciese su voluntad. E después que algún tiempo se aderezaron; el bisrey don Francisco, que lastimado traía su corazón en el secreto de sus entrañas, se partió con su gente para Cananor, adonde se juntaron con la de Alonso de Alburquerque. E de ahí caminaron con diez y ocho velas en busca de los rumes.

Título XXXIV. *Como el bisrey se partió de Cananor en busca de los rumes [e] llegó a Honor, Mergeo e Angediva.*

Don Francisco bisrey con diez y ocho velas a nueve días de diciembre de 1508 años partió de Cananor en busca de los rumes, en que iban mil e trescientos hombres bien aparejados de todas armas a guerra necesarias. E fue la batalla en una muy

the poisonous saliva and die. The King of Cambay was delighted, for they were the very first Christians he had ever seen.
From there they were taken to the city of Diu, where Melik Yas
governed. The Rumis went there also, because it has a good
port, and from there they planned to go to Calicut for reinforcements. The Christians, by the time they had gotten ready☼
and moved into their longboats to go back and help Dom
Lourenço's ship, saw that nothing could be done, for it had gone
down and the men had been killed. Thus, they sadly set sail
for Cochin and the Viceroy. No one dared bring the news
except Francisco de Añaya,☼ captain of a lateen-rigged caravel.
He knew Dom Francisco to be so reasonable that he would not
take offense at something for which they had not been to
blame. Upon hearing the news, with the greatest effort his
heart could muster, he veiled his sorrow, saying that his son's
death left him great glory, for he died a good Catholic Christian
and faithful knight. The Lord gave him and the Lord has
taken him away;☼ His will be done. A short time later, the
Viceroy, hiding his broken heart deep within himself, armed
his men and set out for Cannanore. There they met Afonso de
Albuquerque's men and proceeded with eighteen ships in
search of the Rumis.☼

Title XXXIV. *How the Viceroy left Cannanore in search of
the Rumis and visited Onor, Margão,*☼ *and Angedive.*

The Viceroy Dom Francisco, with eighteen sail on the
ninth of December 1508, left Cannanore in search of the Rumis,
accompanied by thirteen hundred men equipped with all the
necessary weapons of war. The battle took place on a very clear

clara e quieta noche; salió la luna (que era estonces el lleno de
ella) sin dar tanta claridad como una estrella, e estovo [[civ]ᵛ]
así espacio de dos horas, lo cual tomaron ellos por buena señal.
Antiguamente miraban muchos en las buenas señales e fueron
causa de acometer e vencer muchos reyes grandes huestes, batallas e capitanes, a que de otra forma pudieran hallar estorbo.
Como la primera señal que en el mundo se puso fue aquella
águila que en la bandera de Júpiter contra su padre el rey Saturno
se asentó, en venga de la sangre de sus hermanos. Lo cual tovo
por buen agüero, púsola en su bandera e quedó vitoriosísimo
señor. E en la romana monarquía hoy día hay en Roma la principal casa o la de ella que se nombran de *Bonis Auguriis,* lo cual
estando allá noté, e pregunté la causa de su excelente apellido;
e les dije como la principal casa e solar de las generosas
Montañas de Castilla era nombrada de Agüero, descendiente del
conde Fernán González, de sangre real, como a los leídos e
cronistas es manifiesto. Pues el bisrey de Portugal se partió*
[del rey] de Cananor, grande amigo de cristianos e del rey de
Portugal, e aderezáronse† dos naos en el puerto de Mergio,
cercano de allí, que el rey de Garsapa había dado al rey don
Manuel. La gente de esta tierra es bien dispuesta. Adoran los
ídolos. Cuando el marido muere, la mujer de su gana se lanza
en el fuego, que dicen que van a hacer bodas con él al otro
mundo. E de allí se fueron a Angediva, que ahí estaba el
bisrey tomando agua, e de ahí se carteaban Malicayaz e el bisrey,
en que el Malicayaz se excusaba de la muerte de su hijo del
bisrey: porque él no lo conociera e él lo había hecho en su
defensión, porque los cristianos le habían acometido a él e aún

* partido   † aderescaronse

and quiet night. There was a full moon, yet it did not shed as
much light as a star and it stayed that way for two hours, which
they considered a good omen. In olden days many people used
to look for good omens. They led many kings to launch great
battles and conquer enemy hosts and captains, when otherwise
they might have been defeated. For example, the first sign that
appeared in the world was that eagle which perched on Jupiter's
banner✣ as he was about to go against his father Saturn to
avenge his brothers' bloody deaths. Taking it as a good omen, he
placed an eagle on his banner and became a most victorious
sovereign. In the Roman monarchy today there is in Rome an
important family with the name *Bonis Auguriis*.✣ When I was
there I asked them about the origin of their excellent name. I
informed them that the principal estate and manor house of
the bountiful Montaña of Castile is named Agüero. The
Agüeros are descendants of Count Fernán González✣ and of
royal blood, as is manifest to the well-read and chroniclers. Well,
the Viceroy of Portugal took his leave of the King of Cannanore,
who is most friendly to the Christians and the King of Portugal.
In the nearby port of Margão they fitted out two ships the King
of Gersoppa had given to King Manuel. The people of this
land are good-natured. They adore idols. When the husband dies,
the wife willingly throws herself onto the pyre; they say they
are going to celebrate new nuptials in the other world. From
there the Viceroy went to Angedive where he took on water.
From that place Melik Yas and the Viceroy exchanged letters,✣
in which Melik Yas tried to absolve himself in the matter of the
death of the Viceroy's son, because he had not known who it
was and had been forced to act in self-defense because the
Christians had attacked him and were injuring his men. They

tratado muy mal a su gente. E de ahí hablaron sobre paz, e fue en busca de los rumes que mataron a su hijo.

Título XXXV. *Como don Francisco llegó a Dabul e la destruyó.*

[[cv]ʳ] Don Francisco bisrey se partió para Dabul e primero día de enero ancoraron en su puerto, e levantaron con un viento para se llegar más a la ciudad. Fue tanta la artillería de los moros que era muy gran espanto. E quiso Dios que ningún cristiano fue muerto, ante muchas naos dabulesas desbaratadas. E a pesar de los moros, los cristianos salieron en tierra matando en ellos. Do perdió la vida el capitán morisco e otro gran señor que en unas muy ricas andas venía como dueña, que más rico que esforzado debía ser, pues no se preciando de caballero, andaba como mujer, cosa efeminada e que mal parecía a todos, e parecerá do quiera que se usare tan abominable e fea cosa, aquello de andar en andas e jugar por estilo, justas, torneos o cañas o esgrima. Es cosa muy reprobada en los caballeros, que ser amadores honestos curialmente se permite. Así que quedando en el campo e andando vencedores, no supieron quién puso fuego a la ciudad, que ardía con infinita riqueza, que era el mayor placer del mundo. Allí se ahogó un esforzado cristiano, hermano de Martín Coello, capitán que por salir en tierra cayó en la mar, cobrando muerte de doblada vida. E en el puerto quemaron diez naos dabulesas varadas e seis naos grandes encadenadas e veinte no tan grandes llenas de arroz jirasal, que el mejor de la India dicen ser. Dabul está en un valle puesta e sube por unas cuestas o sierras o hasta una cerca vieja que allí está, que ante fue allí muy noblemente edificada e poblada. Luego los cristianos corrieron toda la costa quemando lugares e haciendo grande

also spoke of peace, but the Viceroy continued in search of the Rumis who had killed his son.

Title XXXV. *How Dom Francisco reached Dabul[*] and destroyed it.*

The Viceroy Dom Francisco left for Dabul and anchored in its port on January first, and, as the wind rose, hoisted anchor and moved in closer to the city. The Moorish artillery barrage was terrifying, but God willed that no Christian be killed. Instead, many Dabul ships were routed. In spite of the Moors the Christians charged ashore and killed many of the enemy, including the Moorish captain and another great lord who had shown up in a fancy litter,[*] like a lady. He must have been wealthier than brave, for with no pride in himself as a knight he had himself carried about like a woman. This effeminate behavior seemed bad to everyone, and so it must seem, wherever men practice such abominable customs as going about in litters, stylish sham battles, jousts, tourneys, playing with reed spears, or fencing. It is a thing to be condemned in knights, for in courtly circles only honest love is to be permitted. So the Christians carried the field and were triumphant. They did not know who set fire to the city,[*] which burned amidst infinite riches, the most pleasurable sight in the world. One brave Christian, a brother of Captain Martim Coelho, drowned as he fell overboard trying to get ashore, gaining new life through this painful death. In the port they burned ten Dabul ships they had driven aground, six large vessels they had found chained together, and twenty smaller ones loaded with *jirasal* rice,[*] said to be the best kind in India. Dabul is situated in a valley and

estrago. Hay allí hortaliza asaz, cañas de azúcar, vacas, gallinas, muchas fuentes de sabrosas aguas. E en la ciudad [[cv]ᵛ] de Guoa vieron tantos saltigallos que apenas se parecía el sol e el cielo, los cuales destruyen aquella tierra; e es manjar que los moros usan e tienen tinajas e otras vasijas llenas de ellos en conserva. Por aquella ribera grandísimo estrago hicieron los españoles* e en los† pozos do habían de beber los moros les dejaban asaz cuerpos muertos. Aquella ciudad era del reino de Guoa, que estaba lejos de la mar. E después de siete días partiéronse del puerto e vieron un batel en que iban un rume principal con trece hombres e dos mujeres. Los cuales acometidos de los cristianos pelearon reciamente, hiriendo más de veinte cristianos; e fueron todos los rumes muertos, que no quedó sino una mujer, porque la otra más principal murió abrazada con el rume su marido, que tovo por consolosa muerte.

Título XXXVI. *De como camino de Dio‡ en busca de los rumes fueron el bisrey e su gente e de lo que hicieron.*

Partidos fueron los cristianos de la ciudad de Caúl por la costa e viaje de Cambaya, do en catorce leguas con las muchas mareas tardaron ocho días, que dista el puerto de Caúl del reino de Cani, que se parte con el de Cambaya. E es allí un río do está una población, de Maín, al cual llegaron. E la hondura del agua era ocho o nueve brazas, e son las mareas tan grandes e tantas que en espacio de dos horas quedaron las naos en dos brazas sino que se apartaron de allí. E el bisrey envió su mensaje

---

    * españoles   † les   ‡ Die

rises through hills to an old wall; it had formerly been populous and nobly built. Then the Christians went raiding along the coast, burning and ravaging many settlements. There are plenty of vegetables thereabouts, as well as sugar cane, cattle, chickens, and many fresh water springs. In the city of Goa they saw so many locusts that one could hardly see the sun or sky. Locusts destroy the land. The Moors consider them a delicacy and preserve them in jars and other containers. The men of Hispania created enormous havoc along that shore and put dead bodies in the wells the Moors used for drinking. That city belonged to the kingdom of Goa,❋ a good sailing distance away. Seven days later they left the port and sighted a longboat carrying an important Rumi, thirteen men, and two women. When attacked by the Christians, they put up a fierce battle, wounding more than twenty. All the Rumis were killed; only one woman survived, for the other, of higher status, died embracing her Rumi husband, which she considered a happy death.

Title XXXVI. *About what the Viceroy and his men did as they traveled toward Diu in search of the Rumis.*

The Christians left the city of Chaul and moved along the coast toward Cambay. On account of heavy seas, they were eight days in sailing the fourteen leagues from Chaul to the kingdom of Thana,❋ which borders on Cambay. They went to a settlement called Mahim,❋ located on a river, where the water was eight or nine fathoms and the tides are so extreme❋ that two hours would have found them in two fathoms had they not moved away. The Viceroy sent a message ashore asking that

a tierra: que le dejase por sus dineros tomar mantenimientos e agua fresca, pues no les hacían daño por ser del rey de Cambaya, de que ellos poco se curaron. E don Francisco mandó armar toda su gente e salieron a tierra que despoblada estaba, matando vacas [e] búfalos, de que abunda esta ciudad de Maín. Fue antiguamente muy populosa; tiene un [[cvi]ʳ] castillo cabo la agua de cantería e cuatro esquinas con cubos e hermosas almenas, los muros fortísimos, de diez pies en ancho. Dentro hay una rica mezquita, la antigua,* e otras mezquitas con adros que duran media legua, grandes e hermosos, de imaginería las sepulturas. Esto vieron el capitán e su gente en aquel lugar noche e día, tomando mantenimientos, los que pudieron haber, agua e arroz. Destrozaron cuatro mil palmares e más e no hicieron daño a la ciudad por no enojar a Malicayaz e al rey de Cambay porque a los rumes echase de sus puertos. De ahí se partieron para la ciudad de Dio, por un terrible golfo espacio andando de quince días que no sabían dónde eran. Pero quiso Dios que vino un necesario viento de noche que en amaneciendo los puso a vista de Dio. E llegando al puerto, las naos de los rumes salían, que las dañó mucho, porque como el puerto se cierra con cadena no les pudieran entrar. Dentro del cual había más de trescientas velas, e para llegar, las naos de cristianos habían de ir junto a la ciudad, que por allí va la canal de la corriente. Día era de Santa María, de febrero de quinientos e nueve† años, dos días del mes, ordenaron entrar donde los rumes estaban.

    * atigua   † ocho

he be allowed to buy supplies and fresh water. Since they belonged to the King of Cambay, he would not harm them, but
they paid no attention. Therefore, Dom Francisco had all his
men take up arms. They landed on a deserted shore and slaugh-
tered many cattle and buffalo, in which this city of Mahim
abounds. Long ago it had been very populous. A castle of
hewn stone stands at the water's edge, with turrets and beautiful
crenelations on each of the four corners. The walls are
tremendously strong, ten feet thick. Inside the city stand the
elegant old mosque and several others, with beautiful large
atriums half a league long. Imagery adorns the sepulchers. The
Captain and his men saw these sights during the night and day
they were there, taking on all the provisions they could, namely
water and rice. They destroyed more than four thousand palm
trees, but they did not damage the city in order not to anger
Melik Yas and the King of Cambay:* and cause them to expel
the Rumis from their ports. From there they set out for the city
of Diu, traveling through such a terrible empty gulf:* that for
fifteen days they did not know where they were. But God
ordained that one evening the necessary wind should arise, and
with the dawn it put them in sight of Diu. As they approached
the harbor, the Rumi ships came out a short distance, which
caused considerable damage because, since the harbor closes
with a chain, it was not possible to get in after them. Inside were
more than three hundred vessels, and to get them the Christians
would have to follow the channel current right alongside the
city. On the Feast Day of Our Lady,* the second day of the
month of February 1509, orders were given to go in against the
Rumis.

Título XXXVII. *Como fueron desbaratados los rumes e las armadas de Malicayaz e del rey de Calicut por los cristianos.*

Otro día por la mañana los cristianos se ataviaron de todas las armas que llevaban e aderezaron* sus naos con facas de algodón e colchones por amparo de los tiros de bombardas, tomando sobre las naves redes por cubierta para defensión de las pedradas de las gavias, lo cual era asaz útil e necesario. Tres [[cvi]ᵛ] días† de febrero, fiesta de Sant Blas, entraron dentro por la canal a aferrar las naos de los rumes, que bien apercibidos estaban. E el delantero fue Nuño Vaz Pereira, do fueron muchos los tiros de pólvora de ambas partes, los cristianos llamando a nuestra Señora, Santiago e a San Blas, cuya fiesta celebraban. De los cuales los moros mataron nueve personas de Portugal, que como católicos e leales dieron las vidas aquel día e cobraron otra inmortal de que gozarán *in eternum*. E con un tiro de bombarda fue sorbida de la mar una gruesa nao de rumes, dándoles luego los cristianos gran grita; que también, si no llevaran cubierta, de cierto recibieran gran detrimento de las piedras e saetas que estaban asaces encima las cristianas naos. E aferraron otra nao de rumes en que, puesto que bien defendida, matando muchos moros entraron. E algunos moros saltaban en los bateles e otros se lanzaban en la mar, pero los leales defendían por dentro o por de fuera su nao. Los albaxís, que son de tierra del Preste Juan, cautivos herrados en la frente en tres lugares a manera de cruz, huían, que de la muerte de los rumes no les pesaba mucho. Donde Nuño Vaz Pereira hizo tan señaladas e vitoriosas hazañas e su espada era tan cebada en las carnes de los enemigos que mereció eterna corona e bien por

* aderezara   † día

Title XXXVII. *How the Rumis and the fleets of Melik Yas and the King of Calicut✻ were defeated by the Christians.*

Next morning the Christians took up their weapons and fitted their ships with cotton padding and mattresses, as protection against mortars, and stretched nets over the decks to defend against stones thrown from the topsails, which was very useful and necessary. On February third, Feast Day of Saint Blaise,✻ they sailed through the channel to grapple with the well-prepared Rumi ships. Nuno Vaz Pereira went in the vanguard,✻ and there was heavy firing from both sides. The Christians invoked Our Lady, Saint James, and Saint Blaise, whose feast they were celebrating. The Moors killed nine Portuguese, who as Catholics and loyal patriots gave their lives that day in exchange for a greater and immortal one which they shall enjoy *in eternum.* With one mortar round a sturdy Rumi ship was sent to the bottom, whereupon the Christians gave a great cheer. And certainly, had it not been for the protective coverings, they too would have suffered grave damage from the stones and arrows that rained down upon the Christian ships. They grappled with another Rumi vessel, and, although it was well defended, they boarded it, killing many Moors. Some of the Moors jumped into their longboats, and others threw themselves into the sea, but the loyal ones stayed to defend their ship above decks and below. The Abyssinians,✻ from the land of Prester John, captives branded on the forehead in three places in the form of a cross, ran off, for the death of the Rumis did not bother them very much. There Nuno Vaz performed outstanding and victorious deeds. His sword was so steeped in the enemy flesh that he merited an eternal crown and proved

señal la cruz e brazo que la* defiende en campo sangriento con las orladas quinas de sangre de reyes de Portugal, de que es† claro e esforzado descendiente. Allí lo hirieron a él, por más vitoria le dar, con una flecha en el pescuezo que él con alegre cara recibió, sintiéndola más por placer que por enojo; yendo sintiendo la llaga, dando gracias a nuestro Señor que lo crió, de ahí a tres días, como católico cristiano, valiente e muy esforzado caballero, murió, quedando su nombre inmortal e la fama de gentes en gentes eternalmente publicando con lágrimas las claras hazañas e muerte de tal perso- [[cvii]ʳ] na, que cubrió de luto, que hizo llorosos los de su compañía e, con la estima que de él había, a sus contrarios, los que algún conocimiento de caballería o de virtud tenían. Bien aventurado fue el día en que nació, pues en tal hora e tiempo feneció. Dichosos se ternían muchos de los vivientes ser muertos quedando de sí tan inmortal memoria como de él. E porque hombre humano no es suficiente loarlo, callo. E sabréis que ahí jarretaron una pierna a un cristiano e cayendo en el suelo, los rumes‡ lo mataron crudamente. Con la muerte de los buenos e vida de los esforzados, más prósperos estaban los cristianos, que osaban entrar en las naos de los enemigos. Ese día un caballero portugués cuyo nombre era Figueredo probó a subir a la tolda de los rumes,§ e por un forado que estaba junto con el mastel de la nao le dieron con una pica por entre las piernas e salió la punta de ella al pescuezo. Quedó espetado e con un garfio cruel lo derrocaron abajo; por lo cual no merece menos, que tanto cuanto fue cruda la muerte, tanto es más excelente su gloria. Que otro tanto hiciera‖ al mejor de España su enemigo, queriendo destruir los¶ que allí

* quel   † el   ‡ rimes   § rimes
‖ hicieran   ¶ los destruir

worth of his coat of arms:* the cross and the arm that defends it on a bloody battlefield, bordered by the *quinas* which represent the blood of Portuguese kings, of whom he is a famous and brave descendant. That he might gain greater glory, they wounded him in the neck with an arrow. He accepted it with happy countenance, feeling pleasure rather than pain over the wound and giving thanks to Our Lord his Creator. Three days later he died, a Catholic Christian and brave valiant knight, his name remaining immortal,* his fame eternally proclaiming from generation unto tearful generation the famous deeds and death of such a person. His death covered with mourning and left tearful the men of his company and also, by virtue of their esteem for him, those of the enemy who recognized chivalry and virtue. Blessed was the day of his birth, for at such an hour and moment did he pass away. Many of the living would consider themselves fortunate to die as he did, leaving behind such an immortal memory. But, since human effort is insufficient to praise him, I shall say no more. You must know that the Rumis hamstrung one Christian, and, as he was falling to the ground, they viciously killed him. By virtue of such good men who died and other brave men who remained alive, more prosperous were the Christians, who ventured to board the enemy ships. That day a Portuguese knight by the name of Figuereido* tried to climb onto the aftercastle of one of the Rumi ships, but through an opening near the mast they speared him between the legs with a pike. The point came out through his neck, as if he were on a spit, and they viciously hooked him and dragged him down. He is no less worthy because of this, for, if the manner of his death was horribly crude, so much

tomaran. Cuanto fue grande el martirio, mereció corona de buen caballero e ilustró las cinco hojas de higuera cercadas* con el cordón que por la batalla de las doncellas leonesas que de los moros los principales hermanos libertaron el esclarecido gallego solar mereció. Mataron los rumes† otrosí a Pero Can que subir quería, e derrocaron al hijo de Manuel Pazaña; finalmente que la tolda e nao por los cristianos con la artillería fue sola agua, en gloria de España e vituperio de los rumes‡ E yéndose al hondo§ una de las naos de Portugal en que Nuño Vaz iba o fuera por capitán, en un mastel de la nao se salvó Martín Fernández Figueroa, al cual dieron una lanzada en una pierna, que ató con un paño de algodón como pudo e se fue a la nao *Sancti Espiritus.* Él lo hizo tan esforzadamente aquel día que por ser vi- [[cvii]ᵛ] vo aún, a tocarlo no me atreveré; e como yo escribo loores de otros, no faltará quien allá o acá los escriba de él, que tan bien los merece como los que allá se hallaron, aunque tuviese mayores encomiendas que él. Después de esto aferraron las naos, otras con la artillería metiendo so el agua sangrienta, crudamente peleando, los rumes descayendo, los cristianos viniendo en la nao de Malicayaz. Murieron trescientos e cincuenta hombres. Duró la pelea desde hora de tercia hasta la noche. De los cristianos murieron cuarenta e cinco, heridos quinientos e más. E de la gente rumesa no se libró excepto Miliacén, capitán con veinte rumes que en una barquita se salieron. Los barcos de Calicut e caravelas, viendo el desbarato, huyeron para Calicut. Meliacén fue herido de una saeta en la

---

* cercados   † rimes   ‡ rimes   § hondon

more excellent is his glory. The enemy would have liked to
destroy all the best men of Hispania in the same way. So great
was his martyrdom that he earned the good knight's crown and
honored the fig leaves surrounded by the cordon. This is the
coat of arms that those distinguished brothers merited during
the battle of the Leonese damsels, in which they freed their
illustrious Galician manor house from the Moors. The Rumis
likewise killed Pero Cão* as he tried to climb up and pulled
down the son of Manuel Paçanha.* Finally, to the glory of
Hispania and vituperation of the Rumis, the aftercastle and the
entire ship were driven into the sea by the Christian artillery.
As one of the Portuguese ships, on which Captain Nuno Vaz
was sailing, began to sink, Martín Fernández de Figueroa saved
himself by grabbing onto one of the masts. He had received a
lance thrust in the leg, which he bandaged with a strip of
cotton as best he could, then swam over to the *Sancti Espiritus.*
Because he is still living, I shall not venture to describe the
brave deeds he performed that day. But, since I am writing the
praises of others, surely there will not lack someone somewhere to write about him. He deserves as much praise as anyone there, even though others may have enjoyed greater favor.
After this, they grappled with the Rumi ships and with their
artillery sent others into the bloody waters; fighting fiercely, the
Rumis faltering, the Christians boarded Melik Yas's ship. Three
hundred and fifty men died; the battle lasted from the third
hour until nightfall. Of the Christians, forty-five died and more
than five hundred were wounded. Of the Rumis, only the
captain, Emir Hocein, got away in a small boat with twenty of
his men. The Calicut boats and caravels, seeing the defeat, fled
toward home. Emir Hocein was wounded in the leg by an

pierna, de forma que quedaron por vencedores los cristianos en el puerto e los rumes muertos e vencidos (de quien estaba la mar cuajada). Así quedó el puerto por el bisrey e su gente, el cual cerraron luego con la cadena.

Título XXXVIII. *Como el bisrey hizo paces con Malicayaz e se dieron uno a otro los cautivos que tenían.*

Habida la dicha vitoria, quién cree que no le temblase la contera a Malicayaz por los pasados trances. Contemplando los que le podrían avenir, entendieron sus farautes en concertar las paces, así que le envió los cristianos que cautivos tenía e arriba dijimos en la muerte de don Lorenzo, lo cual porque es larga cosa de contar abrevio. E el bisrey dio a Malicayaz cuatro moros que solamente quedaron de la batalla. E ordenó de se partir de la ciudad de Dio para invernar en Cochín, bien proveído de todos mantenimientos e cosas necesarias, e la muerte de su hijo con la salsa cual pudo hacer. De ahí envió a Alonso de Noroña a don Alonso, que estaba en Sacatora por capitán, con vituallas. A nueve días de febrero alzaron áncoras e fueron para la India. Es razón [[cviii]ʳ] que sepáis cual se llama India, e es desde el reino de Cambaya hasta el cabo de Comarín. E la otra tierra de Cambaya es guzarates, e de Persia al estrecho de Hormuz es Arabia *Felix,* los mantenimientos como España. La seta que tienen: de Mahoma en Persia e Arabia, que en Guoa, Cambaya, Caúl e Dabul adoran los ídolos e son los más negros. Estonces enviaba el rey don Manuel con Diego de Sequera en cuatro naos a descubrir clavo, porque de la pimienta asaz hay en Malabar, Calicut, Cananor, Cochín, Coilán, Caliculán, reinos

arrow. Thus the Christians were triumphant in the port and the Rumis killed and vanquished,✤ the sea filled with their bodies. Having conquered the port, the Viceroy and his men then sealed it off with the chain.

Title XXXVIII. *How the Viceroy made peace with Melik Yas, and how they exchanged the prisoners they were holding.*

After this victory had taken place, who doubts that Melik Yas was trembling in his boots over the defeats he had suffered. Contemplating what might still happen to him, he sent his interpreters to arrange a peace. He sent back the Christians✤ he had taken captive (as we mentioned above) when Dom Lourenço was killed, which, since it is a long story, I shall abbreviate. The Viceroy gave Melik Yas four Moors, the only survivors of the battle. He then issued orders to leave the city of Diu and proceed to Cochin for the winter. He carried off a good supply of things they might need, assuaging his son's death as best he could. From there he dispatched Afonso de Noronha to Dom Afonso✤ the captain on Socotra with a shipment of food. On the ninth of February they weighed anchor and set sail for India. It is appropriate that you know just what is called India.✤ It extends from the kingdom of Cambay to Cape Comorin. The land of the Gujarati lies to the other side of Cambay. Arabia *Felix* runs from Persia to the Strait of Hormuz, where the food is like that of Hispania. In Persia and Arabia the people are of the Mohammedan sect. In Goa, Cambay, Chaul, and Dabul they adore idols and most of them are black. It was at that time that King Manuel was sending Diogo Sequeira✤ out with four ships to discover cloves,

suyos, e de la isla Samatora. La canela viene de la isla Ceilán,* donde las puentes, casas e edificios son de madera e árboles de la canela, que no hay otra en aquella tierra. E allí hay piedras preciosas, rubís, safiros e otras de rico valor. El clavo nace en la isla Maluco, que dista de Melaca doscientas e cincuenta leguas. El bisrey ordenó partirse de Cochín con cuatro naos de especiería a Portugal e que quedase su poder e fuese gobernador de la India Alonso de Alburquerque, que estaba en Cananor. E luego vino el mariscal, sobrino de Alonso de Alburquerque, con diez e seis velas, e hizo que luego el bisrey le dejase toda la gobernación de la India. De lo cual él holgó, que se quería ya venir a su tierra. E partióse de Cananor con tres naos para Portugal, quedando Alburquerque gran señor e muy próspero, que luego determinó ir sobre Calicut e destruir la ciudad, rey e gentes de ella.

Título XXXIX. *Como Alonso de Alburquerque se partió para Calicut a destruirla.*

Partidos para Calicut Alonso de Alburquerque capi[tán] mayor [e el mariscal], dejando mandado o rogado a Rodrigo Rebello en reguarda viniese con ciertas velas, llegaron al puerto; do saliendo de mañana, [[cviii]ᵛ] fueron sentidos los cristianos, a los cuales gran grita los moros dieron. Pero con el gran

* Cuilan

because there is an abundance of pepper along the Malabar coast in Calicut, Cannanore, Cochin, Quilon, Colachel,✤ kingdoms of his, and on the island of Sumatra. Cinnamon comes from the island of Ceylon, where the bridges, houses, and buildings are made from the wood of the cinnamon tree since there is no other kind in that land. Ceylon also has precious stones such as rubies, sapphires, and others of great value. Cloves grow on the island of Molucca,✤ which is two hundred and fifty leagues from Malacca. The Viceroy made plans to leave Cochin and return to Portugal with four spice ships and to delegate his authority to Afonso de Albuquerque, who was in Cannanore, as governor of India. Right then the Marshal, Afonso de Albuquerque's nephew,✤ arrived with sixteen ships and made the Viceroy relinquish all command in India at once. He was delighted to do so, because he was most anxious to return home. With three ships he departed Cannanore bound for Portugal, leaving Albuquerque a mighty and prosperous lord. The latter then resolved to go and destroy the city, the king, and the people of Calicut.

Title XXXIX. *How Afonso de Albuquerque set out to destroy Calicut.*✤

Captain Major Afonso de Albuquerque set out with the Marshal for Calicut, after arranging for Rodrigo Rebelo,✤ either by force of orders or by pleas, to follow along with several ships as the rear guard. The Christians reached the port, and as it began to grow light they were discovered, whereupon the Moors set up a great clamor. The Indians were so

temor de la artillería de cristianos, iban huyendo por los palmares los indios. E los españoles seguros en tierra salir osaron, quemando muchos edificios e matando cruelmente muchos de los enemigos, que no en capitanía mas de diez en diez o veinte en veinte andaban, haciendo certeros tiros con sus arcos, de que mucho se atavian en lid. Son gente ligera; andan en carnes excepto las partes vergonzosas, que con una toca ciñen. E fueron don Antonio, sobrino del capitán mayor e Rodrigo Rebello a quemar ciertas naos que estaban en la costa, que eran catorce por todas. E Alonso de Alburquerque, el mariscal e Manuel Pazaña e otros capitanes, caballeros e hombres de bien cristianos entraron por las calles de Calicut triunfando vitoriosamente, con la bandera de la cruz ante sí e tras ella las de Portugal. La población de la Calicut no está cercada de muros, pero dura su habitación cinco leguas. Los palacios del rey distan una legua, que son de rico muro e piedra cercados e fortalecidos; ante los cuales está una plaza que mucha hermosura causa a la fortaleza. Donde estaba en ella un *coimal,* que es como en España conde, con gran multitud de naires, que así dicen allá a los caballeros. Por los cuales quiso el mariscal entrar, haber e tomar los palacios, cuya vista compró por la vida: que fue allí una grandísima batalla, la más esquiva a los cristianos que en las Indias hobo, muy cruda, en que la gente portuguesa fue desbaratada; mucha se recogió a las naos. Mataron ende al excelente e magnánimo mariscal, que su sangre vertiendo por la fe de Cristo e honra de su tierra, hazañosas cosas haciendo, olvidando su propria vida por el honor de todos, dio la ánima a Dios que lo crió. Hirieron otrosí en el pescuezo con una flech[a a A]lonso de Alburquerque capitán mayor, porque no quedase de la compañía quejoso. Mataron al bueno e esforzado caballero Vasco de Silvei-

afraid of the Christian artillery that they went running away through the palm groves. The men of Hispania confidently surged ashore,⁜ burning many buildings and cruelly slaying many of the enemy. The latter move not in captaincies but in tens and twenties, making accurate shots with their bows, which they use a lot in battle. They are a nimble folk and go about naked, except for their shameful parts, which they girdle with a cloth. Dom Antonio, the Captain Major's nephew, went with Rodrigo Rebelo down the coast to burn certain ships, fourteen in all. Afonso de Albuquerque, the Marshal, Manuel Paçanha, and other Christian captains, knights, and gentlemen moved through the streets of Calicut in glorious triumph, with the banner of the Cross leading the way and the Portuguese standards right behind. The city of Calicut is not walled but spreads over five leagues. The King's palaces are a league away, enclosed and fortified within handsome stone walls. In front of the palaces is a square that lends much beauty to the fort. A *coimal,* the equivalent of a count in Hispania, was stationed there with a great multitude of Nairs,⁜ the name they give to their knights. The Marshal wanted to enter and take the palaces, the sight of which he purchased with his life. For an awful battle took place there,⁜ the most disastrous for the Christians that ever occurred in the Indies. It was a very rough battle, the Portuguese were routed, and many of them took refuge in the ships. They killed the excellent and magnanimous Marshal who, shedding his blood for the Faith of Christ and honor of his homeland, working strenuous deeds, and disregarding his own safety for the honor of all, gave his soul to the God who had created him. Captain Major Afonso de Albuquerque was also wounded in the neck by an arrow; he could not complain of

[d^r] ra, que ante sí con una lanza tenía por su mano muertos siete indios, digno que no fenezca su fama, pues puso la vida por nuestra fe e su muerte dio por buen ejemplo. No se quedó en la posada Manuel Pazaña, dignísimo capitán que maravillosamente peleaba, trazando cabezas a los pérfidos indios por ganar la honra que mereció, envuelta en la sangre de su muerte. E otros capitanes e esforzadas gentes trocaron el mal del cuerpo por el bien de la* alma. La crueldad fue grande que con el mariscal usaron porque le deceparon las piernas, pero la gloria la excede, por el martirio merecida. Había en† Calicut nueve mil hombres de pelea. De allí el capitán mayor envió sus desculpas de aquel desconcierto al rey de Portugal. Las‡ cargadas naos fueron a Cananor e de ahí a Lisbona, e Alonso de Alburquerque se fue a Cochín.

Título XL. *De la ciudad de Calicut e sus gentes.*

Calicut es así dicha de cal e piedra e *catdar,* que acá se dice cutir§ o tocar, así que se interpreta toque de piedra. Era antiguamente imperio, aunque sólo uno debía ser en el mundo como un pontífice. Ahora es reino, su puerto el más célebre de India, donde naos de canela, pimienta, gemgibre e otras mercancías se cargaban para toda la redondez de las tierras. Lo cual después de la mortandad [que] en ella hobieron los portugueses magnánimos cesó, que no tan cumplidamente es

---

* del la   † e   ‡ los   § cutix

not sharing his men's fate.* They killed the good brave knight Vasco da Silveira,⁂ he who had singlehandedly killed seven Moors with his lance. He is worthy of unending fame, for he offered his life for our Faith and crowned it with an exemplary death. Not hiding behind the door either was Manuel Paçanha, who fought magnificently, severing many heads of those perfidious Indians in order to gain the deserved honor, swathed as it was in his death's blood. Other Captains and brave men exchanged the trials of the body for the glory of the soul. They were very cruel with the Marshal, for they chopped off his legs, but the glory earned by his martyrdom exceeds it by far. In Calicut there were nine thousand fighting men. The Captain Major then sent his apologies to the King of Portugal for that misfortune. Those ships which had a full cargo proceeded to Cannanore and thence to Lisbon, and Afonso de Albuquerque went to Cochin.

Title XL. *About the city of Calicut and its people.*

Calicut comes from "cal,"⁂ which means stone, and "catdar," which we would say as "cutir," to touch; thus it should be interpreted as meaning touchstone. It was formerly an empire, although only one person in the world should be like a pontiff.⁂ Now it is a kingdom, its port the most celebrated in India, where cinnamon, pepper, ginger, and other merchandise were loaded aboard ships bound throughout the world. Nowadays, after the carnage inflicted by the magnanimous Portuguese, this trade has ceased, and the port is not so frequently

---

* porque no quedase de la compañía quejoso. The Spanish is not clear here.

visitado. Hay en Calicut e sus tierras multitud de pimienta, la cual como dije se halla en Cochín e Cananor asaz. Es frutice como yedra *in arboris,* yerba que se retuerce o enlaza en cadena en los árbores. La pimienta es en racimos verdes cogida que al sol seca, se vuelve negra, cual a estas partes viene. La canela nace en la ínsula de Ceilán,* que tiene la hoja cual de laurel; la casca de sus árbores es la canela que acá se dice. El clavo nace en la isla que Maluco† se nombra en árbores pequeños cuya flor es clavo de [[d]ᵛ] cabeza, e las nueces moscadas es el fruto del árbol; el cuerecico de las nueces se dice maza. En Calicut e en muchos reinos de India son gentiles que adoran ídolos, animales e sus figuras. Crian en casa bueyes e vacas; el matador de ellas tiene pena de muerte. En esa tierra no hay judíos, las gentes negras, las tetas de las mujeres chicas, por lo cual parecen mejor. Los varones traen oro pendiente de las orejas, las espadas sin vainas, e adargas mayores que rodelas. Hay muchas suertes de estados e gentes. Los principales son naires, que son caballeros, a los cuales no llegan los otros estados, salvo siendo cristiano, moro o judío: así que no sea de su seta. E aún no querían tratar con muchos de los cristianos, e decían que bien conocían ellos ser los cristianos que allí estaban‡ tan buenos e mejores que ellos, pero porque trataban con la gente más baja que de aquella tierra, no querían que llegasen a ellos, mayormente cuando venían lavados. No escupen dentro en casa, que lo tienen por sucia cosa. Comen con la mano derecha, que con la siniestra se lavan. Burlaban de los cristianos porque comían con ambas manos. Adoran los indios de Calicut al diablo, con el cual hablan e se aconsejan. Dicen que creen haber un Dios movedor de

---

  * Cerlan   † Naluco ‡ estaban ser

visited. Calicut and its lands abound in pepper, which, as I have said, is found in great quantities in Cochin and Cannanore. It is a perennial shrub that grows like ivy, *in arboris,* wrapping and entwining itself around the trees. The pepper when picked is in green branches, and as it dries in the sun it turns black, which is how it comes to these parts. Cinnamon grows on the island of Ceylon. It has a leaf similar to the laurel, and the bark of the trees is what here is called cinnamon. Cloves grow on small trees on the island called Molucca. The flower bud of the tree looks like the head of a nail; the tree's fruit holds the nutmeg, and the tiny external covering of the nut is called mace. In Calicut and many kingdoms of India the people are pagans; they adore idols, animals, and representations of animals. They raise oxen and cows inside the house; he who kills one suffers the death penalty. In that land there are no Jews; the people are dark-skinned; the women are small-breasted, which makes them better looking. The males wear golden earrings. They carry unsheathed swords and shields larger than bucklers. There are many kinds of classes and peoples. The highest are the Nairs, knights, whom the other classes do not approach unless they be Christian, Moor, or Jew, that is, someone not of their sect. Even so, they did not wish to deal with many of the Christians. They declared that they knew the Christians who were there to be as good or better than they, but, because the Christians dealt with the lowest classes of the land, they, the Nairs, did not want them to come near them, especially after they had just bathed. They do not spit inside the house, for they consider it a dirty habit. They eat with the right hand because they clean themselves with the left and they would poke fun at the Christians for eating with both hands. The Indians in

los cielos, criador de las criaturas, bueno, e que no hace mal. Pero porque el diablo es malo e perverso que les puede dañar, lo honran e adoran. Pero el diablo es mal amigo e así pierden el servicio; comunícansele más para acrecentarles de pena [que] lo que les muestra de amor.

Título XLI. *De la forma que llegaron a Goa e de sus habitadores.*

Sano de la herida, el capitán Alonso de Alburquerque se partió para el estrecho de Meca. [Luego que] llegase junto al reino de Honor, Timogi,* que era gran hombre de armada o gran cosario por lar mar, [dii^r] de seta gentil, hizo entender al capitán mayor como Sabayo, rey de Guoa era muerto, e cerca la sucesión, por tener muchos herederos que† había grandes revueltas en el reino, que podría ligeramente tomarlo. Lo cual determinaron hacer los cristianos, e Timogi en su ayuda. Guoa quiero que sepáis como es una fuerte e hermosa ciudad asentada en una breve isla inexpugnable. Pasan a ella por pasos en los cuales torres almenadas con capitanes e gentes están. Los que entran o salen en ella van en barcos. Es de mucho arroz, ganados, mantenimientos e aguas sabrosas, dulces e sanas. La fortaleza es fortísima, con cavas muy hondas llenas de agua. *Intra muros* hay dos hermosos castillos, sobre el río uno e otro cara a la ciudad. Adoran sus habitadores al sol e a la luna e animales; cuyo abominable uso (que ellos por santo tienen) es

* Tinogi   † e

Calicut adore the devil,✳ with whom they converse and take counsel. They say they believe there is a God, the Mover of the heavens, Creator of all creatures, who is good and does no evil; but since the devil is evil and perverse and has the power to harm them, they honor and adore him. But surely the devil is a false friend, and they only waste the service rendered him. He communicates with them more to increase their sufferings than to show any love.

Title XLI. *About how they reached Goa and about its inhabitants.*

As soon as Captain Afonso de Albuquerque recovered from his wound, he set out for the Strait of Mecca.✳ As he reached the kingdom of Onor, Timogi,✳ the commander of a great fleet of corsairs, a pagan, informed the Captain Major that Sabayo the King of Goa had died.✳ There were many heirs, and the kingdom was in such turmoil over the succession that it could be taken easily. The Christians resolved to do this, with Timogi's aid. Goa,✳ I want you to know, is a strong beautiful city located on a small unassailable island. One approaches it through passes that have merloned towers manned by captains and troops. Those who enter and leave the island go by boat. Goa abounds in rice, other foodstuffs, cattle, and tasty, clean, fresh water. The fort is extremely strong, surrounded by deep moats filled with water. *Intra muros* stand two beautiful castles; one commands the river, the other faces the city. Its inhabitants adore the sun, the moon, and animals. Theirs is that abominable custom,✳ which they consider holy, whereby when the husband

que muriendo el marido, la mujer se ha de ir luego a quemar de
voluntad ganosa. E espacio de tres días la traen por las calles
principales con muy dulces músicas e canciones, muy vestida e
ricamente apuesta. Se van a la hoguera, la cual en un hoyo
está bien inflamada e grande, donde como llega, da alrededor del
fuego tres vueltas e apartada del fuego, corriendo se mete en él
muy crudamente; adonde sus parientes con ollas de manteca e
aceite le ayudan por la consolar entre las vivas llamas. Los
hombres en aquella tierra andan desnudos por los grandes
calores que hay. Las mujeres traen en las narices pendientes
joyas de oro. Llegados, pues, Alonso de Alburquerque e Timogi
a Guoa, ancoraron ante su río e después entraron por él; contra
los cuales los infieles tiraron mucha artillería que en los almenados baluartes [tenían]. Lo cual como de los cristianos fue
visto, soltaron sus bombardas, de forma que desbarataron la
más gente de los baluartes, entrando por las bombarderas, que
bien se defendían. [[dii]ᵛ] Pero poco les aprovechó porque
sin temor de ellos fueron entradas. De que se maravillaron, diciendo: aquellos no hombres sino diablos debían ser, pues tan sin
temor de la muerte por los más peligrosos lugares hacían su
próspero aunque fatigoso viaje. Los moros, como ya gente cristiana vieron en tierra, huyeron, a las cuales los españoles fueron
en el alcance; e volvieron por la artillería de los baluartes,* que
en sus bateles a las españolas naos llegaron. Otro día ancoraron
ante la ciudad sus naos, que distaban dos leguas, donde los
infieles, muy bravos se mostrando con su espesa e presurosa artillería, en defensión se pusieron. Pero Dios nuestro Señor, defensor e amparo de los cristianos, mostró aquí por ellos un gran
misterio: que en la ribera estaban diez e seis naos grandes, entre
las cuales había una, la mayor que dicen jamás se hizo. E

* baluaris

dies the wife must go straightaway and willingly burn herself.
Three days after his death they bring her through the main
streets, very handsomely dressed and adorned and accompanied
by sweet music and songs. They go to the pyre, which is burning
fiercely in a large pit. Reaching the pyre, she goes around it three
times, draws back, then runs and wildly leaps right in. Her relatives help it with jars of grease and oil to console her amid the
burning flames. The men of that land go about naked on account of the great heat, and the women wear gold jewels in
their noses. Well, when Afonso de Albuquerque and Timogi
reached Goa,* they anchored outside the river. As they started
in, the infidels shelled them from artillery emplacements in
the merloned bulwarks. They drove most of the defenders back
from the bulwarks, entering through the mortar ports. They
were well defended, but to no avail, for the Christians fearlessly
stormed them. The defenders marveled at this, saying that those
must have been devils, not men: so unafraid of death did they
make their prosperous though fatiguing journey through the
most perilous places. When the Moors saw that the Christians
had gotten ashore, they broke and ran. The men of Hispania
pursued them, then returned for the artillery of the bulwarks and
carried it back to the ships of Hispania in their longboats. Next
day they anchored their ships about two leagues from the city;
there the infidels, acting ever so brave behind the defenses of
their heavy and swift artillery, prepared to defend themselves.
But Our Lord God, Defender and Protector of Christians,
worked here a great mystery* on their behalf. For along the
shore stood sixteen large ships, among which was one said to
be the largest ever built. As the vicious battle progressed, a
youth set fire to the ship, which was in the middle of all the oth-

andando la cruda batalla, un joven puso fuego a la nao principal, que en el medio estaba; e como los infieles lo vieron, toda su gente fue a amatar el fuego, desamparando el más necesario paso. Iban por matar el joven, el cual, pensando que en las manos tenían, desapareció. Esto contaban los de Guoa, aunque otros, por no confesar el misterio que sabían, decían: uno que capitán de ella quisiera ser por no se la haber dado la quemara. Lo cual no era así, según después bien luego se descubrió. Había de los rumes cuatrocientos carpinteros haciendo las naos que habían de ir en busca de los cristianos e en su socorro venían del soldán catorce mil rumes si necesarios fuesen. Así aquel día fue grande la liza que entre ellos hobo, hasta que la obscura noche cerró otro día que el sol descubriese las caras a los enemigos.

Título XLII. *Como hicieron los de Guoa paces con Alonso de Alburquerque e fue entrada la ciudad.*

Los de Goa visto el daño que dec[laradamiente]* recibían, otro día dos de los más honrados moros o infieles vinieron a pedir paces al capitán [diii^r] mayor. A los cuales respondió no ser su voluntad si el reino e ciudad de Guoa no le era entregado cual lo había Sabayo, rey de ella, poseído. E le habían de dar las naos que los rumes habían hecho para ir contra ellos e doscientos rumes que en la ciudad estaban. Donde no, que a ninguno de ellos daría vida e mandaría abrasar toda la ciudad, casas, gentes e tierra sin misericordia. En lo cual vinieron los moros, dándole las llaves de la fortaleza. E el capitán Alonso de

* delaradamiente

ers. As soon as the infidels saw this, all their men ran off
to kill the fire, leaving the most crucial pass unprotected. They
were out to kill the youth, who when they thought they had
him in their hands disappeared. The Goans told about this, although others, so as not to admit the mystery which they well
knew, said that a man who had sought to be captain of the ship
and had been turned down had set it afire. This was not so,
as was soon after definitely discovered. Four hundred Rumi
carpenters were in Goa building the ships that were to have
gone in search of the Christians. If need be, the Sultan was
going to send fourteen thousand Rumis in their support. Therefore it was an important engagement which had taken place
that day, until the dark night brought to a close another day
during which the sun had uncovered the faces of the enemy.

Title XLII. *How the Goans made peace with Afonso de Albuquerque, and how the city was entered.*

The Goans saw the damage being so relentlessly inflicted
upon them, so the next day two of the most honored Moors or
infidels came to the Captain Major to sue for peace. He replied
that he did not want it unless the kingdom and city of Goa were
delivered up to him just as King Sabayo had possessed it. Further, they were to hand over the ships the Rumis had built to
go against him, as well as two hundred Rumis who were in the
city. If they did not, he would leave no one alive;✳ he would
order the entire city, its buildings, people, and lands, burned
without quarter. The Moors acceded to all this and gave him
the keys to the fort.✳ Captain Afonso de Albuquerque came

Alburquerque salió en tierra poderosamente con las banderas e estandartes de Portugal, con sonidos regocijados de atabales e trompetas. Vieron las fortalezas e castillos, en las cuales dejaron gente; e otra fortaleza edificó Alonso de Alburquerque en aquella ciudad. E de la mudanza de los manjares murieron cuarenta hombres de los cristianos. Tomaron de los rumes caballos muchos, artillería, armas de malla e de hierro, una casa de flechas e pólvora, aceite, pescado, cobre e plata e otras cosas de rico valor. Sabido por el Soltán Sabaín, hijo del rey Sabayo, ayuntó grandes gentes de guerra e vino contra los cristianos. E este rey de Goa había* sido del rey de Aquen, e Sabayo su vasallo se había levantado contra él. E viendo todas las cosas como pasaban en Goa, fue avisado el rey de Aquen, e envió luego un gran capitán que se decía Camalcán e al hijo del rey Sabayo con gran ejército, que serían sesenta mil hombres de pelea, más de diez mil de caballo e ochocientos espingarderos. Asentaron, pues, sus tiendas fronteras de un paso en que estaba† por capitán García de Sosa, que con su industria e esfuerzo los hizo levantar de allí e pasarse a otra parte, por miedo que [habían]‡ de la artillería e del lugar. Bien mostró e dio a entender los de Sosa venir de la real casta de Portugal, como es verdad e sus armas, que son las quinas e cru- [[diii]ᵛ] zadas lunas, descubren. Con la cual vitoria, sin detenimiento salieron en tierra hasta nueve o diez de los cristianos tras los infieles. E los otros de García de Sosa venían en pos de ellos, que por las§ corrientes no desembarcaron tan presto como era razón para socorrer a los delanteros. De los cuales diez fue Martín Fernández de Figueroa que, esforzada e animosamente peleando, matando e hiriendo en los contrarios, le dieron con una flecha que le

---

    * habían   † estaban   ‡ abiaon   § los

ashore in full force, the banners of Portugal waving to the joy-
ous sounds of kettle drums and trumpets. They inspected the
forts and castles and placed men in them. Afonso de Albuquerque also erected another fort in that city. As a result of the
change in diet forty of the Christians died. From the Rumis
they seized many horses, artillery, suits of mail and iron, a
building full of arrows and powder, oil, fish, copper and silver,
and other things of great value. When Sultan Sabaín, King
Sabayo's son, learned of these things, he assembled a large force
of fighting men and came against the Christians. The King of
Goa had formerly been a vassal of the King of the Deccan, but
Sabayo had risen against him. Seeing how everything was going
at Goa, the King of the Deccan was informed, and he immediately sent a great captain named Khamil Khan* and King
Sabayo's son with a vast army: about sixty thousand infantry,
more than ten thousand cavalry, and eight hundred musketeers.
They set up their tents opposite a pass guarded by Garcia de
Sousa,* who with industrious efforts forced them to pick up
and move to another place out of fear of his artillery and the
emplacement. He certainly gave ample proof that the Sousas
come from the royal caste of Portugal. This is true as their
coat of arms, which depicts the *quinas* and crossed moons, reveals. Immediately following this victory, some nine or ten
Christians leaped ashore after the infidels.* The rest of Garcia
de Sousa's men started after them, but the currents kept them
from disembarking as rapidly as was needed to assist the first
group. One of the ten was Martín Fernández de Figueroa, and
he fought bravely and vigorously. As he went killing and
wounding among his adversaries, he was hit with an arrow
that broke the side of his helmet and drove right through his

rompió el borde del capacete e le traspasó el rostro de parte a
parte; la cual tomó por el hierro e la sacó del rostro. Acabada
de sacar, le dieron una pedrada en la pierna e otra en el capacete
muy cruel, que aína arrodillara si el grande e valiente esfuerzo
que llevaba por escudo no le socorriera hasta que a los bateles
llegaron e socorridos fueron. Mataron allí un cristiano e hirieron
a todos aquellos que acometieron tan gran hazaña de ánimo,
a que no diez pero ciento no hicieran cara. E así de aquella vez
se volvieron a la fortaleza en los bateles e los heridos fueron
bien curados.

Título XLIII. *Como hobo grandes batallas, lides e recias peleas
entre los cristianos e infieles.*

Grandes fueron las cuestiones, saltos, encuentros e batallas
que entre ellos hobo, de la una parte e de la otra, que serían
largas de contar, en que Timogi hizo hazañosas cosas contra
los enemigos aunque los moros que el capitán había hecho de
gente le fueron traidores e se pasaron a los contrarios del capitán
mayor; e aún muchos de los de Timogi fueron contra su señor.
En el cual conmedio* los m[uchos ene]migos quisieron entrar
en tierra, do fueron desbaratados e muchos muertos, así que se
lanzaban huyendo en el† mar' [div^r] do se ahogaban otros
muertos, los cristianos quedando‡ con gloriosa vitoria. Jorge
de Acuña, al cual mataron alguna gente, García de Sosa e
Timogi hicieron maravillosos vencimientos en que fueran bien
empleados los ringlones de *Amadís,* que ocupan loores que
muchos merecieron. Después de lo cual, ido García de Sosa a

     * comedio   † enl   ‡ quedano

cheek. He simply took it by the shaft and pulled it out. As soon as he had removed it, one stone hit him on the leg and another really severe one dealt him a cruel blow on the helmet. These would surely have brought him to his knees had not his great and valiant courage—which served as his shield—sustained him until they could reach the longboats and be helped. They killed one Christian there and wounded all those who had undertaken such an intrepid feat (which one hundred would not have dared face, let alone ten). After that encounter they boarded the longboats and returned to the fort, where the wounded were well cared for.

Title XLIII. *How there were great battles, clashes, and fierce struggles between the Christians and infidels.*

The Christians and infidels engaged in many disputes, assaults, encounters, and battles, and it would take quite long to describe them. Timogi accomplished remarkable feats against the enemy throughout, even though the Moorish troops the Captain had assigned him proved traitorous and went over to the enemies of the Captain Major. Even many of Timogi's own men went against their chief. At that point the large enemy force tried to land but were routed. Scores were killed, and many more drowned as they threw themselves into the sea trying to escape. The Christians thus obtained a glorious victory. Jorge da Cunha,✳ some of whose men were killed, Garcia de Sousa, and Timogi prevailed and triumphed so marvelously that one might well apply to them the lines of the *Amadis,*✳ which contain the caliber of praise so many of these men merit-

Benesterí defendiendo e amparando el paso esforzadamente, le fue mucha de su gente muerta e desbaratada. Él fue herido e un hermano suyo muerto, digno de no ser puesto en olvido según defendía a los infieles la entrada. García de Sosa hobo de perecer en un peligroso batel que las aguas llevaron a puerto de sus enemigos, pero como Dios remedia en las necesidades prestamente, remando con la más fuerza que los cristianos pudieron, se salvaron por el paso que Francisco Pereira guardaba. Dice Figueroa que parecía el día del juicio, según las cosas que avinieron. E las casas de Benesterí abrasaron los infieles, por lo cual don Antonio, que en las galeras estaba, fue forzado recogerse a la fortaleza. E una nao suya que se llamaba *La espera* metió so la agua con toda la artillería, que después sacaron los moros.* E el capitán mayor envió una nave por mantenimientos, la cual al salir de la barra se perdió.

Título XLIV. *Como los moros enviaban los cristianos† renegados a los cristianos por les hacer enojo.*

La causa de las tan recias batallas fue que había hecho el capitán mayor seis mil moros de pelea soldados de Goa e hicieron traición, por lo cual todos [los] daños que allí se recrecieron, habidos muchos encuentros, se causaron. Asaz veces los moros en sus bateles venían a la orilla del río haciendo se-
[[div]ᵛ] ñales de paz, a las veces por rescatar moros, e otras porque viesen los cristianos a los renegados, como los traían a caballo con pajes e mozos de espuelas e ataviados, de que gran pesar había Alonso de Alburquerque e su gente. Un día los

* maros   † christanos

ed. After this, when Garcia de Sousa had gone to Bana-starim,❉ vigorously defending and protecting the pass, many of his men were killed and routed. He was wounded and a brother of his killed,❉ and the way he defended the pass against the enemy will never be forgotten. Garcia de Sousa very nearly perished in a longboat that the current carried dangerously close to the enemy shore. But, since God is quick to remedy in moments of need, rowing as hard as they could, the Christians pulled away to safety through the pass guarded by Francisco Pereira.❉ Figueroa says it seemed like Judgment Day, so many terrible things were befalling them. The infidels burned the houses at Banastarim, which forced Dom Antonio and his galleys❉ to pull back to the fort. And one ship, the *Espera,* he scuttled with all her guns, but the Moors later pulled them up. The Captain Major sent a ship after provisions,❉ but it was lost trying to cross the bar.

Title XLIV. *How the Moors would send renegade Christians to harass the Christians.*

The reason for such fierce battles was that the Captain Major had made six thousand Moorish fighting men❉ mercenary troops in Goa, and they committed treason, which caused all the subsequent troubles and battles that took place there. Often the Moors would come to the river's edge in their longboats under a flag of truce. Sometimes they came to ransom Moors, others so the Christians could see the renegades,❉ how they came riding horses, with pages and footmen and all dressed up, which greatly upset Afonso de Albuquerque and his men. One

moros vinieron a la orilla del río con camisas blancas, haciendo señales que los cristianos viniesen con ellos seguramente a hablar. E el capitán mayor envió allá un batel, de que iba por capitán Johan Núñez. E estando cuasi juntos, habló un renegado a los cristianos, preguntando cómo estaban e les había sucedido en aquellos trances. Johan Núñez le interrogó que quién era. El renegado replicó que se llamaba Juan Deras, físico del capitán mayor. Al cual Johan Núñez, haciendo de ojo que armasen un tiro de espingarda, dijo que porqué se había ido a los infieles e había renegado. Estando en palabras, diole por mitad del corazón la espingarda, que cayó renegadamente muerto; e duró aún tres días pero a cabo de ellos malaventuradamente feneció. E vuelto Johan Núñez, buen capitán e católico varón, lo contó al capitán mayor, el cual hizo dar al espingardero cincuenta cruzados.

Título XLV. *Como los moros quisieron combatir las naos cristianas e mataron a don Antonio, sobrino del capitán.*

Los infieles sabiendo la mucha flaqueza que [entre los] cristianos había de gente e socorro (¡excepto el del cielo!), mandó Malcán combatir las naos cristianas, de que Alonso de Alburquerque fue avisado. Fue contra las galeras e bateles que el capitán envió por tentarlos e los que en su am[paro vinie]ron gran liza e pelea, así de artillería como de personas. Simón de Andrada e Fernán Pérez su hermano con ocho ca- [[dv]ʳ] balleros en una galera de los enemigos saltaron, do esfuerzo e sangrientas espadas eran testigos de sus virtuosas obras e claras hazañas. Aquel día fue herido el buen caballero don Antonio, sobrino del capitán mayor, muy esforzado e católico, que seis

day the Moors came to the shore signaling with white shirts
for the Christians to come and talk in safety. The Captain
Major sent in a longboat captained by João Nunes.✳ When they
were almost there, a renegade called out to the Christians, asking how they were and how they were getting along in those
difficult straits. João Nunes asked him who he was, and the
renegade replied that his name was Juan Deras, a physician of the
Captain Major. João Nunes, signaling with a wink for a
musket to be loaded, asked Deras why he had gone over to the
infidels and become a renegade. While they were talking, the
musket shot hit Deras right in the heart, and he fell to die a
renegade, for even though he lingered on for three days, he
perished wretchedly. Upon his return, the good captain and
Catholic gentleman João Nunes reported this incident to the
Captain Major, who rewarded the musketeer with fifty cruzados.

Title XLV. *How the Moors attempted to attack the Christian
ships and killed Dom Antonio, the Captain's nephew.*

Since the infidels knew of the Christians' grievous lack of
men and assistance (except for that of Heaven!), Khamil Khan
ordered an attack on the Christian ships, of which Afonso de
Albuquerque was informed.✳ There was a great attack, including artillery and hand-to-hand fighting, against the galleys and
longboats the Captain Major had sent to observe the enemy and
the ships he then sent to support them. Simão de Andrada, his
brother Fernão Peres,✳ and eight other knights leaped aboard an
enemy galley, where determination and bloody swords attested
to their virtuous deeds and outstanding feats. That day the good
knight Dom Antonio, the Captain Major's brave Catholic

días después murió, siendo causa de asaz tristeza porque entre las muchas virtudes que tenía, era bienquisto. Murió gran gente de los contrarios, entre los cuales un sobrino de Melcán desesperadamente hobo, e dos capitanes, los mejores de su hueste.

Título XLVI. *Como se partió de Guoa a Cananor e de los capitanes e gente de Portugal e de sus mudanzas.*

En el mes de agosto era cuando el capitán mayor, viendo la triste vida que en Guoa hacían, salió del río para Cananor a proveerse de viandas, que no tenían. E aunque los moros o infieles (aunque diga algunas veces moros, entiéndense gentiles o infieles* do está ya declarado) quisieron resistir e desbaratar los cristianos en la salida, no pudieron, donde sólo un cristiano murió. Fueron camino la vía de Angediva. Vieron venir a ellos doce naos: cuatro iban a Melaca, ocho iban a la India, e un navío del mariscal. Capitán de las ocho era Gonzalo de Sequera, las cuales habían de volver en Portugal con especiería. Así que conocidos, hobieron mucho placer e fueron a Cananor. Ahí vinieron Gonzalo de Sequera e Duarte de Lemos con otras cuatro naos, el cual venía de Hormuz. Las cuales, sabiendo que había guerra contr[a el] rey de Cochín, fueron a lo favorecer contra el príncipe, hijo de su hermana, que allá hereda; e porque él se había de entrar en la cueva do el rey su antecesor había muerto e él no quería (que es una costumbre que allá tenían, que no reina más el rey de [cuanto] vive el otro rey que está en la cueva, e muerto, ha de entrar el sucesor en ella e el sobrino heredar). Allí fue desbaratado el príncipe e le tomaron

* infielens

nephew, was wounded. His death six days later caused great sadness, because among his many virtues he was well liked.⁜ A great number of the adversaries were killed, among them a nephew of Khamil Khan who died to eternal despair, plus two of the best captains of his host.

Title XLVI. *How he left Goa and went to Cannanore and about the captains and crews newly arrived from Portugal and their adventures.*

It was in the month of August⁜ when the Captain Major, seeing the sad life they were leading in Goa, sailed out of the river toward Cannanore to secure food which they needed. Although the Moors or infidels (although I sometimes say Moors, where I have done so you should understand it to mean pagans or infidels) tried to stop and defeat the departing Christians, they could not, and only one Christian was killed. Proceeding toward Angedive, they sighted twelve ships approaching; four were bound for Malacca,⁜ and eight for India. One of the Marshal's ships also appeared. Captain of the eight, which were supposed to take on spices and return to Portugal, was Gonçalo de Sequeira.⁜ Once recognized, they were all very pleased and went to Cannanore. Gonçalo de Sequeira went there, as did Duarte de Lemos⁜ with four other ships en route from Hormuz. The latter, learning that there was a war against the King of Cochin, went to his assistance against the prince, his sister's son. This is the person who inherits the throne there. The king was supposed to go into the cave⁜ where his predecessor as king had just died, but he did not want to. For it is the

el galeón en que iba, e aún [[dv]^v] otro tanto hicieran a él si no estuviera presto en tierra. De allí determinó Alonso de Alburquerque ir para Goa e mandó que todo hombre se recogiese a las naos dado caso que tuviesen licencia de se ir para Portugal ya en aquel año. Determinaron algunos de se asconder e no ir más en su compañía, pues habían visto a Guoa e estaban ya* hartos de ella. Mayormente que si† no fueron con él por espacio más de tres años, habían ido ya siete e algunos de ellos nueve que estaban en las Indias, puesta al tablero la vida cada rato e momento como habéis visto. Uno de los que con mucha causa se quedaron fue Martín Fernández Figueroa, que maravilloso ejemplo de bondad dejó en aquellas partes e trajo a éstas. De allí fue partido el capitán mayor para Guoa. Adonde llegando, algunos fueron mal heridos, e con valientes e magnánimas fuerzas de Diego Méndez de Vasconcelos, capitán mayor para Melaca, e de Manuel de la Cerda, del linaje de los reyes de Francia, e de Simón de Andrada e Fernán Pérez su hermano, juntamente con la venturosa muerte del caballero don Jerónimo, capitán de veinte e cinco cristianos, se tomó e triunfó Goa poderosamente. En los infieles fue tal el estrago que no hay papel al presente prompto para tan largamente escribir. De lo cual todo avisó por una caravela que envió a Cananor a Duarte de Lemos, que tenía siete naos cargadas para Portugal, en que trajo hasta Lisbona a Figueroa e a otros caballeros e hombres de bien, puesto que otra cosa le enviara rogar el capitán mayor.

* estabayan   † s

custom there that the king reigns only as long as the former
king who is in the cave lives. When the latter dies, the incumbent must enter the cave, and the nephew succeeds to the
throne. They routed the prince, seized his galleon, and would
have caught him as well had he not quickly gotten ashore. From
there Afonso de Albuquerque resolved to set out for Goa. He
ordered all those who had permission to return to Portugal
that year to go aboard the cargo ships. Some resolved to hide
and not continue in his company any longer. They had seen
Goa and had had their fill of it. Moreover, not only had they
been with him for more than three years, but it was seven and
for some even nine years that they had been in the Indies, risk-
ing their lives every moment of every day, as you have seen. One
of those who with ample reason stayed behind⁜ was Martín
Fernández de Figueroa, who left in those parts the same
marvelous example of goodness he brought back to these. From
there the Captain Major set out for Goa. As they arrived, some
of the men were seriously wounded, but, thanks to the valiant
and magnificent efforts of Diogo Mendes de Vasconcelos, Captain Major for Malacca, and Manuel de la Cerda,⁜ of the lineage
of the kings of France, and Simão de Andrada and his brother
Fernão Peres, and Dom Jerónimo,⁜ who died a blessed death
at the head of twenty-five Christians, Goa was seized in mighty
triumph. Among the infidels the devastation was such that there
is not enough paper at hand to describe it fully. They were
informed of all this by a caravel sent to Cannanore, where
Duarte de Lemos had seven ships loaded for his return to
Portugal,⁜ in which he brought to Lisbon, Figueroa and other
knights and gentlemen, even though the Captain Major had
entreated him not to.

Título XLVII. *De las cosas que en Melaca había.*

Cuatro naos había el rey de Portugal enviado a descubrir clavo, ruibarbo e otra especiería, en las cuales por capitán iba Diego Sequera. E llegó do el bisrey estaba, [cuando]* García de Sosa capitán en un buen navío envió. Fueron a Melaca por el cabo de Comerín, bien edificado de templos e muros [[dvi]ʳ] de mármor con historias de bulto muy ricas. Figueroa dice que son mejores que en Roma, pero como los romanos yo haya visto,† creo no las excederán las de Comarín. Hay allí un templo en el cual tal costumbre guardan que él que en él entra no ha de comer por tres días que de él saliere. Es muy rico templo de grandes rentas que da de comer a más de cinco mil vírgenes‡ que siendo de edad casan, e las que no quieren ser casadas pueden allí estar para siempre como beatas. En aquella tierra son idólatras. Hay brámenes que duermen con las reinas aunque no quiera su marido el rey, por lo cual el rey se volvió§ brámene, porque con mujer de uno otro no puede yacer. Es tierra de muchos mantenimientos excepto de trigo, que no se da allí. Yendo, pues, a Melaca, pasaron por Ceilán, do nace la canela como asaz dije, e por Samatora, do nace la pimienta, los dineros de cuya tierra son pimienta e medidas de ella. Es de muchas riquezas e piedras preciosas. En la cual isla hobo paces entre el rey de ella e los cristianos. E de allí partieron para Melaca, dejando a la mano siniestra contra el norte ciertas islas

---

* q̄uedo. Although it is difficult to determine exactly what this combination of letters represents, "quãdo," rendered in this edition as "cuando," best fits the context. When Sequeira arrived, Almeida did assign Garcia de Sousa to accompany him.

† vstio   ‡ virgines   § selvio

Title XLVII. *About what took place in Malacca.*

The King of Portugal had sent four ships in search of cloves, rhubarb, and other spices, with Diogo Sequeira in command. He paid a visit to the Viceroy,✠ who assigned Captain Garcia de Sousa✠ and a good warship to his company. They went to Malacca by way of Cape Comorin, which is well adorned with temples and walls covered with very handsome legends carved out in marble. Figueroa says they are better than in Rome, but, as I have seen Roman carvings, I believe that those of Cape Comorin cannot surpass them. There is a temple there in which they observe a certain custom whereby he who enters does not eat for three days after coming back out. It is a very wealthy temple; its great income feeds more than five thousand virgins, who, when they come of age, may marry, or, if they do not want to, may remain there forever as holy women. The people of that land are idolators. There are Brahmans who sleep with the queens even though her husband the king be opposed. For this reason the king became a Brahman, for no man should lie with the wife of another. It is an abundant land except for wheat, which does not grow there. Proceeding toward Malacca, they passed by Ceylon, where cinnamon grows as I have already said several times. They went to Sumatra, where pepper grows, and money consists of pepper and varying measures thereof. It has many other riches and precious stones, and its king was at peace with the Christians. From there they set out toward Malacca, passing certain islands to their left,✠ to the

en las cuales unos a otros se comen: su manjar no es sino carne
humana. Aportaron a Melaca, distante de Cochín cuatrocientas
leguas poco más o menos, isla muy rica e abundosa asaz, do
contrataron paces. El clavo viene allí de Maluco, que lo traen
los chines, gente cercana de Melaca, cuyo calzado son botas de
cuero, blancos como cristianos. A lo que comen no llegan con
las manos, excepto con unos palos de muy olorosa madera.
Beben por escudillas muy limpias que ellos dicen por más lindas
que de cristal; las cuales son doradas e de diversas colores. En
la isla de Melaca hay gentes de divers[as tie]rras por las
muchas mercancías con que tratan, sus faciones anchas, blancas,
como las de Antilla del cristianísimo e más que poderoso rey
de Castilla. [[dvi]ᵛ] Sus armas son de hierro, los hierros de
las lanzas ondeados e en forma de lenguas; tiran flechas con
cebratanas. Los cristianos estovieron allí algunos días proveídos
de sus mercancías, confiando en la paz de los enemigos, la cual
no guardaron. Ante mataron muchos e fueron los portugueses
desbaratados e a sus bateles recogidos. Se partieron al cabo de
Camarín en la cual cargaba Diego de Sequera, llegando ahí con
tres naos, que otras dos perecieron: una que metieron so la
agua, e otra en una obscura noche en la isla Polvoreda se robró;
de las cuales la gente se salvó. De allí fueron dos capitanes en
dos naos a Cochín, García de Sosa e Jerónimo de Tejeda, que
del capitán mayor fueron bien recibidos e tratados hasta que
volvieron en Portugal. E Diego de Sequera se partió para
Lisbona.

north, where the people devour one another; their only food is human flesh. They made port at Malacca, a very rich and abundant island situated some four hundred leagues from Cochin, and there concluded a peace treaty. Cloves come there from Molucca, brought by the Chinese,✳ a people who live near Malacca, wear leather boots, and are white like Christians. They do not pick up food with their hands, but with sticks fashioned from a very fragrant wood. They drink from sparkling clean bowls which they consider prettier than crystal. These are gold-plated and multicolored. On the island of Malacca there are peoples from many lands on account of all the items traded there. Their features are broad, and they are white, like the people of the Antilles✳ of the most Christian and more than mighty King of Castile. Their weapons are made of iron; the lance shafts are curved in the shape of tongues. They fire arrows with blowguns. The Christians were there several days, loading their goods and trusting that their enemies would keep their word,✳ which of course they did not. On the contrary, they killed many, and the Portuguese were routed and had to withdraw to the longboats. They then made their way to Cape Comorin, where Diogo Sequeira secured a cargo. He arrived with three ships, for two others had been lost, one that they scuttled, and another that broke up on a dark night near the island of Pulo Brasse.✳ The men of both ships were saved. From there two captains, Garcia de Sousa and Jerónimo Texeira,✳ took their ships to Cochin, where they were welcomed and well treated by the Captain Major until their return to Portugal. And Diogo Sequeira set out for Lisbon.✳

Título XLVIII. *De los elefantes indios e sus diferencias e propriedades.*

Cuenta Figueroa, testigo de vista, las condiciones, precios e estima de los elefantes de las Indias que quiero sepáis. En las Indias de Persia e Arabia* hay muchos de ellos, domésticos, mansos e tratables e de mucho trabajo, cuyo precio es dos mil ducados. Son muchos de ellos tan prudentes animales que no les falta de más de ánima racional sino la habla para tener entendimiento de sabios varones. Entienden la lengua e voz india e lo que les manda† hacer el que va encima él pone en execución con su trompa; e hace tan cuerdamente cuanto otro [animal pudi]ese echar e levantar fácilmente. Tiene coyunturas como otros animales e fuerza de ochenta hombres. Sacan bateles del mar, bombardas o masteles mejor que cient hombres poniendo todas sus mayores fuerzas en ello. [En guerr]as arman sobre ellos castillos, en que iban seis o siete flecheros. Dos espadas le atan en los cuernos con que hacen cru- [[dvii]ʳ] damente adó le mandan. Aunque cient cuchilladas en las piernas un elefante reciba, no cae ni se jarreta, por tener grandes carnes en ellas. Es el mayor animal del mundo. Para subir en él, mandándoselo inclina las piernas traseras. Su color es de ceniza; tiene poco pelo, las orejas como adargas, los ojos chicos como de un puerco, poco pescuezo. Sus dientes son cuernos aunque salen por la boca, nacientes de la cabeza; son huecos hasta el medio, de los cuales es el marfil. La cola del elefante como de puerco, los pies anchos e redondos como de buey. Son pesados e no ligeros; su mantenimiento es arroz cocido con manteca, hojas de palma e yerbas,‡ su ayuntamiento como de varón a mujer. Tienen gran acuerdo o memoria; de lo que se hace muestra

* arabin   † mandan   ‡ yerbos

Title XLVIII. *About the elephants of the Indies and their different properties.*

Figueroa recounts as an eyewitness the characteristics, prices, and high esteem of the elephants of the Indies which I want you to know. There are many of them in the Indies of Persia and Arabia, domesticated, tame, manageable, and hard-working. The price for one is two thousand ducats. Many are such prudent animals that they lack only a rational soul and the ability to speak to have the understanding of wise men. They understand the spoken word of India, and what the man who rides on top commands they execute with their trunk, and do so as soundly as any other animal might easily lie down and get up. It has joints like other animals and the strength of eighty men. It can haul longboats, mortars, or masts out of the sea better than one hundred men exerting all their strength. In time of war castles capable of carrying six or seven bowmen are mounted on them. A sword is affixed to each tusk, and they use them to fierce effect wherever directed. Even if an elephant receive a hundred cuts on its legs, it will not fall or be hamstrung, for they are quite thick and tough-skinned. It is the largest animal in the world. To mount one, it lowers its hind legs on command. It is ash gray in color, with very little hair, ears like shields, small eyes like a pig, a short neck. Its teeth are horns, for though they protrude through the mouth, they start up in its head. Hollow for half their length, they are the source of ivory. The elephant's tail is like a pig's; its feet are wide and round like those of oxen. They are ponderous animals, not nimble. They feed on rice cooked in lard, palm leaves, and grass, and they copulate like man and woman. They have an

gozo o tristeza. En Goa hay tigres, puercos monteses, leones, unzas, venados e otros* animales que España desea criar. En Cochín hay culebras e tienen un capillo delante los ojos, e cuando alzan el capillo muestran gesto como de mujer, en la cual figura afirman haber tentado el diablo, enemigo de natura humana,† a Eva. Tienen en muchos reinos de las Indias tal costumbre, si alguno acreedor encuentra el deudor, lleva un ramo en la mano, verde, e hácele un círculo alrededor, en el cual pone el ramo verde. E así so grandes penas no puede el deudor salir de allí sin le pagar lo que le debe o concertarse con el acreedor. En otras partes e provincias las mujeres tienen cuantos maridos quieren; e en otras cosen las naturas a las niñas en naciendo hasta ser para casar, una de las cuales trajo Tristán de Acuña a la reina de Portugal. Lo cual se debía guardar en todas partes, si a ellas [no] les hiciese agravio, porque estuviesen más seguras sus honras.

Título XLIX. *De la venida de Duarte de Lemos en Portugal.*

[[dvii]ᵛ] Después que Duarte de Lemos cargó siete‡ naos que llevaban, un martes, once de diciembre de mil e quinientos e diez§ años del nacimiento de nuestro salvador Jesucristo, partieron de Cananor. E [fueron] por la costa a Angediva e otros lugares, en los cuales e su venida hobo muchos encuentros e recios pasos. Fueron por la isla de los Azores e por otra llamada de las Flores. Fueron a la Tercera, que de ella dista cincuenta

---

* otras   † humna   ‡ site   § once

accurate memory and show joy or sorrow over things done to them. In Goa there are tigers, wild boars, lions, ounces, deer, and other animals which Hispania would be fortunate to possess. In Cochin there are serpents, and they have a little fold of skin over their eyes. When they raise this fold they appear to be gesturing much as would a woman, in which form it is affirmed that the devil, the enemy of mankind, tempted Eve. In many of the kingdoms of the Indies they have a certain custom whereby, should a creditor encounter his debtor, he takes a branch in his hand, a green one, and draws a circle around him in which he places the green branch.* The debtor under severe penalties may not leave the circle without paying what he owes or making some arrangement with the creditor. In other parts and provinces the women have as many husbands as they please; while in others girls' genitals are sewed up at birth and kept that way until marriage. One of these girls Tristão da Cunha brought back to the Queen of Portugal.* This might well be done everywhere, if it did them no harm, so as to safeguard their honor more effectively.

Title XLIX. *About Duarte de Lemos' return to Portugal.*

Once Duarte de Lemos finished loading his seven ships, on a Tuesday, the eleventh of December, fifteen hundred and ten years after the birth of Our Savior Jesus Christ, he left Cannanore and sailed for Angedive and other places. At each stop there were many battles and difficult situations. They sailed by the island of the Azores* and another called Flores, then to Terceira, fifty leagues away. Anchoring there, they sighted the

leguas. Allí ancorando, vieron las otras naos que de India venían, los cuales fueron bien recibidos. E contaron como, habiendo salido a proveerse de agua junto al cabo de Buena Esperanza en la agua de Saldaña, vieron muchas cabezas de muertos, sepulturas, pedazos de vestidos; e conocieron ser gente del bisrey, cuya cabeza e cuerpo hallaron cavando en una sepultura o hoya que por almohada una piedra tenía, lo que no había en otras, que bien conocieron en los dientes e faciones. E recogiéndose a sus naos, supieron o habían sabido como los negros de aquella tierra habían muerto al bisrey, a Jorge Barreto e Pero Barreto, Manuel Tellez, Antonio de Ocampo, Martín Coello e Lorenzo de Brito e otros muchos, que fueron sesenta personas, las más católicas, valientes, generosas* e esforzadas de Portugal; que con la muerte de sus cuerpos mártires inmortales hicieron sus ánimas. De esto fueron los cristianos muy pesantes e maravillados, sabien[do] los muertos e pocos que quedaron con las naos de aqu[ellos que] eran idos a Portugal. E luego vieron venir las naos de Duarte de Lemos que se quedaran atrás de las de su compañía con las tempestades del cabo de Buena Esperanza, de que todos fueron muy contentos e al[egres. Combi]nando ya juntos, vieron tierra de Portugal a veinte e cuatro [días] de junio,† víspera de Sant Juan, año del Señor de mil e qui- [[dviii]ʳ] nientos e once. Entrando en Lisbona a tres días de julio, miércoles, salieron en tierra con harto deseo de ella. La nao de Gonzalo de Sequera decían haberse perdido en la tormenta del cabo de Buena Esperanza, que otro año ante en aquel viaje perecieron tres naos, cuyos nombres eran *Sant Gabriel* e *Sant Raphael* e *La India,* cuyo‡ capitán fue el honrado varón Fernán Suárez.

---

* generosos   † janio   ‡ curo

other ships coming from India and bade them welcome. These men told of having gone ashore for water near the Cape of Good Hope, at the Saldanha✜ watering place. There they saw many skulls, graves, and bits of clothing which they realized had belonged to the Viceroy's men. His head and body they found by digging in a grave or rather ditch that had a stone for a headrest, which the others did not have; they recognized him by his teeth and other features. Returning to their ships, they realized that the Negroes of that land had killed the Viceroy, Jorge Barreto, Pero Barreto, Manuel Telles, Antonio do Campo,✜ Martim Coelho, Lourenço de Brito, and many others: sixty of the most Catholic, valiant, generous, and brave men of Portugal had through the death of their martyred bodies rendered their souls immortal. The Christians were grief-stricken and amazed, knowing how many had died and how few had sailed on to Portugal. Then they sighted Duarte de Lemos' ships that had fallen behind the rest of the company because of the storms at the Cape of Good Hope; they were all happy and pleased to see one another. Sailing together now, they sighted the mainland of Portugal on the twenty-fourth of June, the eve of Saint John's Day, 1511. They entered Lisbon on Wednesday, the third of July,✜ and finally stepped out onto their avidly longed-for land. Gonçalo de Sequeira's ship was said to have been lost during the storm at the Cape of Good Hope. The year before on that same voyage three ships had perished, the *Saint Gabriel,* the *Saint Raphael,* and the *India,* captained by the honorable gentleman Fernão Soares.✜

Título L. *Del placer que hobieron* en Portugal con la venida de las naos de las Indias.*

Grande fue el placer que en el puerto e en la tierra e corte del rey de Portugal hobo por la venida de las naos, cuyos capitanes e gentes el rey don Manuel remuneró sus trabajos e cuitas pasadas en el viaje de las Indias. E de Lisbona Figueroa se partió para Salamanca, su patria e natural habitación, a ruego de Luís Godínez, esposo de doña Catalina de Cárdenas su hermana, que le escribió. Trajo un libro excelente como en el proemio dije, e en forma de que† en esta historia habéis conocido por teórica [lo] que él vio por experiencia. Lo cual todo aprueban los muchos testigos que de vista hay, así en Portugal como en toda España.

Deo gracias.

Fue impresa la presente obra en la
muy noble e leal ciudad de Salamanca
en casa de micer Lorenzo de León de
Dei. Acabóse primero día de setiembre
de 1512 años.

* obieyon   † de lo que

Title L. *About the joy in Portugal over the arrival of the ships from the Indies.*

Great was the pleasure in the port, within the court, and throughout all the King of Portugal's realm over the arrival of the ships, whose captains and crews King Manuel remunerated for the tribulations and hardships suffered during their voyage from the Indies. From Lisbon, Figueroa set out for his fatherland and native city of Salamanca at the behest of Luís Godínez,⸸ the husband of his sister Doña Catalina de Cárdenas,⸸ who had written him. He brought with him an excellent book, as I said in the Proem, and in this history you have come to know in theory what he saw and experienced. Everything he says is attested to by the many eyewitnesses to be found in Portugal as in all Hispania.

Thanks be to God.

This present work was printed in the
very noble and loyal city of Salamanca
in the shop of Master Lorenzo de León
de Dei. It was completed on the first
day of September 1512.

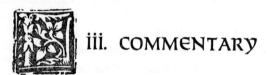 iii. COMMENTARY

The principal sources of information on Portuguese activities in the Indies during the period of Figueroa's travels are the sixteenth-century historians Fernão Lopes de Castanheda, João de Barros, Damião de Góis, and Gaspar Correia. In the interest of greater ease of reference and comparison, a table indicating the chapters of their histories which correspond to each title of the *Conquista* has been included as Appendix A.

The Illustration

Emerging from what appears to be a body of water, the Angel is depicted carrying the Portuguese coat of arms through a portal intended perhaps to represent the Gates of Heaven. Eight castles instead of the now standard seven border the royal device, recalling the seizure of strategic cities in the Algarve during the Portuguese Reconquest. The five shields or *quinas*

symbolize the five Moorish kings defeated by Afonso Henriques at Ourique in 1139, the feat that Portugal celebrates as marking its birth as an independent nation. Each *quina* bears five coins, and Camões explains their meaning:

> Aqui pinta no branco escudo ufano,
> Que agora esta victoria certifica:
> Cinco escudos azues esclarecidos,
> Em sinal destes cinco Reis vencidos.
>
> E nestes cinco escudos pinta os trinta
> Dinheiros, porque Deos fora vendido,
> Escreuendo a memoria em varia tinta,
> Daquelle de quem foy fauorecido,
> Em cada hum dos cinco, cinco pinta,
> Porque assi fica o numero comprido:
> Contando duas vezes o do meio,
> Dos cinco azues que em Cruz pintando veio.*

(Canto III, 53-54)[1]

* 'Twas then they painted on the proud white shield
  What still our claim to victory has sustained,
  The azure targes five, emblazoned fair,
  In token of the five kings conquered there.

  On those five shields the thirty pence he drew,
  For which aforetime our dear Lord was sold,
  Blazoning memorial, in various hue,
  Of Him Whose favor could so well uphold.
  Five he limned on all five. And that the due
  Number of pence may properly be told,
  Of five blue shields, the midmost men count twice,
  With the pence drawn cruciform in the device.

Title

Conquest of the Indies of Persia and Arabia. In his role as editor, Juan Agüero made several notable changes in the title of Figueroa's manuscript, which appears to have been *La historia del viaje, i armada queel Rei D. Manuel de Portugal mando facer paralos reinos de Persia i Arabia . . .*[2] He has introduced the element of conquest, giving an aura of national military achievement to Figueroa's account of the Portuguese armada. More significantly, he has substituted the word *Indias* for the manuscript's *reinos.* The Spanish reading public of 1512 was keenly interested in books dealing with the Indies; their own recent overseas accomplishments as well as those of Portugal made that part of the world an exciting theme of discussion and reading. Agüero no doubt expected that the Salamancan reader, in whose city the *Conquista* was published, would be especially drawn to a volume devoted to the Portuguese Indies, for the bonds linking Salamanca and Portugal ran strong and deep, nurtured by physical proximity and sustained by close family ties. Agüero's desire to focus Castilian attention on Portuguese activities evidently impressed itself upon the original cataloguer of the Colón Library, for he listed the book as *Conquista de las yndias de portugal de arabia y persia . . .*[3] As a result of Agüero's modifications, the Spanish reader of the *Conquista* could expect to learn about the Portuguese Indies, in implicit contrast to those of Castile. The difference becomes explicit in **Title I,** as reference is made to "the Indies we now-adays call Portuguese."

King Manuel of Portugal. Manuel I succeeded to the throne in 1495, at the age of twenty-six, and ruled until his death in 1521. The brilliant accomplishments of such captains as Gama,

Cabral, Pacheco Pereira, Almeida, and Albuquerque set the vast riches and territories before his throne that inspired historians to name him Manuel the Fortunate.

Proem

At great expense. The Portuguese Operation Indies was primarily a monopoly enterprise conducted at the King's expense, with profits accruing directly to the Crown. Royal officials directed and supervised every aspect, from initial planning of a fleet and detailed instructions to ships' captains, through to the return to Portugal and final disposition of cargo. In the particular case of the 1505 fleet, however, foreign investment was welcomed, and Italian and German financiers were quick to take advantage, realizing a handsome return on their investment. This experiment did not succeed in establishing a precedent, and the Crown managed subsequent voyages.[4]

Pedro de Añaya. Like many of his countrymen, Pedro de Añaya sided with Afonso V in his campaign for the Castilian throne. Hernando del Pulgar reports that a Pedro de Añaya was captured by the Castilians in 1479, during the battle of Albufera.[5] At the war's end he evidently left Castile, for João de Barros says that Añaya was a Castilian who had moved to Portugal after having aided Afonso V. The Catholic Kings, Fernando and Isabel, took careful note of Pedro de Añaya's devotion to the Portuguese cause. In a letter dated June 1, 1479, they listed him among a group of Castilians to be excluded from the general amnesty by which they invited those who had supported Portugal to return to Castile.[6] What must have been competent and continued service to the Portuguese is reflected in

Añaya's being charged with the important and lucrative responsibility of establishing the Sofala captaincy. One of the more salient characteristics of the *Conquista* is its attempt to vindicate the name and memory of this Castilian who had gone over to the Portuguese.

The cosmography of Poggio the Florentine and Marco Polo the Venetian. This is a clear reference to Rodrigo Fernández de Santaella's 1503 *Cosmographia.*

And likewise with a letter. The King Manuel newsletters provide excellent documentation of the first three years of Figueroa's stay in the Indies. The letter Juan Agüero consulted was written on June 19, 1508, and is quite similar to one written in Latin on June 12. Tristão da Cunha returned from the Indies in early June, and his report supplied the information for both letters. The Latin letter, addressed to Pope Julius II and entitled *Letter about Provinces, Cities, Lands, and Places in the Eastern Part,* deals with Portuguese activities in East Africa and India during the years 1506 through 1508. Addressed to the town of Évora, the Portuguese letter that Agüero read contains essentially the same information.[7]

Hispania. In the *Conquista* the name *España* has the meaning of the Latin *Hispania* and follows the latter in designating the entire Iberian peninsula. The same accommodation to the Latin model was made in another early-sixteenth-century travel narrative, the *Libro del infante don Pedro de portugal* of Gómez de Santisteban. The sixteenth-century Portuguese historians did likewise; *Espanha* signifies the entire peninsula. The *Conquista*

uses *Castilla* and *castellanos* to distinguish between Portugal and her Christian neighbors to the east.[8]

The wise Marqués' advice. In 1437, Iñigo López de Mendoza, Marqués de Santillana, completed a collection of proverbs he had been preparing for the instruction of the young prince who was later to reign as Enrique IV of Castile. Santillana selected his proverbs from the stock of classical wisdom, and the one to which Agüero refers figures among his reflections on *Fortaleza,*[9] and reads as follows:

> Los casos de admiraçion
> Non los cuentes,
> Ca no saben todas gentes
> Cómo son.
> Ca non es la perfection
> Mucho fablar;
> Mas obrando, denegar
> Luengo sermon.*

Title I

The invention and conquest of the Indies. The use of *invención* in this context denoting finding or discovery has a precedent in similar employment of the Latin model *invenire.* The second *Inter Caetera,* in 1493, one of the papal bulls devoted to discovery, refers to lands *inventas et inveniendas,* found and to be found. In the *Conquista, descubrir* sometimes denotes discovery, as in the phrase *siete años después del descubrimiento*

---

* Do not tell about wondrous events, for not all people know what they are like. Perfection lies not in many words; rather let deeds replace the lengthy sermon.

primero (Title IV), but more often it refers to the act of uncovering or revealing something already known to exist. Thus, Gaspar lies to Gama *por no descubrir tantos bienes* (Title II), and Diogo Sequeira is sent out *a descubrir clavo* (Title XLVII).[10]

    King João of Portugal. Born in 1455, João II, known as the "Príncipe perfeito," reigned from 1481 to 1495. He was especially devoted to the cause of overseas exploration, and his chronicler, Rui de Pina, praised him as a "muy solicito investigador dos secretos do mundo." [11]

    Over his seas. In 1455, Pope Nicholas V in his bull *Romanus Pontifex* awarded to Portugal exclusive rights of conquest in the area extending southward from capes Bojador and Nun on the west coast of Africa "as far as to the Indians who are said to worship the name of Christ." Portugal's claims in this area were further strengthened by provisions of the 1479 Treaty of Alcaçovas that ended the war with Castile. In spite of these concessions, actual advances southward had slowed considerably during the reign of Afonso V. João II, however, stabilized Portuguese internal affairs and gave new and vigorous encouragement to the voyages of discovery. In 1482, Diogo Cão reached the Congo River and Cape Santa Maria, setting the stage for Bartolomeu Dias' voyage.

    In addition to sending men and ships out over his seas, João also dispatched expeditions overland. In May of 1487, Afonso de Paiva and Pero da Covilhã set out on their long journey. Paiva died, but Covilhã reconnoitered the Malabar coast, Hormuz, and East Africa as far south as Sofala, ending up a long-staying guest of the Emperor of Ethiopia, the fabled

"Prester John." Before reaching there, however, Covilhã did manage to send back to Portugal a valuable account of his travels. He was still in Ethiopia when the Lima expedition arrived in 1520.

When Bartolomeu Dias returned to Lisbon in 1488 with the news of his successful rounding of the African mainland, the route to India was open. Knowing this and prompted by Columbus' discoveries in the west, King João willingly signed the Treaty of Tordesillas in 1494, which confirmed Portuguese rights to control and development of the southern and eastern routes to India.[12]

They reached the Cape of Good Hope. Although the *Conquista* does not mention Dias, this is an obvious reference to his voyage. He and his men were actually blown around the cape during a storm; they had their first view of it on the return leg of their journey.

They all turned back. The *Conquista* shows no awareness of the fact that Dias had sailed up the East African coast as far as the Great Fish River before acceding to the exhortations of his weary and frightened crews to turn back. If this was known, it was no doubt omitted in order to make Gama's feat that much more important.

Vasco da Gama (who later became an admiral). A member of the Portuguese gentry, Gama, though familiar with the ways of the sea, was not a professional mariner when chosen to lead the first expedition bound for the Malabar coast in India. Manuel wanted his emissary to possess other skills, which helps to explain why he bypassed the available Bartolomeu Dias.

Gama was considered to have the military and diplomatic competence required for successful dealings with the Indian rulers. He received the rank of admiral in 1502, on the eve of his second voyage to India; Manuel at the same time took to himself the resounding title of "Lord of the Conquest, Navigation, and Commerce of Ethiopia, Arabia, Persia, and India." [13]

Said to King João. This is an error. Gama sailed for India in 1497, and King João died in 1495.

Finis Tormentorum. Bartolomeu Dias is credited by his contemporaries Duarte Pacheco Pereira and Christopher Columbus with naming the cape Good Hope. Some fifty years later, João de Barros offered a different explanation, saying that Dias and his men "gave it the name *Tormentoso,* but King João when they returned to the realm gave it another more illustrious name, calling it Cape of Good Hope, by virtue of what it promised for the discovery of India, so hoped for and so sought after for so many years." [14] It is worthwhile to note that the rounding of the cape, though intrinsically important, was considered but a preliminary step; its importance lay in "what it promised for the discovery of India." The *Lusiads* reflects this attitude, in that Camões forges his epic around Gama's first voyage, and the cape has already been rounded when the poem begins.

Malindi. This was not Gama's first port of call in East Africa. He had been opposed and attacked at Mozambique and then at Mombasa. The friendly welcome received at Malindi must be seen in terms of the rivalry between the ruler of Malindi and his counterparts in Mombasa and Kilwa.

Title II

A Moor to act as navigator and interpreter. Gama was exceptionally fortunate in obtaining as his navigator Ahmad bin Mâdjid, the best Arab pilot and authority on navigation of his day. He led the Portuguese safely and quickly across the Indian Ocean to their destination at Calicut, the principal port on the Malabar coast.[15]

Gaspar. This version of Gama's encounter with Gaspar is a clever distortion designed to attack the Jews. By placing their meeting prior to the fleet's arrival in Calicut, it is plainly implied that the Portuguese had first to outwit and defeat the cunning and avaricious Jew before they could go on to uncover the riches and wealth of the Indies. The available facts indicate a wholly different situation. A Jew did board Gama's ships, and there was trouble, but this happened as they were homeward bound with a cargo of spices, after their stay in Calicut. Historians variously indicate his origin as Granada or Poland. Placing it in Seville makes him a more immediate target of hatred and resentment on the part of the Spanish reader. The Portuguese were informed that the Jew had come to spy on them for the ruler of Goa, and under torture he did admit to his intelligence mission. Gama astutely realized the potential value of his guest, brought him back to Portugal, and christened him Gaspar da Gama. Better known to history as Gaspar da India, he made repeated voyages to the Indies and rendered important services to the Portuguese.

Strait of Mecca. Gaspar would have sailed down the Red Sea, through the Gulf of Aden, then across the Indian Ocean

to the Malabar coast. In the *Conquista,* the term *estrecho de Meca* generally refers to the Red Sea, although in **Title XXV** it appears to indicate the Gulf of Aden. In **Title XXII,** the term *golfo de Meca* is employed, which in that context denotes the Indian Ocean.

Which is a shadow of many tribulations. "For we are but of yesterday, and know nothing, because our days upon earth are a shadow" (Job: 8, 9).

He and his company returned to Portugal. Gama and his crews, depleted by more than half, reached Lisbon in September 1499.

Title III

The Indians killed the men who remained in Calicut. Pedro Álvares Cabral had established a factory at Calicut in 1500. While he was away visiting other ports, a crowd of Moslems stormed the factory and killed the factor and fifty men. Cabral bombarded the city in retaliation before returning to Portugal. Gama also shelled Calicut during his second voyage and treated the prisoners he captured with extreme cruelty. Faced with the constant hostility of the Zamorin of Calicut, the Portuguese decided to move down the coast to Cochin. There they were welcomed, the ruler being an enemy of the Zamorin, and Cochin became the main Portuguese headquarters on the Malabar coast.

Title IV

All men-at-arms. In addition to the normal ships' comple-

ments, King Manuel recruited some fifteen hundred men for the 1505 fleet. These men, and Figueroa as well, obligated themselves for three years. Officers' appointments, such as that of Añaya, were also of three years' duration. In contrast to the two measures of pepper offered the men-at-arms, Almeida as commander of the expedition was authorized fifteen hundred.

Sofala. Located a short distance from the coast on the Revue River, Sofala lies in the southernmost portion of Portuguese East Africa. Pero da Covilhã had visited Sofala in 1490, and it was probably his optimistic report on the amounts of gold to be obtained there that encouraged the Crown to establish the Sofala captaincy.[16]

Tristão da Cunha. The precise cause of Cunha's blindness has not been determined. Barros attributes it to an "attack of vertigo," which may mean that it was caused by a fall resulting from a fainting spell or delirium. As the *Conquista* later reports, the blindness was temporary, and Cunha was able to sail for the Indies the following year, during which voyage he discovered the remote islands that bear his name. After returning to Portugal, Tristão da Cunha continued to serve and advise Manuel on Indian affairs and in 1514 led the Portuguese delegation sent to Rome to render Manuel's obedience to the new Pope, Leo X.

Dom Francisco de Almeida (who became viceroy in India). Almeida had long been a close confidant to Portuguese kings when chosen to replace Cunha. He had accompanied Afonso V to Paris during the latter's unsuccessful bid for French support against Castile. Given permission to assist Fernando and Isabel in the campaign against Granada, he was present

when the last Moorish state in Iberia fell in 1492. According to Manuel's orders, Almeida was to assume the title of Viceroy once he had effectively established himself in India. He did so at Cannanore in October 1505.

One of the ships, of Biscayan make, floundered. The *Conquista* neglects to mention that it was Pedro de Añaya's ship that sank. Some historians say a storm was to blame; Correia reports that it simply sprang a leak. Almeida and Añaya sailed on the exact dates indicated. Añaya was aboard the *Santo Espírito,* and it may be assumed that Figueroa, as one of the Captain's men, sailed on the same vessel.

Title V

Bezeguiche. This was originally the name of a chieftain encountered by the Portuguese in the latter part of the fifteenth century. They gave his name to the area he ruled, near Cape Verde.[17]

Canary Islands. Portuguese fleets bound for the Indies did not normally put in at the Canary Islands. Long a source of dispute between Portugal and Castile, the archipelago was awarded to Castile by the Treaty of Alcaçovas.

On their left. As a soldier of the sea, not a sailor, Figueroa evidently spoke in terms of left and right rather than the nautical port and starboard. According to Castanheda, there were so many landlubbers among Almeida's crews that one exasperated captain resorted to the more meaningful terms of "garlic" and "onions" to designate port and starboard.

Cape Correntes. A constant menace to Portuguese shipping, Cape Correntes lies at twenty-four degrees South latitude, about one-third the distance between Lourenço Marques and Sofala.

Title VI

Chiloane. This is a small settlement located a short distance to the south of Sofala.

Shipwrecked Christians. These survivors were off one of Almeida's ships, commanded by Lopo Sanches, that had been destroyed at Cape Correntes. Castanheda and Barros place the number of survivors at five, Correia at twelve; Damião de Góis makes no mention of the incident. The drowning of the captain and seven others through greed would appear to indicate an unsuccessful attempt on their part to get ashore with heavy valuables. The *Conquista* presents a vivid account of the survivor's sufferings and provides more detail than do the historians, thanks to the firsthand report Figueroa must have received from the survivors. One is reminded in this instance of Camões' account of the travails of the shipwrecked Manuel de Sousa Sepúlveda and his lovely wife, she of the "cristalinos membros" and "pes delicados." When Añaya and his company reached Sofala, they found twenty more survivors from Sanches' ship.[18]

Francisco de Añaya. After a short stay with his father in Sofala, Francisco de Añaya left East Africa and proceeded to join Almeida in India, where he spent the remainder of his service in various activities along the Malabar coast.

His coat of arms. In the *Triunfo Raimundino,* Juan Agüero

describes the coat of arms of three branches of the Añaya family. The one that most closely corresponds to his picture of Francisco's belongs to a Pedro de Añaya and speaks of *los armineos de limpieza / con bandas de fortaleza*. I have been unable to find any reference to a castle on the Añaya coat of arms.[19]

Title VII

The nineteenth of September. Pedro de Añaya and his men reached Sofala on September 19, 1505, after a journey of four months.

Coco or India nuts. Coco was first used as an infantile expression for head. In India the Portuguese applied the term to the nut they found to have many of the features of a human head.

Poggio the Florentine. Juan Agüero refers here to Poggio Bracciolini's treatise, published by Santaella in 1503. Having seen a coconut with his own eyes, Agüero does not hesitate to contradict the Papal Secretary's secondhand account.

Title VIII

To meet with the King of Sofala. This description of Añaya's meeting with Yusuf, the King of Sofala, is significant both for what it reveals and for what it does not. It provides information unavailable elsewhere on Añaya's alert security measures and discusses in detail the circumstances of the actual interview. On the other hand, there are several important omissions. The historians emphasize the majestic bearing and bravery of the highly respected Yusuf, who was seventy years old and

blind. None of this information appears in the *Conquista*. Damião de Góis was especially impressed with Yusuf's kind treatment of Añaya and his company. Among his fellow historians, he stands out for his ability to look at events from the perspective of the natives as well as from that of the Portuguese. In the case of Sofala, he claims that the Portuguese often abused their welcome.

Title IX

Sofala. This description, obviously based on Figueroa's long stay in Sofala, is quite similar to the account given by Duarte de Barbosa in his travel narrative.[20]

Monomotapa. The history of Monomotapa, empire and emperor, is a fascinating blend of fact and fiction. The Monomotapa ruled a kingdom of the same name situated inland from Sofala. Although an area of active gold mining, in actual fact it was no more powerful or wealthy than many of its neighbors. By the time the Portuguese had reached Sofala, however, legend had linked Monomotapa with the fabulous mines of King Solomon and had attributed to its king wealth and power scarcely less than that of Prester John.[21]

Title X

They wanted to go and risk their lives. The historians have little to say about living conditions in Sofala, no mention at all of the men's understandable desire to move on.

Wood sinks in water, but stones float. "If you take a stick or a straw and throw it into one of the lakes, it sinks at once;

and if you throw a stone or piece of iron, it floats on the water contrary to nature." According to Gómez de Santisteban, this is what he and his companions observed at Sodom and Gomorrha as they accompanied the Infante Dom Pedro of Portugal to "the four parts of the world." [22]

Title XI

In this title the *Conquista* summarizes Francisco de Almeida's activities in East Africa prior to his arrival in India.

Mozambique. Almeida rounded the Cape of Good Hope in late June and proceeded up the African coast. He put in at Mozambique for provisions and fresh water, but no military action took place.

Kilwa. Kilwa was the scene of Almeida's major effort in East Africa; in seizing and fortifying this port, he was carrying out explicit instructions issued by King Manuel. As the *Conquista* reports, the attack took place on July 25. To commemorate the victory, Almeida, himself a *comendador* of the Order of Santiago, named the fort in honor of his patron.

Abraham, Mohammed Ankoni. Mohammed Ankoni had actually replaced Abraham as ruler of Kilwa shortly before the arrival of Almeida. Abraham did run off, and in an elaborate ceremony Almeida gave the crown to Ankoni, who in turn pledged his allegiance to Portugal.[23]

Pero Ferreira. Ferreira, who almost drowned when his ship sank en route to the Cape, is known to Portuguese scholars

as Pero Ferreira Fogaça. In depicting his coat of arms and calling him Pedro de Herrera, Juan Agüero links him to the Herreras of Salamanca; as in the case of Francisco de Añaya, the description is taken from the *Triunfo Raimundino*.[24]

Mombasa. Almeida burned Mombasa on the exact day and under the same circumstances as reported. His goal was to leave Kilwa the only strong point along that coast. As the *Conquista* later reveals, he would have done the same to Malindi had not opposing winds and seas driven him off.

Title XII

Nangabe. My search for the precise location and present name of this place has been unsuccessful.

Cidi Akoti. According to João de Barros, Cidi Akoti was an Ethiopian Christian who had been captured by Moslems at the age of ten. When the Portuguese arrived in Sofala, he was the principal advisor to King Yusuf and thus privy to his plans. He did warn Añaya of the impending attack, and the Sofalese evidently discovered his treason. Shortly before the attack, Cidi Akoti found it prudent to betake himself and three wives to the Portuguese in order to avoid capture.

The King of Sofala and the Kaffirs came against the Christians. The attack occurred sometime prior to May 19, 1506. On that day, after the battle, Pedro de Añaya wrote a letter directing his factor to record the value of gifts given to Akoti's wives upon their arrival at the fort.[25] Although Añaya and his men had little trouble withstanding what Barros labels a rather half-

hearted Kaffir siege, Camões in the *Lusiads* (Canto X, 94) notes that Añaya defended the fort *com destreza*.

Charge! This explosion of rhetoric is intended to confer elegance and dignity on the heroic deeds of Pedro de Añaya. Aware, however, of the ethereal quality of such a lofty harangue, the *Conquista* hastens to add the delightful rejoinder of the fighting man concerned with the immediate demands of battle.

Title XIII

The latter had said these things. This title contributes entirely new information on events at Sofala. None of the historians mentions Añaya's adroit stratagem prior to the counterattack.

Title XIV

Cutting off his head. Manuel Fernandes, the factor who was shortly to succeed Pedro de Añaya in the captaincy, is credited with the actual killing of Yusuf. King Manuel later commemorated the deed by awarding Fernandes a coat of arms depicting a severed Moorish head.

Title XV

Añaya fell sick and died. The historians report that about half the original garrison fell victim to the fever that claimed Pedro de Añaya. His death occurred in early June 1506, for captaincy documents show Manuel Fernandes signing himself as captain later that month.[26]

Title XVI

In the month of April. This statement is somewhat ambiguous, since there is no mention of April in the body of the title. However, this remark indicates that initial work on the fort must have begun in April 1506.

God forbid. The *Conquista* is alone in reporting the Portuguese attempt to acclaim Yusuf's eldest son as king. From the detail with which his rejection is reported, Figueroa was probably one of the emissaries sent to him. He obviously admired the son's courageous and honorable reply.

Sultan Sulema. In the absence of other information, it must be accepted that this is the name of the son whom the Portuguese succeeded in placing on the throne of Sofala.

Buene. This is Buene Island, located a few miles south of Sofala.

Title XVII

Nuno Vaz Pereira. Pereira had come out to India in 1505 with Almeida. When the latter learned of Añaya's death in September 1506, he named Pereira to replace him. He reached his new command in November. In **Title XXXVII** the *Conquista* reports Nuno Vaz Pereira's heroic death during the battle of Diu. Accompanying him to Sofala was Ferdinand Magellan, who had also come out in 1505.

Mokondi. The ruler who had sent the force of Kaffirs to

support Yusuf's attack on Añaya, he must have come to the fort around February 1507. The historians credit Nuno Vaz Pereira with a high degree of diplomatic ability, and his adroit handling of Mokondi, not recorded elsewhere, shows that his reputation was well earned.

Title XVIII

Vasco Gomes de Abreu. Abreu had initially appeared in India in 1505 as commander of a cargo ship in the Almeida fleet. His stay was brief, just long enough to secure a cargo of spices and head back to Portugal. In April 1507, he was sent out again, this time with a warrant for the captaincy of Sofala. Arriving on September 8, he immediately demanded that Pereira hand over to him the gold which had accumulated during his tenure in office. Correia says that Pereira was right in refusing to comply. This refusal no doubt led to Abreu's harsh treatment of the garrison, not reported elsewhere, and his peremptory orders for their departure.[27]

Toward the end of September. On September 19, 1507, Figueroa sailed out of Sofala; he had been there exactly two years.

Diogo de Melo. Melo commanded one of the ships which sailed with Abreu in April 1507. His orders were to proceed to Afonso de Albuquerque and place himself under his command. As **Title XXXII** reveals, Diogo de Melo was killed in the fall of 1508, during Albuquerque's second campaign against Hormuz.

Title XIX

Mozambique, where they wintered that year. Figueroa

reached Mozambique in late October, after a very danger-filled voyage. An attempt to cross over to India was frustrated by the weather, and he and his companions remained in Mozambique until March 1508.

Their language. The languages spoken in East Africa are part of the Bantu family. The Kaffirs were considered one of the more powerful and intelligent groups among the Bantus.

Title XX

Vasco Gomes was lost at sea. There appears to be no first-hand source of information on the circumstances of Abreu's death; the historians report only that he sailed from Sofala shortly before Christmas and, never heard from again, was presumed drowned. Of importance here is the reaction to the news. Proud of the way men had fought and died at Sofala, the death of the royal favorite who had callously seized the fruits of their labor is seen as divine punishment.

São Lourenço. Diogo Dias discovered São Lourenço, the present day Madagascar, in 1500. The Portuguese thought they had found a rich source of spices, but their expectations were not fulfilled. Abreu's expedition was one of several early attempts to find spices there.

Angoche. Better known as Antonio Enes, Angoche is a small port about one hundred miles south of Mozambique.

Title XXI

Tristão da Cunha arrived at Mozambique. After recovering

from the malady that had kept him from India the year before, Cunha sailed from Portugal in the spring of 1506, accompanied by Afonso de Albuquerque. In the succeeding titles, the *Conquista* recapitulates Tristão da Cunha's activities in the Indies prior to his arrival at Mozambique on January 8, 1508.

Cunha and his ships remained at Mozambique until January 17, and during this interval Figueroa may well have had the opportunity to meet and exchange impressions with the great Italian traveler Ludovico de Varthema. After years of adventure-filled escapades in the East, Varthema was returning to Europe with Tristão da Cunha. Two years later, in 1510, he was to publish the well-known account of his travels, the *Itinerario*.[28] While resting at Mozambique, the Italian no doubt entertained his hosts with tales of his recent experiences with their compatriots in India. Figueroa may have listened with great care, for in the coming titles many striking similarities between the *Conquista* and the *Itinerario* will be noted.

Title XXII

This title presents a general summary of Portuguese activities in India during the period from September 1505 to December 1507.

Cannanore had been besieged. An account of the siege of Cannanore is presented in greater detail in this same title; after mentioning it briefly here, Cunha proceeds to order his account chronologically.

Kilwa and Mombasa. These engagements have been described in **Title XI.**

Saint Helena. A watering place located about fifteen miles north of Malindi, Saint Helena appears on modern maps as Mambrui.

Angedive. This island is located close to the Indian coast, about sixty miles south of Goa. Work on the fort began in September 1505, but it was dismantled a year later in favor of strategically and commercially more important sites.

Manuel Paçanha. Paçanha had come out with the 1505 fleet and served as first captain of the Angedive fort. He was with Almeida at Diu and was one of the leaders of the group of officers who continually exhorted him not to allow Albuquerque to become governor. He signed the statement they composed to show that Albuquerque was unfit for the position. As is reported in **Title XXXIX,** he was killed during the Portuguese defeat at Calicut in 1510.

Onor, Gersoppa. Onor is the present-day city of Honavar, just north of Gersoppa; both are on the Malabar coast south of Goa. The battle to which the *Conquista* refers took place on October 16, and Francisco de Almeida was hit in the foot, in the toe according to Castanheda.

The King of Narsinga. Like the Portuguese historians and Varthema, the *Conquista* confuses the "kingdom" of Narsinga with the actual person of King Narsinga, who ruled the Hindu state of Vijayanagar between 1505 and 1509. Vijayanagar was the strongest Hindu force still opposing the Moslem advance into India.

In his stable there are more than fifteen hundred horses.
Varthema was also impressed by the size and value of the
royal stable; he credits the King with a cavalry of forty thousand.[29]

Cannanore. The first Portuguese factory at Cannanore had
been established by João da Nova in 1501. Good relations with
local rulers and populace was the rule at Cannanore, and only
the extreme circumstances described below could provoke open
war.

Lourenço de Brito. Brito and Almeida came to India together, left together, and died together. As the *Conquista* accurately indicates, Lourenço de Brito died at his commander's side
at Saldanha in March 1510.

*In Quilon the Jews had murdered Antonio de Sá and all
the men with him.* Immediately upon his arrival in India,
Almeida sent instructions to the Portuguese factories to begin
assembling cargoes for his merchant ships. He selected an
exceptionally vehement captain by the name of João Homem to
take the message to Quilon, an active port located at the southern end of the Malabar coast. Reaching his destination, Homem
was infuriated to discover that the desired spices were already
being loaded into Moslem ships. His remedy for the situation was
simple if not diplomatic; he summarily confiscated the sails and
rudders of the Moorish ships and blithely sailed away. Antonio
de Sá, the factor in Quilon, paid the price for his countryman's
highhanded action. No sooner had Homem cleared the harbor
when a mob of outraged Moslems stormed the factory, killing
Sá and his twelve companions.

There is no evidence of Jewish involvement in these events, nor do the historians implicate Jews in any way. In much the same manner as the erroneous account of Gaspar, blaming the Jews for what happened at Quilon appears to represent but another instance of strong anti-Jewish bias.

His son Dom Lourenço. Lourenço de Almeida was a very popular and competent commander; he served his father well in a wide variety of assignments. The *Conquista* records his major accomplishments in India: victory over the Calicut fleet in 1506 and again in 1507, and his leadership in the first Portuguese expedition to Ceylon. The circumstances of his death are depicted in detail in **Title XXXIII.**

They burned twenty-seven Moorish ships. In the course of this punitive expedition, Lourenço did burn twenty-seven ships in Quilon harbor, while back at Cochin the Viceroy relieved João Homem of his command.

The King of Calicut assembled an armada. The war fleet assembled by the Zamorin of Calicut represented his attempt to destroy the Portuguese before they could fully establish themselves as a permanent force in India. The Portuguese, however, possessed accurate advance knowledge of the Zamorin's intentions. The ubiquitous Varthema had been living comfortably in Calicut under the imaginative guise of a Moslem holy man. In February of 1506, deciding that it was time to return to Christendom, he made his way to Cannanore and the Portuguese, bringing with him detailed information on the Calicut fleet. Before the battle Varthema was involved in a daring but unsuccessful plot. With money provided by Francisco de Al-

meida, he attempted to induce two repentant Italian renegades, expert cannonmakers in the employ of the Zamorin, to leave Calicut and come over to the Portuguese. Unfortunately, the scheme was discovered and the Italians killed.[30]

Eighty heavy ships, one hundred and twenty smaller ones, and one hundred longboats, which they call paraos. These figures correspond closely to those given by the historians and Varthema, who listed "two hundred and nine sail, of which eighty-four were large ships, and the remainder were rowing vessels, that is, paraos." [31]

Dom Lourenço amply demonstrated his industry and courage. Varthema participated in this battle and also emphasized Lourenço's brave leadership.[32]

He was greeted with huge celebrations. "I leave to you to imagine how great was the joy of the Viceroy and the king of Cochin, who is a true friend of the King of Portugal, on seeing us return victorious"; so speaks Varthema of the triumphant return to Cochin.[33]

To explore the islands off Cochin. The Portuguese had heard that Moslem traders were attempting to bypass the Malabar coast, shipping their merchandise from Malacca to Aden and Hormuz through the Maldive Islands. At the end of the monsoon season, early in August, the Viceroy sent his son to investigate these reports.

Ceylon. Castanheda claims that Lourenço visited Ceylon in

November 1505. The *Conquista* places the Portuguese arrival in
Ceylon after the defeat of the Calicut fleet in March 1506, as
does Barros.[34] This expedition did not yield the important
results claimed for it in the *Conquista;* Lourenço merely pursued preliminary contacts with the local rulers before returning
to his father.

One hundred and eighty thousand Moors from the entire
Malabar coast of India descended upon Cannanore. A varied
chain of events led to the siege of Cannanore, which lasted from
March through August 1507. Moslem merchants were incessant-
ly intriguing and agitating against the Portuguese and were
able to intensify their activities when the Portuguese fleet of
1506, commanded by Tristão da Cunha, did not reach India that
year. To further weaken the Portuguese position, the ruler of
Cannanore who had originally befriended Vasco da Gama
died. His successor was unfriendly to the Portuguese and listened more favorably to Moslem protestations. In March the
increasingly tense situation was exacerbated when a Portuguese
captain attacked a Cannanore vessel that carried a safe-conduct
signed by the Viceroy. Not content merely to disregard this,
he seized passengers and crew, sewed them up inside the vessel's
sails, and threw them overboard. One of the victims was a
prominent Moslem merchant residing in Cannanore, and as
soon as the atrocity was discovered open warfare began. To
supplement the Conquista's summary account of the siege, one
again turns to Varthema's *Itinerario.*[35] As a reward for his
services during the battle of March 1506, Varthema was named
Portuguese factor at Cannanore; he was present throughout the
long and arduous siege. The siege was lifted and peace restored
when Tristão da Cunha arrived in late August.

A great miracle. According to Castanheda, it was discovered after the siege that "Santiago was there." The other historians make no mention of the incident. Varthema writes: "Four days being past, there came two merchants of Cannanore, who were friends of mine before war had been made, and they spoke with me in this manner, as you shall understand. 'O factor, show me a man who is a yard larger than any of you, who every day has killed ten, fifteen or twenty of us . . .' I answered him in this manner . . . 'that knight whom thou hast seen is not a Portuguese, but he is the God of the Portuguese and of all the world.' " [36]

Ponnani. For Tristão da Cunha and his men the attack on Ponnani, located to the south of Calicut, was essentially a raiding expedition, a last taste of action before starting home. According to Barros and Damião de Góis, it was a costly venture; they say that eighteen Portuguese were killed and more than sixty wounded. In its claim that there were no fatalities the *Conquista* is supported by the *Itinerario,* for Varthema was at Ponnani and was knighted after the battle.

Since the *Conquista* makes no mention of Varthema, it is not possible to affirm that Figueroa knew him or his book. Nonetheless, there remains the strong probability that Martín Fernández de Figueroa met and talked with Ludovico de Varthema at Mozambique in January 1508, and that their conversations are reflected in this and other titles of the *Conquista.*

Title XXIII

Martim Coelho. Coelho had come to the Indies in April 1507 with Gomes de Abreu and Diogo de Melo; like Melo his

orders were to serve with Albuquerque. Figueroa accurately reports his subsequent death with Almeida at Saldanha.

Babylon. Albuquerque's mission in the Red Sea area was to halt the flow of Moslem shipping between the Indian Ocean ports and Cairo, known in the later Middle Ages as Babylon.

Songo. In this and the immediately succeeding references, Figueroa enumerates the places encountered as he moved up the African coast toward Malindi. The area described lies between about nine and two degrees south latitude. Songo is the principal settlement on the island of Songo Manara, located about one mile south of Kilwa.

Songo Songo. This island lies about thirty miles north of Kilwa.

Mafia. Mafia Island actually is some thirty miles beyond Songo Manara, and thus lies thirty miles north of Kilwa.

Tomagunda, a land of pomegranates, and Kwale. Kwale is located on the mainland opposite the southern end of Zanzibar, close to Dar-es-Salaam. The Tomagunda of the *Conquista* may be the mainland area near Kwale, called Bogamoyo.

Zanzibar. Zanzibar was first visited by Vasco da Gama in 1499, en route back to Portugal; he signed a treaty of friendship with the local ruler. With Tanganyika, Zanzibar is the second major component of the recently formed Tanzania.

Another very verdant island. Figueroa is probably referring to Pemba, located to the north of Zanzibar.

A mainland called Tanga. This appears to be a reference to the coastal areas of Tanganyika, between Cape Delgado and Mombasa.

Gujarati. Varthema also comments on the Gujarati, calling them "a certain race which eats nothing that has blood and never kills any living thing." [37] As is explained in **Title XXXVIII,** the land of the Gujarati corresponds to the modern state of Pakistan. European travelers, and especially the Portuguese, often confused the Gujarati with the Indian Brahmans. The Gujarati in Malindi may have been merchants.

Francisco de Tabora. Tabora sailed from Portugal in 1506 in command of one of the ships of Albuquerque's squadron. In **Title XXIV** he is erroneously called Diogo. Often at odds with Albuquerque, at one point during the 1507 siege of Hormuz he was relieved of command. He must have enjoyed returning to India in 1515 with Lopo Soares de Albergária, when the latter was to replace Albuquerque in the governorship.

Brava . . . Socotra. The seizure of Brava and Socotra and the rest of Albuquerque's actions from his arrival in the Indies in 1506 through March 1508 are the subject of **Titles XXIV** through **XXXII.**

Title XXIV

Brava. Located in the Somali Republic, Brava was assaulted by the combined forces of Albuquerque and Tristão da Cunha early in 1507.

Severe cruelty. The *Conquista* sternly condemns the atrocities committed at Brava, although it finds some mitigation in

the knowledge that only the most reprobate elements were involved, and in the fact that many virtuous men had intervened to protect the women. Castanheda and Damião de Góis report that from two to eight hundred women were mutilated before Tristão da Cunha managed to bring the men under control. They do not, however, voice any special criticism. Barros roundly censures the wrongdoers and notes with satisfaction that they were quickly punished: "But since such things which humanity cannot tolerate do not please God, those men and their bracelets ended up at the bottom of the sea" (Barros, *Asia,* II, i, 2). In checking Figueroa's account against the King Manuel letter of June 19, 1508, Agüero evidently rejected the latter's version. It could not be expected that an official newsletter would acknowledge atrocities; it merely notes in passing that some jewelry was obtained from the arms and legs of the dead.

Mogadishu. Located to the north of Brava, Mogadishu is the capital of the Somali Republic.

Socotra. This description of the Jacobite Christians of Socotra follows the June 19, 1508 letter almost verbatim. Damião de Góis also relied heavily on this letter for his description of Socotra. Figueroa's personal observations appear in **Title XXVI.**

Although it gives the honor to Tristão da Cunha. The seizure of Socotra took place in April 1507, and Tristão da Cunha was in over-all command; for this reason the Manuel letter rightly credits him with the victory. The *Conquista's* reservation is based on the fact that the Portuguese attacked in two groups, and Afonso de Albuquerque's was the first to get ashore and assault the enemy fort. Tristão da Cunha himself acknowledged Albuquerque's special military prowess and effective leadership,

for after the battle he asked him to perform the ceremony
knighting him and his son Nuno.

Leonel Coutinho. This brave captain, who came out with
Albuquerque in 1506 and distinguished himself here on Socotra,
was later killed during the defeat at Calicut in 1510.

Fartak. Cape Fartak is located across the Gulf of Aden
on the Arabian peninsula, opposite Cape Guardafui. The historians, especially Castanheda, praise the heroic defense offered
by the Fartak garrison.

When winter passed. Leaving behind a strong garrison,
Tristão da Cunha left Socotra for India in August 1507; Albuquerque set sail toward Hormuz. His campaign against Hormuz, alluded to here, is discussed fully in **Titles XXVII**
through **XXXII.**

Of Castilian ancestry. When Afonso IV ascended to the
Portuguese throne in 1325, he banished his half brothers from
the country. One of them, Afonso Sanches, moved to Castile
and married into the Castilian nobility; the castle of Alburquerque near Badajoz was part of the dowry. Afonso de
Albuquerque is eventually descended from this marriage and
others involving Castilians and is therefore "of Castilian ancestry." This remark no doubt reflects Juan Agüero's interest
in genealogy and his native Castile.

Title XXV

Honorably welcomed. As honorable as their reception may
have been, Figueroa and his companions found their new com-

mander in an angry mood; a three-month vigil at Cape Guarda-fui had netted but one small Moslem merchant ship.

Arabia Felix. Arabia was traditionally divided into three parts, *Deserta, Petrea,* and *Felix,* with Arabia *Felix* embracing the coastal areas of the Arabian peninsula, particularly the Yemen, and, as noted in **Title XXXVIII,** coastal regions of the Persian mainland. There appears to be no precedent for the *Conquista's* etymology, that of a town called *Felix.* Santaella in the *Cosmographia* explains *Felix* in terms of "the incense which comes from there."

Title XXVI

Good-natured men. Although Figueroa censures the Soco-trans' libidinous sexual behavior, he is generally sympathetic toward them. Unlike **Title XXIV,** which follows King Manuel's letter in questioning the orthodoxy of people who "consider themselves Christians," Figueroa does not raise the question at all here. Santaella emphatically criticized the Socotrans' religious beliefs and practices, calling them "Nestorian heretics."[38]

The Trinitarian Order. The cross of the Trinitarians, an order dedicated to freeing Christians captured by the Moors, consists of a red upright and a blue crossbar. Founded by the Frenchman Saint John of Matha, the order was formally authorized by Innocent III in 1198.[39]

Title XXVII

The other coast. This refers to the east coast of Africa, whence Figueroa has just come and where word of Albuquerque's exploits had not yet reached.

Swiss mercenaries. In describing the Fartak defenders of Socotra, the King Manuel letter reports that "they serve for a salary, in the manner of the Swiss."

Set out in search of provisions. Shortly after leaving Socotra, Albuquerque decided that the seizure of the rich and strategically located Hormuz would serve Portuguese goals more effectively than patrolling the approaches to the Red Sea. He thus set course for the Persian Gulf and Hormuz. The Portuguese knew of its importance from several sources, including Pero da Covilhã, who had been there before going on southward to Sofala.

Kalhat. Part of Albuquerque's design for the capture of Hormuz was to attack several of its ports along the way. Kalhat, located near the easternmost tip of the Arabian peninsula, was his first stop. He hoped that the news of his approach, such as the bombardment of Kalhat on August 18, would demonstrate his power and determination; more than the isolation of Hormuz, he sought to weaken its inhabitants' will to resist.

Quryat. Proceeding northward, Albuquerque assaulted and sacked the port of Quryat, a few miles from Kalhat, in the manner indicated. He was there from August 19 through 21.

Masqat. Masqat is located on the Tropic of Cancer, in the Gulf of Oman north of Quryat. The local ruler had come aboard ship to talk with Albuquerque and had agreed to his demands. After returning ashore, however, Moslem reinforcements arrived and together with the town's Moslem residents they persuaded him to disregard his agreement. In the ensuing

encounter, which took place on Sunday, September 5, the Portuguese bombarded, assaulted, and sacked the town.

Suhar. Albuquerque's strategy was proving effective. The ruler of Suhar, a town located northwest of Masqat, had heard of the Portuguese depradations to the south; as soon as they arrived, he hastened to declare himself a vassal of King Manuel. The Portuguese flag was raised peacefully.

Title XXVIII

Khor Fakkan. The Portuguese stormed ashore at Khor Fakkan, located just north of Suhar, on September 22. The inhabitants had indeed abandoned the town rather than face the Portuguese squadron in battle. Albuquerque was now ready to move against Hormuz itself.

Title XXIX

Off the Arabian coast. Hormuz actually lies but a few miles off the Persian coast; otherwise the description is quite accurate.[40]

Qeshm. This island, many times the size of Hormuz, lies close to it and the Persian mainland.

Bahrain. The Bahrain Islands are still famed for their rich pearl beds. They lie well up into the Persian Gulf, close to the coast of Arabia.

Larak. Larak is a small island several miles south of Hormuz.

Title XXX

The King of Cambay's ship. The Sultan of Cambay consistently opposed the Portuguese, and in this instance his ship, the *Meri,* was the largest facing Albuquerque.

Coje Atar. An astute and intelligent eunuch, Coje Atar was the effective power in Hormuz; Castanheda called him a tyrant. In these conversations with Albuquerque, he sought to delay the Portuguese attack until the arrival of expected reinforcements. He paid little heed to a condescending peace offer from Albuquerque.

An infinite number of Moors were killed. One of the most unusual aspects of the conquest of Hormuz was the discovery after the battle that many of the enemy had been killed by their own arrows, an incident duly recorded by the historians and celebrated by Camões:

> Ali verão as setas estridentes
> Reciprocarse, a ponta no ar virando,
> Contra quem as tirou, que Deos peleja
> Por quem estende a fe da madre Igreja.
>
> (Canto X, 40)*

The Red Sea. Fernández de Enciso's *Suma de geographia* offers a similar explanation: "this water of the Red Sea is not naturally red, but they say that the soil of the banks is red, as well as that of the bottom."

---

* But they will see the whistling arrow flight
Wheel right around, recurving in the sky
On him who shot. God fights upon his side,
Who faith of Mother Church spreads far and wide.

A great Moorish astrologer. There is no mention of the astrologer or his prediction in the historians' accounts. Since the information is offered by one of Albuquerque's officers, it no doubt is authentic.

Title XXXI

The relationship between the kings of Portugal and many knights of Salamanca. This quite inaccurate digression into genealogies has but one purpose—to exalt the various branches of the Remón family; and Juan Agüero, who also bore the name Remón, will share in their glory.

Alfonso VI of León and Castile had invited Raymond of Burgundy to the peninsula and had given him his daughter Urraca in marriage. In 1102 Alfonso commissioned Raymond to undertake the repopulation of Salamanca. A son of Raymond of Burgundy and Urraca eventually ruled as Alfonso VII in León and Castile (1126-1157); in 1135, Alfonso VII claimed the title of "Emperor of the Peoples of the Two Religions," referring to his sovereignty over Christians and Moors. Raymond of Burgundy's brother Guy enjoyed a short reign as Pope Calixtus II (1118-1119). Shortly after his arrival in Castile, Raymond invited his cousin Henry of Constantinople to join him. He did so and in 1094 married another of Alfonso VI's daughters, Teresa. Their son became the first King of Portugal, Afonso Henriques.

The third person mentioned by Agüero was Raymond of Saint Gilles; he married yet a third daughter of Alfonso VI. This Raymond was the fourth Count of Toulouse and was blind in one eye.

In his discussion, Juan Agüero has confused Raymond of Burgundy and Raymond of Toulouse as well as their respective

characteristics. He has the latter rebuilding Salamanca when he was actually off on a Crusade in the Middle East. Although this confusion makes it impossible to determine to which illustrious predecessor our genealogist has attempted to trace the various branches of the Spanish Remones, the purpose of the digression is quite clear.

Jorge Barreto. Barreto was one of the Portuguese captains who later sided with Almeida against Albuquerque over the succession to command in India. No doubt as a result of this, he accompanied Almeida when he left India. As is reported in **Title XLIX,** Barreto was another of the many victims of the Saldanha massacre.

Title XXXII

Many disagreements among the captains of Hispania. Directly following the seizure of Hormuz, Albuquerque began work on a fort which he later named in honor of Our Lady of Victory. Working on a fort, however, was not a labor of love for the officers of his squadron. They were anxious to collect a tribute from Hormuz, leave the island, and get back to the more lucrative activity of prize-hunting at sea. The fact that Albuquerque obliged officers to perform manual labor right alongside the men further enraged and alienated them. They repeatedly exhorted him to abandon the fort, and on one occasion a furious Albuquerque threw one of their petitions into the open foundation of an incomplete entrance to the fort. The gateway was immediately dubbed "Porta dos Requerimentos," Gate of the Petitions.

Four Christians. The four who deserted were enlisted men,

valuable artillery experts. In addition to bringing Coje Atar their much needed skills, they informed him of the dissension among the Portuguese officers. This inspired Coje Atar to seek an open break with Albuquerque, and fighting was renewed late in November when Coje Atar refused to return the four renegades.

The battles were many, large, and diverse. Albuquerque's strength lay in his ships and artillery; on land his forces were too small to hold and control Hormuz. Therefore, he decided to force the island into submission by cutting off the flow of needed supplies, especially water. The blockade proved effective; by January the inhabitants were clamoring for Coje Atar to surrender. He might well have yielded had not three of Albuquerque's captains solved his problem. Without warning, they abandoned Albuquerque and sailed for India, forcing him to leave Hormuz. Figueroa joined Albuquerque at Cape Guardafui after the lifting of the blockade and was an eyewitness to the subsequent events described in this title.

The Christians took Kalhat a second time. Albuquerque was especially severe when he attacked Kalhat the second time, in August 1508, for the Kalhat merchants had deceived him the year before with false and rotten supplies.

A written assurance. Realizing that Albuquerque was sure to return to Hormuz at the end of winter, Coje Atar and the Sultan wrote to the Viceroy in India requesting aid against the impending attack and declaring their loyalty to Portugal. The captains who had deserted Albuquerque were serving under Almeida when the Hormuz envoy arrived, and they encouraged

the Viceroy to write the letter of friendship to the rulers of Hormuz.

Naband. A port on the Persian mainland, Naband was the main source of Hormuz' water supply. While respecting the authority of Almeida's letter, Albuquerque used Coje Atar's refusal to hand over the four renegades as a pretext to raid this port and other surrounding areas.

They were all pleased and happy to see each other. Albuquerque sailed for India in November 1508, fully expecting to assume the governorship upon arrival. However, Almeida had been exhorted by many not to relinquish his authority, and he did not do so until a year later. Figueroa would certainly have been pleased to reach India, but it is equally certain that the meeting between Almeida and Albuquerque was far from pleasant.

Title XXXIII

Chaul. Chaul lies about thirty miles south of Bombay, near the larger city of Alibag.

Dabul. Castanheda and Barros offer a radically different version of Lourenço's actions at Dabul. They report that although young Almeida wanted to attack the Moslem ships, he in fact did not. His father had instructed him to consult with the other officers of the squadron before undertaking any major action. When he did, they rejected his proposal. Upon his return to Angedive, Lourenço was admonished by his father for not having attacked.

Pero Barreto. This is Pero Barreto de Magalhães; he sailed with Lourenço and his father in 1505 and according to Castanheda had acquired the nickname *O lião* by virtue of having killed a lion in Africa. Although there was no major engagement at Dabul, there were several minor forays ashore during one of which Barreto must have distinguished himself. He too perished at Saldanha, as is reported in **Title XLIX**.

Diogo Pires. Lourenço's tutor, Pires was one of the officers who had supported the idea of a major attack against the ships in the Dabul harbor.

A fleet of Turks. By 1507, Portuguese successes in the Indies had diverted sufficient amounts of spices from Cairo to arouse the immediate concern of the Sultan of Egypt. He devoted the greater part of 1507 to organizing a fleet to be sent into the Indian Ocean against the Portuguese. The Mameluke fleet reached Diu early in 1508 and, after being briefed by the friendly ruler there, moved out in search of the Portuguese. The first force encountered was Lourenço de Almeida's squadron at Chaul in March. According to the historians, the Portuguese recovered quickly from the initial supposition that the approaching craft represented the arrival of Albuquerque. Almeida aggressively seized the initiative and moved to attack the Egyptians. Casualties were heavy on both sides in an engagement which lasted throughout most of the afternoon. Then, as the sun was beginning to set, the Portuguese were dismayed to see the Cambay fleet start to move into the harbor.

Melik Yas. Governor of Diu, the wily Melik Yas was a constant thorn in the side of the Portuguese. Although he had

counseled the Egyptians and had accompanied them from Diu, he had withheld his own forces throughout the afternoon battle until he could determine whether the Egyptians appeared to be winning. Seeing them with the advantage over the smaller Portuguese force, he moved in with his fleet and took up position against the Portuguese.

The Christians resolved to leave the harbor. Lourenço's captains advised him to leave Chaul harbor that evening, under the protective cover of darkness, but he refused. Mindful of his failure to engage the enemy at Dabul, the young commander proudly replied that he was not about to sneak away in the night, for "where he comes from they call that running away."

Dom Lourenço de Almeida was killed by two mortar shots. Lourenço was a commander who led by example. His ship was the last to weigh anchor the next morning. As it started for open water and safety, it took a hit at the water line and became enmeshed in a cluster of fishermen's stakes close to shore. Hopelessly outnumbered in a foundering ship, he and his men put up a determined defense but were no match for the eager attackers. Figueroa correctly reports Lourenço's death from two mortar shots. Only eighteen of his crew survived to be taken prisoner.

Champanel. Located some one hundred miles north of Cambay, near the city of Baroda, Champanel is now in ruins but was a thriving city in the early sixteenth century. Duarte Barbosa visited it; he reveals that the Sultan was introduced to poison as a child so that as an adult he would not be vulnerable to assassination by poisoning. Although he makes no mention

of the Sultan's using his condition for punitive purposes, its effects were no less lethal, for "as many women as slept with him perished." Varthema also takes note of the sad plight of the Sultan's harem as well as the use of poisonous saliva on his enemies. As for the Sultan's shirts, he merely notes that they were discarded after wearing and never used again.[41]

By the time they had gotten ready. Adverse winds and currents hindered the other Portuguese ships' attempts to put about. Castanheda adds that several captains and crews were quite frightened and unwilling to try very hard. Pero Barreto did lead a longboat back and managed to secure a line to Lourenço's ship, but his men were so exhausted from the exertions of the previous day's battle that they were unable to tow it free.

Francisco de Añaya. This is no doubt Pedro's son; apparently it was not considered necessary to identify him again. Castanheda infers that Añaya had behaved in a cowardly manner at Chaul and says that he was afraid to deliver the news of Lourenço's death himself, but instead sent a messenger to the Viceroy.

The Lord gave him and the Lord has taken him away. "The Lord gave, and the Lord hath taken away; blessed be the name of the Lord" (Job, 1:21). According to Gaspar Correia, one Duarte Camacho gave the sad news to Almeida, whose reaction was less religious but equally stoic: "he who ate the pheasant must also eat the rooster."

In search of the Rumis. Figueroa accompanied the Viceroy Almeida as he set out on his campaign of retaliation and revenge.

Title XXXIV

Margāo. This small port lies some ten miles to the south of Goa.

Jupiter's banner. According to tradition, Kronos, whose equivalent in the Roman pantheon was Saturn, believed that one of his children would some day overthrow him; to avert this he devoured them as they were born. Zeus, the Roman Jupiter, was spared and later did defeat his father in battle. The eagle is the symbol of Roman power.[42]

Bonis Auguriis. It is difficult to determine to which specific Roman family Juan Agüero may have spoken; there are many with this combination of Latin names.

Count Fernán González. Having already laid claim to kinship with the Portuguese Crown, Juan Agüero now proceeds to link himself with that of Castile. Fernán González was the first independent Count of Castile, and his descendants did become kings of Castile. One of the original founders of the Agüero family in Trasmiera was a Pedro González de Agüero, who may have been related to Fernán González. In the *Triunfo Raimundino,* Agüero specifically states that he is a member of the González family. His attitude here illustrates an observation made by Cadalso in the eighteenth century to the effect that "those of Asturias and the Montaña have the highest esteem for their genealogy." [43]

Meliḳ Yas and the Viceroy exchanged letters. Melik Yas

was very likely sincere in his protestations that he had not sought Lourenço's death. He would much rather have taken him hostage for use in further dealings with the Viceroy.

Title XXXV

Dabul. According to Damião de Góis, Almeida's cruelty at Dabul became proverbial among the Indians: "May the ire of the Franks come upon you, just as it came upon Dabul." Castanheda also notes such atrocities as pulling infants from mothers' arms and smashing them against walls.

Who had shown up in a fancy litter. To show their scorn for the approaching Portuguese, seven wealthy gentlemen of Dabul had themselves carried down to the shore in litters. All seven paid with their lives for this bravado. The *Conquista* seizes the opportunity to criticize similar unmanly practices among Christian knights as well.

Who set fire to the city. Almeida himself gave the order to burn Dabul, to prevent indiscriminate looting and loss of control over his men.

Jirasal rice. Of the various classes of rice cultivated along the western coast of India, Duarte Barbosa says that "the first and best is *girasal.*" The word *girasal* appears to derive from the Marathi language, meaning "like cumin," from the rice's odor, which is similar to that of the aromatic cumin.[44]

Goa. A discussion of Goa is more appropriate to **Title XLI,** to which the reader is referred.

Title XXXVI

Thana. Thana is located immediately to the south of Bombay.

Mahim. This is Kelve Mahim, thirty miles north of Bombay.

The tides are so extreme. The tidal range in the Gulf of Cambay is forty-five feet, a change effected with disconcerting speed. The Portuguese were fortunate to move when they did.

In order not to anger Melik Yas and the King of Cambay. Almeida need not have worried about Melik Yas; he was doing his best to keep the Egyptian fleet in Diu. He knew that the Portuguese were heading for Diu and feared what might happen to him and the city should Almeida not find his quarry there. Melik Yas was perfectly willing to sacrifice the Egyptian fleet in order to keep Almeida from attacking Diu itself.

A terrible empty gulf. Almeida sailed from Kelve Mahim across the Gulf of Cambay toward Diu.

The Feast Day of Our Lady. On February 2, the Purification of the Blessed Virgin Mary is commemorated. Candlemas Day, it also marks the presentation of Jesus in the temple.

Title XXXVII

The King of Calicut. A number of Calicut ships were at Diu when the Portuguese arrived and did take part in the battle against them.

Saint Blaise. Martyred in 317, Saint Blaise is honored as a special protector against afflictions of the throat.

Nuno Vaz Pereira went in the vanguard. Almeida announced that he would lead the attack, but his officers convinced him to concede the honor, and the danger, to Nuno Vaz Pereira.

Abyssinians. This is a clear reference to the Christians of Ethiopia and the practice of baptism by fire. Damião de Góis claims that the Abyssinians fought bravely and well for their captors.

His coat of arms. The Pereira family is another of those whose heraldry is described and praised in the *Triunfo Raimundino.*[45]

His name remaining immortal. Nuno Vaz Pereira is one of the true heroic figures of the *Conquista.* More praise is given him than any other. Figueroa had served with him at Sofala and again here at Diu; he obviously had very special admiration for him. The historians also note that he was an exceptionally popular commander.

A Portuguese knight by the name of Figuereido. Gaspar Correia describes at length a particularly violent encounter involving five Portuguese who had leaped aboard an enemy ship. Making their way to the aftercastle, they found themselves stranded when their ship broke loose and drifted away. Three of the five were killed, and Figuereido may have been one of

them. His coat of arms is described in the *Triunfo Raimundino* under the name Figueroa.[46]

Pero Cão. Pero Cão was one of the five cited by Correia. Castanheda lends support to his account, saying that Cão was killed after being stranded aboard an enemy ship.

The son of Manuel Paçanha. Manuel Paçanha had lost two sons when Lourenço de Almeida was defeated at Chaul, and, according to Barros, he lost two more at Diu. A fifth son was sent home to Portugal so that the entire family would not be wiped out.

The Rumis killed and vanquished. The defeat of the Egyptian fleet at Diu marked the end of the Sultan's influence in the Indian Ocean. Failure to recoup the revenues lost as a result of the interruption of the spice traffic contributed substantially to his final defeat at the hands of Selim I in 1517.

Title XXXVIII

He sent back the Christians. Wisely anticipating the day when he might have to reckon with the Viceroy, Melik Yas had taken good care of the survivors of Lourenço's ship.

Afonso de Noronha to Dom Afonso. There is a mistake in names here. As Almeida was leaving Diu, he dispatched Antonio de Noronha to Socotra. The latter's brother had been in command there since the seizure of the island in 1507. Almeida did not know that Afonso de Noronha had just been lost at sea while en route to India. Both Noronhas were nephews of Albuquerque.

Just what is called India. The *Conquista's* concept of India in terms of the coastal area extending from the Gulf of Cambay to Cape Comorin corresponds roughly to the traditional Second India, India *Intra Gangem.* The *Conquista* makes no mention of the east or Coromandel coast of India, nor does it refer to the Third India, India *Extra Gangem.* First India would appear to be accounted for by the "land of the Gujarati," that is, modern Pakistan. In this title Arabia *Felix* denotes part of the Persian mainland.

Diogo Sequeira. Diogo Lopes de Sequeira sailed from Portugal in the spring of 1508. A full account of his expedition to Malacca is the subject of **Title XLVII.**

Colachel. This port lies between Trivandrum and Cape Comorin.

Molucca. Several groups of islands make up the Moluccas or Spice Islands; the Ternate group was the richest source of spices and hence of principal interest to the Portuguese. Magellan's proposal to reach the East by sailing around South America and across the Pacific, which led to the first circumnavigation of the globe, received Spanish support because he had visited the Moluccas and believed them to lie within the area awarded to Castile by the Treaty of Tordesillas. The islands, however, remained in Portuguese control until the arrival of the Dutch.

The Marshal, Afonso de Albuquerque's nephew. Francisco Coutinho sailed from Portugal in March 1509, believing that his uncle was already installed as Governor of India. To his surprise, he found him in Cannanore a virtual prisoner. When Almeida

saw uncle and nephew sail into Cochin with all the power of
the latter's strong fleet, he realized the futility of delaying his
departure any longer. Handing over the reins of power to
Albuquerque, he sailed from India in late November 1509. The
historians also say that he was about ready to leave and Coutinho's arrival could have done nothing to change his mind.

Title XXXIX

To destroy Calicut. Francisco Coutinho had gone to
India with the sole purpose of destroying Calicut. Albuquerque
tried to dissuade him, on the grounds that such an attack would
be costly and yield no lasting benefits. The newcomer persisted,
however, deriding the fighting ability of the Indians, an enemy
he had yet to face in the field; he also reminded his uncle that
King Manuel had ordered him to support the campaign in every
way possible.

Rodrigo Rebelo. Rebelo captained one of the ships of
Coutinho's fleet. He later distinguished himself during the Goa
campaign and also served as Captain of Cannanore.

The men of Hispania confidently surged ashore. The landing began on the morning of January 2, 1510. As commander in
chief, Coutinho had divided the assault forces into two sections;
he would lead one, Albuquerque the other. He specifically reserved to himself the honor and privilege of landing first. In spite
of their agreement, however, Albuquerque was the first ashore;
he had already secured the beach and port area by the time
Coutinho arrived. Although the *Conquista* does not so state,
Figueroa was probably with Albuquerque's force. The outraged

Marshal bitterly accused his uncle of having betrayed their agreement. The historians give varying accounts of what might have happened. Castanheda says that Albuquerque simply disregarded his promise. Barros, on the other hand, says it was all a mistake: Albuquerque had hurried ahead in order to stop one of his captains who was charging in toward the beach; landing first was thus an accident. Damião de Góis's cryptic remark is probably the most accurate; he reports that Albuquerque "in matters of war was well aware of the opportunities of the moment."

Whatever may have been the reason for Albuquerque's getting ashore first, the results were to prove disastrous for the expedition. Coutinho was determined to regain the honor he felt Albuquerque had perfidiously usurped. Back in Lisbon he had boasted that he would return with the doors of the Zamorin's palaces. Armed with a walking stick and wearing a jaunty green beret, the rather paunchy Marshal started out after his trophies.

Nairs. In **Title XL,** the *Conquista* comments on the rigid separation of the various components of Indian society but mistakenly calls the Nairs the highest class. The warrior caste, they actually occupy the second position in the Hindu caste structure, after the Brahmans.

An awful battle took place there. With Albuquerque reluctantly and warily trailing behind, Coutinho succeeded in reaching and storming the palace, whereupon he allowed his men to wander off in individual looting and sacking. While this was going on, the Calicut forces were reorganizing and converging on the palace. As Coutinho and his booty-laden men

began the three-mile trek back to the beach, they were hit from all sides. The Marshal and most of his men were killed, and Albuquerque was wounded as he attempted to relieve him. A soundly beaten expedition was driven back to the ships.

Vasco da Silveira. Silveira had seen service in the Indies on several previous occasions. He had come out in 1504 with Lopo Soares de Albergária and again in 1508 with Jorge d'Aguiar.

Title XL

Calicut comes from "cal." According to tradition, the name Calicut, meaning "cock-fort," is derived from the manner in which the city's boundaries were established. Calicut was to include all the area within which the crowing of a cock placed in the local temple could be heard. The *Conquista's* venture into the etymology of Calicut, as fanciful as the explanation of Arabia *Felix* in **Title XXV,** closely parallels Juan Agüero's ingenious explanation of the meaning of Salamanca[47] in the *Triunfo Raimundino:*

> Sal, por la sabiduría,
> Y Mancia divinación,
> Será su interpretación
> Por cierta etimología.*

Only one person in the world should be like a pontiff. This is a clear allusion to the ecumenical ideal of one flock and one shepherd.

---

* *Sal* represents wisdom, *mancia* divination: this is its true interpretation through accurate etymology.

The Indians in Calicut adore the devil. Varthema was also impressed by this practice: "they acknowledge that there is a God who has created the heaven and the earth and all the world . . . but that he has sent this spirit, that is, the devil, into this world to do justice." [48]

Title XLI

He set out for the Strait of Mecca. Once recovered from the wounds received at Calicut, Albuquerque set out for the Red Sea, intending to attack Suez and then Hormuz, over which he proposed to reassert Portuguese control; Figueroa accompanied him.

Timogi. There are reports of pirates operating out of Onor as early as the times of Marco Polo. Timogi had first pledged his loyalty to Portugal in 1505 when he met Almeida. Among his many services, he frequently provided reliable information on political conditions within the various Indian states.

Sabayo the King of Goa had died. Shortly before Albuquerque's meeting with Timogi, Sabayo the Sultan of Goa had died. João de Barros offers a comprehensive history of Goa prior to the arrival of the Portuguese in which he mentions, as does the *Conquista,* that the Sultan of Goa had won his independence from the Sultanate of the Deccan. Sabayo's son, Adil Khan, often called Idalcão by the Portuguese and Sabaín in the *Conquista,* was in the process of establishing control over his father's domains when the Portuguese arrived on the scene.

Goa. Figueroa's eyewitness description is quite accurate. In addition to its strategic location on the western coast of India,

Goa was an important port in the lucrative horse trade. Horses were shipped in great quantities from Persia to Goa, then dispatched inland. This traffic was a major source of Goa's wealth and of great interest to the Portuguese.[49]

That abominable custom. Western travelers to the East have been fascinated by the custom of suttee and Figueroa is no exception. His description and Varthema's are similar in many respects.[50]

When Afonso de Albuquerque and Timogi reached Goa. The attack on Goa began in late February 1510. Albuquerque sent Antonio de Noronha and Timogi ahead in two groups; both landed successfully, and by the end of the first day the Goan defenders had been scattered.

A great mystery. This is new; there appears to be no other reference to such an occurrence. There can be no doubt concerning the religious faith demonstrated here; one can but conjecture as to the veracity of the events.

Title XLII

He would leave no one alive. According to Correia, Albuquerque promised that, unless the Goans accepted his demands, "they would see their homes filled with fire and blood."

The keys to the fort. The Portuguese entry into Goa took place on March 1, 1510, and Martín Fernández de Figueroa was among those who marched along behind Albuquerque. Although the Portuguese did obtain the items mentioned, Albu-

querque strictly forbade looting of the city. His actions indicate that from the very start he was thinking in terms of a permanent settlement.

Khamil Khan. Away from Goa at the time of the Portuguese triumph, Adil Khan was determined to regain the city; and the Sultan of the Deccan and several other neighbors agreed to support his campaign against the Portuguese. Adil Khan was so confident that he delayed his return to Goa until the onset of the monsoon season; he did not want the Portuguese to be able to escape by sea. Khamil Khan, referred to as *Camalcão* by the historians, was one of Adil Khan's chief field commanders.

Garcia de Sousa. The coat of arms depicted here is another of those presented in the *Triunfo Raimundino*. In addition to his competent leadership at Goa, Garcia de Sousa previously had distinguished himself with Diogo Lopes de Sequeira at Malacca in 1509, as is pointed out in **Title XLVII.** He gave further proof of his courage during Albuquerque's unsuccessful assault on Aden in 1513.[51]

Nine or ten Christians leaped ashore after the infidels. Adil Khan's army moved into action against the Portuguese in early May. Their first attempts to land on the island were repulsed, and in one of these encounters Figueroa and his companions must have displayed their bravery and eagerness. The historians, and especially Correia, describe many of these skirmishes, but it is not possible to identify in their accounts the specific episode involving Figueroa.

Title XLIII

Jorge da Cunha. The historians praise this captain as an outstanding leader in both the seizure and defense of Goa. He had come out to India with the fleet of Marshal Coutinho.

Amadís. The popular tales of chivalry strongly influenced the Iberian man-at-arms' self-awareness. In **Title XXXV,** unmanly and frivolous aspects of the chivalric world are ridiculed and censured. In this instance, the *Conquista* claims for real men and real deeds the praise given to the fabulous exploits of the best-known embodiment of the chivalric ideal, Amadís de Gaula.[52]

Banastarim. Banastarim is located at the eastern end of Goa island, on the Canal of Combarjua, a backwater channel that connects the Mandovi River with the Zuari, thus completing the separation of Goa from the mainland. Banastarim was considered the most likely avenue of approach for Adil Khan's army, and to defend it Sousa had a command of one hundred infantrymen, ten cavalry, with cannon and mortars in support. Several Portuguese ships patrolled the canal to give aid when required.

A brother of his killed. This was Jorge de Sousa, killed along with thirty others. Increasing pressure from Adil Khan forced Garcia de Sousa to abandon the positions at Banastarim and pull back to the fort.

Francisco Pereira. Francisco Pereira Coutinho was with Albuquerque prior to the taking of Goa and distinguished himself again at Malacca in 1511.

Dom Antonio and his galleys. Antonio de Noronha was in charge of the ships at Banastarim. Once the pass was lost, he also withdrew to the fort. He scuttled the *Espera* because he did not have enough men to handle it.

The Captain Major sent a ship after provisions. The *Conquista* passes over the details of the Portuguese expulsion from Goa. Once Adil Khan had a foothold on the island, he vigorously pursued his advantage. The Portuguese were soon pushed back to the fort, all the passes falling to the advancing Goans. As pressure on the incompleted and under-stocked fort became increasingly severe, Albuquerque decided to evacuate. On May 30, the Portuguese returned to their ships; they were to spend two months anchored in the Mandovi River, confined there by the monsoon. The ship referred to here was one that made an unsuccessful attempt to clear the sandbar and reach another port and provisions.

Title XLIV

Six thousand Moorish fighting men. The historians place special emphasis on the defection of the Goans Albuquerque had armed and hoped to use in the defense of the island. Barros reached the same conclusion as the *Conquista,* that "truly, if these Moors, residents of the island, had not gone against us, as many Moors as landed on the island, no matter how many, would all have perished."

The renegades. The vehement condemnation of Juan Deras shows that this form of psychological warfare was very effective. Men like Figueroa, thoroughly imbued with religious zeal, must

have been repelled and morally affronted by the sight of turn-coats. Yet, more than a few hungry and harassed Christians must have envied them their material comforts. Killing this one had a salutary effect on morale. An incident involving a man named Deras is recorded by the historians, with varying circumstances. He either simply deserted or was stranded aboard an enemy ship during a skirmish, at which point he chose to go over to the enemy. Correia, on the other hand, reports that Juan Deras was the musketeer who shot the renegade.

João Nunes. Nunes had been at Malacca with Diogo Lopes de Sequeira prior to joining Albuquerque early in 1510. He returned to Portugal in the same fleet carrying Figueroa.

Title XLV

Albuquerque was informed. Throughout their enforced stay in the Mandovi River, the Portuguese received important help from a fellow countryman named João Machado. A *degre-dado,* or condemned man, Machado had been left behind at Malindi in 1500 by Pedro Álvares Cabral. After much adventurous wandering, he had succeeded in gaining a position of trust under Adil Khan. Serving as his emissary to Albuquerque, Machado gave warning of the impending attack.

It was common practice for early Portuguese fleets to the Indies to carry one or more *degredados.* They were placed ashore at locations about which information was desired, and survival or death depended upon individual resourcefulness. Time and again the histories cite the timely intervention of a *degredado;* often nameless, they were for the most part consistently loyal to Portugal and proved of great value, as was the case with João Machado at Goa.

Simão de Andrada, his brother Fernão Peres. The naval engagement described here resulted in a clear victory for the Portuguese. The Andradas so distinguished themselves that Adil Khan, who had observed the battle from the shore, sent a messenger next day to congratulate them. They also figured significantly in Albuquerque's successful return to Goa the following November.

He was well liked. An ability to calm his uncle's wrath contributed in large measure to Antonio de Noronha's popularity. According to Barros, Noronha was not only an effective military leader; he also "resolved several disputes between him [Albuquerque] and the captains. Since Afonso de Albuquerque was passionate and rude in the conduct of his affairs, and sometimes hard to please, he always took advantage of a good intermediary through whom he worked to remedy those verbal explosions that marked the initial eruption of his wrath."

It is surprising that the *Conquista* makes no mention of Antonio de Noronha's daring assault on the fort at Panjim. Albuquerque had been forced to select an anchorage that left his ships in range of Adil Khan's artillery emplacements in the Panjim fort. To put an end to the harassing and damaging bombardment, Albuquerque ordered an attack on the fort and entrusted it to his nephew. It was an unexpected and highly successful maneuver. Barros notes that the Portuguese task was made considerably easier by the fortunate coincidence that the Panjim garrison had gotten thoroughly drunk the night before the attack.

Title XLVI

In the month of August. On August 15, when weather final-

ly permitted, Albuquerque led his beleaguered company out of the Mandovi River.

Four were bound for Malacca. In March 1510, King Manuel dispatched Diogo Mendes de Vasconcelos as captain major of a squadron bound for Malacca, unaware that the 1508 expedition under Diogo Lopes de Sequeira had ended in defeat. Albuquerque met with Vasconcelos in Cannanore, informed him of what had happened to Sequeira, and in light of this refused to allow him to proceed. The Governor reasoned correctly that Vasconcelos' force was too small to do any good at Malacca; moreover, he wanted to use him and his ships to support his own return to Goa. Although Vasconcelos did fight well at Goa, he was a reluctant warrior; Albuquerque had to imprison him before the battle to keep him from slipping away to Malacca.

Gonçalo de Sequeira. Gonçalo de Sequeira left Lisbon a few days after Mendes de Vasconcelos. His mission was to take eight cargo ships to the Malabar coast, secure spices, and return to Portugal without delay. Albuquerque, however, commandeered the most seaworthy of the vessels for the upcoming Goa campaign. In **Title XLIX** it is stated that Gonçalo de Sequeira was believed lost at sea during the return voyage to Portugal; actually he had been forced to winter at Mozambique, reaching Portugal safely in 1512.

Duarte de Lemos. Realizing that one man could not effectively control and administer an area of operations extending from the Cape of Good Hope to Malacca, King Manuel in 1508 created the captaincy major for the coast of Arabia, with jurisdiction extending from Sofala to the Gulf of Cambay. Duarte de Lemos was assigned to this new command when he sailed from

Portugal in the spring of 1508. He came to the Malabar coast in 1510 in search of men and supplies.

The king was supposed to go into the cave. In Cochin the senior member of the ruling family was customarily obliged to live in the local temple. The actual ruler remained in office so long as the other remained alive in the temple. When the latter died, the incumbent was supposed to move into the temple and be replaced by a nephew. Succession was through the offspring of the ruler's eldest sister. The situation in which the Portuguese became involved began when the ex-rajah living in the temple— the ruler who had originally befriended Pedro Álvares Cabral— died. The incumbent was reluctant to give up the throne; since he also was friendly to the Portuguese and his would-be successor was not, the Portuguese were quick to intervene on his behalf. The pretender was easily driven off and the cooperative incumbent continued in office.

Who with ample reason stayed behind. Did Figueroa leave the Indies illegally? He had more than satisfied his original three-year obligation, yet it is not clear that he had permission to return to Portugal at that particular moment. The *Conquista* describes quite sympathetically the emotions of men with long years of hazardous service behind them, unwilling to go back to Goa with Albuquerque. It is likely that Martín Fernández de Figueroa was one of those who decided on their own to stay behind and return to Portugal.

Manuel de la Cerda. Another captain whose coat of arms is depicted in the *Triunfo Raimundino*,[53] he is credited with singlehandedly killing eight of the enemy in spite of serious wounds.

Dom Jerónimo. Jerónimo de Lima had been with Albuquerque since 1506 and was one of his staunchest supporters, especially during the disputes with Almeida.

His return to Portugal. Expecting that he would soon succeed Albuquerque as Governor of India, Duarte de Lemos was surprised and chagrined when a ship put in at Cannanore bearing a letter for him from King Manuel, in which he was ordered to relinquish his command and return to Portugal. Lemos had always been on bad terms with Albuquerque and curtly refused his plea to delay departure until after the expedition against Goa. Furthermore, he shielded many of those who had hidden away. Figueroa learned of Albuquerque's victorious retaking of Goa while at Cannanore with Lemos preparing for the return voyage.

Title XLVII

He paid a visit to the Viceroy. The first part of Diogo Lopes de Sequeira's expedition consisted of an exploration of Madagascar. Unable to find sufficient quantities of spices there, he crossed over to India, arriving in April 1509. After waiting out the monsoon season in the company of the Viceroy, he departed for Malacca.

Captain Garcia de Sousa. Almeida directed Sousa to accompany Sequeira's squadron. Since Figueroa later served under Sousa at Goa, he no doubt learned about the Portuguese experience in Malacca from him or his men.

Certain islands to their left. Lying to port as one proceeds toward Malacca from India are the Nicobar and Andaman island groups. Concerning the inhabitants of the Andaman Islands, Marco Polo notes that "they are a most cruel generation,

and eat everybody that they can catch, if not of their own race." [54]

The Chinese. The Portuguese ships were anchored near some of the numerous Chinese junks engaged in trading at Malacca. Dealings with the Chinese were interesting and cordial; they did not take part in the attacks against the Portuguese.

The Antilles. Fernando, although King of Aragon, was but regent in Castile, governing on behalf of his daughter Juana la Loca. As regent, however, he was the effective ruler of Castile's new possessions in the West.

Trusting that their enemies would keep their word. "Item, we remind you that whilst you are in port you should keep careful watch both by day and night against the people of the land and the storms of the sea. . ." (King Manuel's instructions to Diogo Sequeira).

At first the commercially minded Malaccans welcomed the Portuguese and gave them permission to trade, but Moslem intriguers soon convinced the principal minister to move against them. Their first plan was to assassinate Sequeira at a banquet, but he was informed and stayed away, feigning illness. He was not so alert to the next ruse. Under the guise of offering cargo at exceptionally low prices, Moslems and their Malaccan supporters obtained permission to board the Portuguese ships. The historians roundly criticize Sequeira's credulity; Damião de Góis says he behaved "as if he were in the port of Lisbon." Garcia de Sousa sensed the impending attack and sent a messenger to alert Sequeira. The messenger, Ferdinand Magellan, arrived just in time to save the latter's life. The Portuguese were thoroughly routed, however, and forced to leave Malacca. Many

men were stranded ashore during the hasty retreat, which explains why one of the ships had to be scuttled on the way back to India. Albuquerque personally led the successful assault and definitive seizure of Malacca in 1511.[55]

Pulo Brasse. This small island off the northern tip of Sumatra most closely corresponds to the place name *Polvoreda* recorded by Figueroa. The historians also report the loss of one of the returning ships there.

Jerónimo Texeira. Texeira was with Albuquerque during the first attack on Goa, but, more interested in commerce than conquest, he left before the long siege.

Diogo Sequeira set out for Lisbon. Upon reaching Cape Comorin in January 1510, Sequeira learned that Albuquerque had taken over as governor. Since he had actively supported Almeida, he was reluctant to meet up with his successor, especially after an embarrassing defeat. In April, therefore, Diogo Sequeira sailed directly for the Cape of Good Hope, a dangerous voyage at that time of year. He reached Portugal and apparently suffered no punishment for the defeat at Malacca, since he returned to India as governor in 1518.

Title XLVIII

In addition to describing the elephants of the Indies, a favorite topic of all travelers to the East, the *Conquista* includes in this title a random set of observations on flora, fauna, and strange customs. Figueroa may well have seen all these things himself, but literary sources for his observations may be found in Santaella's 1503 edition of Nicolò de' Conti and Marco Polo and in Varthema's narrative.

The green branch. Varthema's description of this method of bill-collecting makes it appear somewhat more difficult than in the *Conquista:* "I . . . shall take a green branch in my hand, shall go softly behind the debtor, and with the branch shall draw a circle on the ground surrounding him, and if I can enclose him in the circle, I shall say to him these words three times: 'I command you by the head of the Brahmans and of the king that you do not depart hence until you have paid me and satisfied me as much as I ought to have from thee.' And he will satisfy me, or truly he will die there without any other guard. And should he quit the circle and not pay me, the king would put him to death." [56]

The Queen of Portugal. Two years after the death of his first wife Isabel in 1498, Manuel married her sister María. Both were daughters of Fernando and Isabel. When María died in 1517, Manuel continued his policy of Castilian marriages, this time with Leonor, the sister of Carlos V.

Title XLIX

The Azores. After rounding the Cape of Good Hope, homeward bound vessels sailed before the Southeast trade winds, then across the Northeast trades. This course would carry them to the Azores. In this case Figueroa reached Flores first, then moved east to Terceira. From there it was due east to Lisbon.

Saldanha. Francisco de Almeida's death at Saldanha, a small watering place on the Atlantic side of the Cape, could hardly have been more senseless. It came during a punitive expedition against a band of natives who had supposedly insulted two Portuguese officers. The *Conquista* is accurate in reporting that some sixty others died with Almeida, and at the

very moment that his rival was entering triumphantly into Goa.

Antonio do Campo. Campo, who had come out to the Indies in 1506 with Albuquerque, was one of the group that vehemently urged and finally convinced Almeida to attack the natives. Pero Barreto and Manuel Telles did likewise, while Lourenço de Brito counseled against the attack.

They entered Lisbon on Wednesday, the third of July. Duarte de Lemos' ships were the first to bring to Portugal news of the seizure of Goa. His report gave Manuel the information for another of his newsletters. On July 12, he wrote to his neighbors in Castile announcing the good news.[57]

Fernão Soares. This brave captain had gone to the Indies with Almeida in 1505 and had played an important part in the burning of Mombasa. According to Castanheda, he left for Portugal in December 1508 and was never heard from again.

Title L

Luís Godínez. Although the Godínez coat of arms is described in the *Triunfo Raimundino*,[58] I have been unable to find specific information on Luís Godínez.

Catalina de Cárdenas. The Cárdenas were a prominent family in Salamanca in the early sixteenth century, but no reference has been found to a Catalina de Cárdenas who might be identified as Figueroa's sister.[59]

iv. THE NARRATIVE IN HISTORY AND LITERATURE

The *Conquista de las Indias de Persia e Arabia,* published in 1512, predates by almost forty years the appearance of the first of the great histories of the Portuguese in India. It was not until 1551 that Fernão Lopes de Castanheda brought out the first book of his *Historia,* and not until the following year was the first "decade" of João de Barros printed. Figueroa's eyewitness account appears to present the earliest printed record of some of the most important events which took place during the years 1505–1510. Most notable of these were Almeida's victory at Diu in 1509 and Albuquerque's initial seizure of Goa in 1510. The *Conquista* thus makes substantial contributions to the historiography of the Portuguese Indies. As the account of a resourceful man's adventurous initiative, it is a significant representative of the literature of travel.

The Portuguese traditionally view the history of their

expansion into the *mares nunca de antes navegados* as a deeply significant and valuable contribution to the ecumenical goal of Christian unity. They, and the non-Portuguese reader as well, find this belief most beautifully and forcefully articulated in what has come to be the most enduring child of Portugal's Eastern dream, the *Lusiads* of Luis de Camões.

The *Lusiads'* evaluation of Portuguese deeds in the Indies is best understood in the light of the development of the ideal of Christian unity in Europe and its particular manifestation in Iberia. The statement of the ideal of Christian unity in politico-religious terms dates from the Roman Empire, when the temporal power of the Emperor was used in close cooperation with the spiritual power of the bishops of the Church. Although this union ceased to be effective after the division of the Empire and its collapse in the West as a result of the barbarian invasions, the dream of ecumenical unity persisted throughout the centuries. In claiming the title of Emperor, the tenth-century kings of León considered themselves successors to and perpetuators of the imperial ideal, and the Carolingian Empire was but another gesture of similar intent. As King in Spain and head of the Holy Roman Empire, Carlos V's avowed goal was Christian unity.

The dream of effective unity of the temporal and spiritual realms found frequent expression in the literature of medieval Europe. The extraordinary tenacity with which the legend of Prester John was believed and circulated attests to the power which this ideal held over men's minds. In the early sixteenth century Hernando de Acuña[1] expressed what the advent of Carlos augured for mankind:

> "Ya se acerca, Señor, o es ya llegada
> la edad gloriosa en que promete el cielo
> una grey y un pastor solo en el suelo,

> por suerte a vuestros tiempos reservada.
> Ya tan alto principio, en tal jornada,
> os muestra el fin de vuestro santo celo,
> y anuncia al mundo para más consuelo
> un Monarca, un Imperio y una Espada."*

With the rise and militant expansion of Islam, the goal of ecumenical unity took on special significance in Iberia, the scene of direct and continued confrontation between Christian and Moor. As the Christian kingdoms of the peninsula slowly gathered strength and consciousness and began to advance southward, the just struggle against the religious enemy became a major theme of Iberian life and literature. When, as so often occurred, recalcitrant and factious noblemen disregarded their sacred obligation to expel the Moor, men of letters were quick to exhort and unremitting in their efforts to remind them of their duty.

In the *Lusiads,* Camões celebrates at length the heroes and battles of the Portuguese Reconquest, and in his eyes Portugal's loyalty to this mission is so complete that Afonso IV can overcome his scorn for Castilians and render the aid which is decisive at the battle of Salado in 1340. The *Lusiads* summarizes Portugal's contribution to the Reconquest in the following verses:

> "Este quis o Ceu justo que floreça
> Nas armas contra o torpe mauritano,

---

* Now draws near, sire, or has arrived, the glorious age in which Heaven promises one flock and one shepherd upon the earth, fortunately reserved for your days. Already such an auspicious start on this journey reveals to you the fulfillment of your holy quest and announces to the world for its consolation one Monarch, one Empire, and one Sword.

Deitando-o de si fora, e la na ardente

Affrica estar quieto o nam consente."*   (III, 20)

Camões thus views the Portuguese advance into North Africa, highlighted by the 1415 seizure of Ceuta, as a logical continuation of the Reconquest. In time, explorations down the western coast of Africa became more important than the military expeditions, but he sees the two together as a further development of the national energy and consciousness forged during the years of battle against the Moor:

"Não sofre o peito forte, usado aa guerra

Nam ter imigo a quem faça dano,

E assi, nam tendo a quem vencer na terra

Vay cometer as ondas do Occeano."†   (IV, 48)

As the voyages of discovery carry the bold sons of Lusus past the dread Adamastor and across the Indian Ocean, Camões praises the new knowledge, developed through research activities at Sagres and personal experience on the high seas, which made such triumphs possible. Recognizing and lamenting that the many statements about Christian unity emanating from national capitals are but empty rhetoric, he confidently finds justification in the belief that Portugal has remained actively loyal to the ecumenical ideal. After criticizing the various nations of Europe for abandoning their duty, he says of Portugal:

* And they [the Portuguese] have flourished, by just Heaven's
    decree,
In arms against the brutal Moorish strain.
They hurled him forth, and they permit him not
To live in peace where Africa burns hot.

† The strong heart used to battle ill can bear
    The lack of enemies to work them woe.
    On land was none to conquer anywhere,
    And Ocean's wave he went to overthrow.

"Mas em tantos que cegos, & sedentos
Andais de vosso sangue, o gente insana,
Nam faltaram Christaos atreuimentos
Nesta pequena casa Lusitana
De Affrica tem maritimos assentos,
He na Asia mais que todas soberana,
  Na quarta parte noua os campos ara,
  E, se mais mundo ouuera la chegára."* (VII, 14)

The Portuguese historians of the sixteenth century were equally proud of their nation's achievements, and their histories are founded by and large on the beliefs sung by Camões. Throughout the works of Castanheda, Barros, and those who followed runs the firm conviction that the Portuguese have surpassed the epic achievements of Antiquity, real or fabled. According to Castanheda, for example: "the feats which the Portuguese accomplished during the discovery and conquest of India were such that in grandeur, fame, and admiration they held great advantage over those described by Titus Livy and Homer" (III, prologue). Moreover, these things have been done for the sake of the worthiest cause, for in a new area of operations Portuguese *fronteiros* aggressively pursue the crusade against the infidel Moor, striking him on the flank and denying him the revenues and strength he had previously obtained from control of trade in the Indian Ocean. In the process the Portu-

---

* But while you are so blind and thirst so hot
  For life-blood of your brothers, men insane,
  Adventurous Christian courage falters not
  Within our Lusitania's small domain.
  Africa's ports have fallen to her lot;
  In Asia more than sovereign is her reign;
    In the world's new fourth part she plows the field
    And there will go, where more shall be revealed.

guese have rendered the equally valuable service of re-establishing contact with long separated brethren, the Eastern Christians.

Men of the caliber of Barros and the humanist Damião de Góis were intelligent and perceptive. Like Camões, they were acutely aware of the often awesome disparity existing between men's ideals and men's actions. The resulting tension is ever-present in their writings. As one calls to mind the harangue of the Old Man of Restelo in the *Lusiads,* one understands the uneasy diffidence with which Barros approaches the dispute between Almeida and Albuquerque. Although the Portuguese historians frequently do criticize individual acts of omission or commission, their final judgment on the history of the Indies reflects their initial assumption that they are recording *gloriosos feitos,* divinely sanctioned. Barros' analysis of Diogo Lopes de Sequeira's narrow escape at Malacca illustrates the providential view of history which he and his colleagues shared: "For it is certain that whoever reflects upon this dangerous encounter and others which our people experienced both previously and afterward must realize how much Our Lord wished to demonstrate that the discovery of these parts was a miraculous process: for whenever our prudence was lacking, He would hasten with His mercy" (II, iv, 4).

Dealing with such a virtuous subject, the Portuguese historians naturally felt that their vocation served a high moral purpose. Not only did they preserve the memory of noble deeds, but in addition they placed before their contemporaries and future generations a portrait of exemplary men and epic achievements worthy of admiration and emulation. Castanheda especially recommends to rulers the careful study of history, "such a profitable human endeavor, for it teaches us those acts we should perform and those we should shun" (I, prologue). In

order to prove that he was qualified to deal with the "majesty and grandeur of the task," Barros reveals that he presented to King Manuel an example of his writing, a romance of chivalry which he characterized as "a metaphorical picture of men's armies and victories" (decada I, prologue).[2] Just as the romance of chivalry is in many ways didactic, so too are the Portuguese histories of the sixteenth century "chivalric."

Proud of their mission, the Portuguese historians worked long and hard at their task. Placing primary emphasis on eyewitness reports, they questioned men who had been in the Indies, and painstakingly elicited information from all who might have something to contribute. They also used written material, including Arab and Indian documents, much of which was kept in the Casa da India in Lisbon. Castanheda states that he used all the "treatises and memoirs" he could find. The critical results of their investigations are organized in chronicle form, a presentation so artfully developed by predecessors such as Fernão Lopes and Zurara. Although each historian composed his history independently, each achieved very much the same results, and the reader of their histories enjoys a detailed and cogent celebration of Portuguese deeds in the Indies.

As informative as their histories are, Castanheda, Barros, and their fellow historians present certain problems. The first results from the original premise, the faith in the unequivocal moral worth of their subject, which encourages them to pass over events which would detract from the fundamental belief. Barros is illustrative here. Writing in the context of the Almeida-Albuquerque dispute, he likens his history to a beautiful building, to which as a conscientious architect he must affix only the most harmonious and appropriate elements. He thus justifies the omitting of certain derogatory information. On the

other hand, Gaspar Correia proposed to tell the truth in each and every case, without favoritism. This commitment, along with a rather unadorned style help explain why the *Lendas* remained in manuscript until the nineteenth century.[3]

A significant limitation of the historical method of these historians lies in the difficulty of verifying their findings.[4] Eyewitnesses cannot be re-examined, and few treatises and memoirs have survived. Afonso de Albuquerque's letters are of significant interest and value,[5] as are the *Commentaries,* account of his activities in India composed by his son Braz.[6] Varthema's *Itinerario,* while delightfully informative, only deals directly with the Portuguese for the period between January 1506, and January 1508. In this context, then, Martín Fernández de Figueroa's narrative is unique. During his travels in the East, Figueroa personally visited almost the entire area of Portuguese operations. Where it was not possible to give a firsthand report, he used the same method that the historians were later to employ: he questioned someone who had been there, someone who did possess firsthand information. Furthermore, the *Conquista* was published barely a year after Figueroa's return from the Indies, when his recollections were still fresh and precise.

Examining the *Conquista* from an historical point of view, one is immediately impressed by its richness and accuracy of detail, leaving aside Juan Agüero's introductory orientation, which the commentary shows to be misleading. On the matter of dates, for instance, there is almost complete agreement with the Portuguese historians, and the same concordance is found in the case of numbers of ships or personnel involved in the various battles. When the *Conquista* reports that a certain captain has distinguished himself in a particular encounter, the historians invariably give the same information.

Sensitive to the reader's interest in events in which he himself was not personally involved, Figueroa thoughtfully interrupts his narrative at convenient and logical moments to go back and bring the reader up to date on activities in other areas of operations. Very briefly, the principal résumés presented in the *Conquista* are the following:

Dom Francisco de Almeida in East Africa, July–September 1505, **Title XI**;

Tristão da Cunha in India, August 1506–December 1507, including a summary of Almeida's activities during the same period, **Title XXII**;

Cunha and Albuquerque in East Africa, with particular emphasis on Brava and Socotra, July–August 1506, **Title XXIV**;

Albuquerque on the south Arabian coast and at Hormuz, August 1506–November 1508, **Titles XXVII–XXXII**;

Events in India, with special emphasis on the death of Lourenço de Almeida, December 1507–November 1508, **Title XXXIII**;

The second seizure of Goa, November 1510, **Title XLVI**;

Diogo Lopes de Sequeira at Malacca, August 1509–January 1510, **Title XLVII**;

Death of Dom Francisco de Almeida at Saldanha, March 1510, **Title XLIX**.

By means of these résumés, Figueroa brings to his narrative an account of virtually every significant occurrence during the period between 1505 and 1510. Based upon information garnered from eyewitnesses, they are in substantial agreement with the later accounts of the historians. Although markedly abbreviated in several instances—Agüero's editorial hand seems to have been especially active in **Titles XXII** and **XXXII**—these summaries combine with Figueroa's personal experiences to produce a

comprehensive and accurate history of his five-year sojourn in the Portuguese Indies.

Although the *Conquista* omits very little of what occurred between 1505 and 1510, it does not offer a complete record of those years. Too many things were going on over too wide an area for Figueroa to have known about and recorded all of them. Many secondary voyages are not mentioned, nor does the *Conquista* take cognizance of numerous minor military actions. We learn very little about Almeida's commercial achievements during his tenure as viceroy. After Albuquerque's first seizure of Goa, he received ambassadors from Hormuz, Diu, Vijayanagar, and many other states. Important conversations took place, all duly treated by the historians yet absent from the *Conquista*. In considering these and similar gaps in the narrative, it must be remembered that Figueroa was not a captain, and therefore was not privy to many of the actions and decisions which later historians would find important. As a frontline soldier, Figueroa was probably quite unaware of many of the activities of his commanding officers.

Figueroa must have known about yet chose not to mention other events. Like the Portuguese historians, he omits certain incidents which would contradict his generally laudatory account. For example, no mention is made of Albuquerque's summary hanging of young Rui Dias during the blockade of Goa harbor. Similarly, the *Conquista* alludes only indirectly to the conflict between Almeida and Albuquerque; and Figueroa no doubt believed that when Coutinho arrived, Almeida was truly anxious to return to Portugal.

The most significant new information presented in the *Conquista* is the account of activities in Sofala from establish-

ment of the captaincy in September 1505 to Figueroa's departure in September 1507. Although the historians dealt with events at Sofala, they understandably considered them subordinate to Almeida's campaigns in India. As the only known record composed by someone who served at Sofala, the *Conquista* presents information unavailable elsewhere. Figueroa is alone in reporting his companions' desire to abandon Sofala because of the unhealthy living conditions. His praise of Añaya's perseverance in the face of adversity has no counterpart. Exclusive to the *Conquista* is the news of Añaya's alert refusal of Yusuf's peace offer after the attack, as is the description of the courageous behavior of the dead king's son. In discussing Vasco Gomes de Abreu's arrival at Sofala, the historians concentrate on the dispute with Nuno Vaz Pereira over the gold. Figueroa evaluates Abreu's actions from the perspective of the men who had struggled to establish the captaincy and were forced to leave it on such short notice.

None of the Portuguese historians presents as much information about Sofala as does Figueroa. In the case of Castanheda and Correia, for example, the more detailed of the historians, it may be assumed that, had they read the *Conquista,* they would surely have incorporated its information into their histories. Primarily on the basis of Figueroa's account of Sofala, it may be concluded that the *Conquista* was not used as a source of information by the Portuguese historians.

Another significant contribution of the *Conquista* is less obvious but equally important in that it enables us to read the Portuguese historians with renewed assurance. When it is seen that there is such consistent and close agreement between Figueroa's narrative, written practically on the scene, and the

histories, compiled forty and fifty years later, one cannot but praise the efficiency of these historians and place greater faith in their accuracy.

Juan Agüero enthusiastically undertook the task of editing Figueroa's manuscript, and in the process frequently and deliberately introduced himself into the narrative. He declares that the desire for knowledge first interested him in Figueroa's account. A man of scholarly background, he was aware of the contribution the *Conquista* would make to Iberian knowledge of the East. He already possessed some knowledge of that part of the world, for he had read the accounts of Marco Polo and Poggio Bracciolini in the sophisticated context of Santaella's *Cosmographia*. In addition, King Manuel's newsletter helped to bring him up to date on the latest developments in the Portuguese Indies. To supplement his reading, he was himself a traveler and would not hesitate to apply his own experience to correct the printed authorities. Having been to Rome and admired its sculptures, he does not accept Figueroa's claim, based on hearsay, that the objects at Cape Comorin are superior.

An equally important reason for collaborating with Figueroa was Agüero's high esteem for Pedro de Añaya. He was deeply concerned that Añaya's accomplishments be properly recognized, and this "good knight" emerges as one of the main heroes of the *Conquista*. He extends the praise of Añaya to embrace all Castilians who have gone forth to the Portuguese Indies to continue the struggle against the Moor. Even Afonso de Albuquerque is remembered as being "of Castilian ancestry."

Although many brave men, Portuguese and Castilian, fought in the Indies, Agüero pays special homage to fellow Salamancans like Añaya. In extolling the feats of members of

noble Salamanca families, he was but continuing the efforts of the *Triunfo Raimundino*. He apparently did no new heraldic research in preparing his edition of Figueroa's narrative, since only those descriptions which may be found in the *Triunfo Raimundino* are present in the *Conquista*. No mention is made of the coat of arms of such distinguished noblemen as Albuquerque or the Almeidas.

Agüero wanted the *Conquista* to contribute to an increase in faith and renewed dedication to Christian ideals. Unfortunately, this ambition did little to mitigate a strong anti-Semitic bias present in the narrative. Agüero follows traditional anti-Semitic attitudes in depicting Jews as avaricious, perfidious, and cowardly in the Gaspar incident. Jews are later accused of murder at Quilon. It is quite possible that Martín Fernández de Figueroa shared his friend's feelings.[7]

As anxious as Agüero was to preserve the fame of worthy men, he was equally determined to secure his own fame and honor. He identifies himself with the oldest and highest ranks of Iberian aristocracy. As Juan Remón, he traces his lineage back to the first king of Portugal, and as Juan Agüero he claims to descend from Fernán González and Castilian royalty. More important than the truth or falsehood of such assertions is the motivation behind them, the desire to be known as a member of such illustrious families. Agüero shared this concern with many of his fellow writers, anxious to be accepted by the nobility about whom they wrote.[8]

Juan Agüero was much the man of his times. Keenly interested in the progress of the overseas discoveries of Castile and Portugal, he was glad to participate in the publication of the *Conquista*. As a man who disliked Jews and wanted to be known as a descendant of ancient nobility, he shared views wide-

ly held in the Castile of the early sixteenth century. Above all, he sought to praise the Salamancans who had answered King Manuel's call to service in the Indies.

In spite of the many instances wherein Juan Agüero places himself or his previous literary works directly in the foreground —all the first-person references indicate Agüero, not Figueroa— neither he nor the reader ever lose sight of the true protagonist of the *Conquista*. One does not forget that Martín Fernández de Figueroa actually traveled and fought in those distant lands, and that the printed word is the result of personal experience and action. Through reminders such as *dice Figueroa testigo de vista* or *según lo cuenta Figueroa que allí estaba,* Agüero repeatedly stresses that Figueroa personally gathered the information he is reporting. The value of personal experience is once more impressed upon the reader in the final title, when Agüero concludes with the reminder that Figueroa compiled his book in such a manner that his reader has come to know in theory "what he saw and experienced."

Just as Figueroa must have respected the literary skills of the man to whom he entrusted his manuscript, Agüero on his part sincerely admired his friend's accomplishments. Notwithstanding his own strong aristocratic pretensions, Agüero is quite generous in his praise of the nonaristocratic Figueroa. It is significant that Agüero made no attempt to associate him with the Figueroa family whose coat of arms he depicted in the *Triunfo Raimundino;* evidently Figueroa was not of sufficient social standing to be authorized such a device. On the other hand, it is readily seen that Figueroa created his own nobility, earned by valiant deeds on the field of battle. In place of hereditary distinctions, "his great and valiant courage—which

served as his shield—" led him to accomplishments equal to those of any man, "even though others may have enjoyed greater favor." When departing from the Indies, Figueroa is credited with leaving "in those parts the same marvelous example of goodness he brought back to these."

The vital perspective of the *Conquista* is that of the *hombre de armas,* and the reader sees events through the eyes of the soldier. Figueroa's world is that of the Christian engaged in the centuries-old struggle against Islam, and the terms employed to describe what he saw and heard are those which evolved during that struggle. Just as the Portuguese historians apply the medieval concept of *fronteiro* to their countrymen in the Indies, the *Conquista* invariably pits *cristiano* against *moro;* and the heroic Pedro de Añaya is praised as a "relentless foe of the Moorish enemies of our Faith." This outlook imparts to the *Conquista* many of the characteristics of a medieval chronicle, as Figueroa and his companions in arms enter battle invoking Santiago, *matando moros e robando grandes riquezas.* His faithful report of Santiago's timely intervention at Cannanore is but the enactment in a new setting of the countless occasions when Santiago had aided his followers against the Moor in Iberia.

Although the *Conquista* discusses varied aspects of the Portuguese enterprise in the Indies, it is primarily oriented toward military operations. For example, the way of life at Sofala is well described and mention made of the gold trade, yet one feels that the factor at Sofala would have described events there with a different emphasis, stressing the commercial aspects of the captaincy. Figueroa describes his stay at Sofala from the point of view of "men who anticipate war and make ready to fight it."

Believing the Portuguese expansion into the Indies to be a form of religious crusade, Figueroa is free to criticize his fellow Christians while never doubting the righteousness of their "good and worthy goal." Although he sternly censures the excesses committed at Brava, he never questions the Portuguese right to subjugate the Indies. As part of his soldier's code, Figueroa is capable of appreciating and commending bravery on the part of the enemy and does so on several occasions. Similarly, when the enemy flees rather than offer battle, he condemns them as *canina e perra gente*. It is the same soldier's code which calls for severe criticism of Vasco Gomes de Abreu and unremitting scorn for the effeminate gentlemen of Dabul.

The soldier's life is precarious and fraught with peril, and one of the principal characteristics of the *Conquista* is the theme of danger, of death constantly at hand. This point is emphasized repeatedly from the moment Figueroa and his companions sail into the "hateful sea." A soldier's life is always *puesta al tablero*, and men like Figueroa must be ever on their guard—*apercibido* is a term which occurs frequently in the *Conquista*.

Although Figueroa accompanied the Portuguese during the years of their most striking victories, and although he himself returned to tell the tale, he was profoundly impressed by the number of fellow Christians who lost their lives in the Indies. This is especially evident in his astonished reaction to news of the slaughter at Saldanha. As a result of his experiences in the Portuguese campaigns, Figueroa was confirmed in beliefs widely held among his contemporaries. He saw life as an unfathomable alternation of joy and sorrow, of fortunes "prosperous or adverse." This outlook is succinctly expressed in the description of Pedro de Añaya's death: "All great joys are but harbingers of imminent sorrow, for fickle fortune never permits a man to be either always sad or always happy. Thus . . . since he was

mortal and his lord the King of Portugal had not the power to guarantee him life, he fell sick with fever" **(Title XV)**.

Asceticism and renunciation accompany a life characterized by instability and impermanence. Life is a "shadow of many tribulations," a "perilous and stormy sea." Those Christians who die give up the "trials of the body in exchange for the glory of the soul." In this spirit of stoic resignation is Almeida's reaction to the news of his son's death: "the Lord gave him and the Lord has taken him away." [9]

Although there can be no *seguro de vida,* Figueroa is sure in the knowledge that he has volunteered for a just war, one in which Divine assistance can be called upon in moments of need. He shares with the Portuguese historians the belief that their Operation Indies is a Divinely endorsed enterprise; and it is logical that God should come to the aid of His militant followers. In the initial assault on Goa, "Our Lord God, Defender and Protector of Christians," intervenes on their behalf. When later blocked in the harbor, the Christians are completely without help, "except for that of Heaven!" Garcia de Sousa was able to escape certain death "since God is quick to remedy in moments of need."

Death does come to the fighting man and has for him a special meaning. Death in battle against the Moor merits eternal salvation in Heaven. Nuno Vaz Pereira's death justifies his entire life: "Blessed was the day of his birth, for at such an hour and moment did he pass away." On the other hand, the heinous crime of Juan Deras is rewarded with eternal condemnation, for he died *malaventuradamente.*

There are many other moments in the *Conquista* wherein a fighting man attains salvation by faithful adherence to the demands made upon his particular vocation, just as would the peasant or the cleric. Yet, along with saving his soul, the soldier

is preoccupied with another matter, that of his honor and fame.[10] In the *Conquista* death in battle brings with it everlasting fame and glory. Just as Jorge Manrique's father departs this life, which is but *temporal perecedora,* leaving behind *otra vida más larga / de fama tan gloriosa,*[11] Lourenço de Almeida is assured of being *a los parientes eterna corona,* and Nuno Vaz Pereira shall never be forgotten, *quedando de sí tan inmortal memoria.*

Whereas in Jorge Manrique's beautiful *Coplas* the testament of fame that a man leaves behind among his fellows is subordinate to true glory which is eternal life in Heaven, no such conscious distinction is made in the *Conquista.* Dying heroes earn both earthly and heavenly glory; in the case of Diogo de Melo, "in heaven and on earth perpetual glory shall be his." The men at Diu "gave their lives that day in exchange for a greater and immortal one which they shall enjoy *in eternum."*

The coexistence of asceticism and the desire for earthly and heavenly glory is similar to the "combined ascetic and chivalrous points of view" which María Rosa Lida finds in the chivalrous novels produced in Iberia, such as the *Caballero Cifar, Tirant lo Blanch,* and *Amadís de Gaula.*[12] In his preoccupation with fame to be gained in a new setting, the Indies, Figueroa has created in the *Conquista* a work much in the spirit of the *Amadís,* which has been characterized as "a work of synthesis, composed of ancient ideals and illuminated by the approaching Renaissance."[13] Figueroa's "ancient ideals" are those of medieval Iberia and its struggle against the Moor, and it was the new knowledge forged by the Portuguese which carried them to the Indies.

A comprehensive document of travel experiences, the *Con-*

quista is replete with various kinds of information. Like many another returning traveler, Figueroa hastens to regale his audience with news of things which he hopes will most interest them, that is, things most removed from their everyday life. He compiles an extensive store of observations: fellow Christians living and worshiping in lands beyond Islam; black peoples who go about naked; widows who cast themselves into fiery pits; kings who wear poisonous shirts; magic staffs to aid in the collection of debts; and huge elephants with the strength of one hundred men. These and many more items of exotica amply satisfy Agüero's introductory promise of great quantities and diversity of information.

The chronological arrangement of the *Conquista* corresponds to Figueroa's sincere and unpretentious desire to inform. He and his narrative belong to the long tradition of travelers who later write of their adventures, great travelers like Marco Polo, Clavijo, Pero Tafur, and the contemporary Ludovico de Varthema.[14] Varthema sought to entertain as well as inform, while Figueroa concentrates almost exclusively on the latter. Whereas the Italian traveler quite consciously seeks to excite and intrigue the reader in his version of the Queen of Aden's attempt to seduce him, Figueroa, who probably experienced similar temptations on Socotra, stolidly and piously brands "abominable" any departure from established norms of behavior. Nor is Figueroa polemical in the manner of the later Bernal Díaz. His is a straightforward narrative, simply and plainly told. His primary purpose is to praise the accomplishments of the Portuguese and report on them and the new lands he has seen to his fellow Castilians.

When virtually nothing is known about a man who has

written a valuable and interesting book, one is inevitably
tempted to conjecture about him. In the case of Martín Fernández de Figueroa and the *Conquista,* three items of information make the temptation all the more appealing. In 1535, in
Salamanca, a Martín de Figueroa, *arcediano de Santiago,* is reported to have donated the funds for construction of a hospital
to be called San Bernardino y Nuestra Señora de la Paz; it was
to be built on the ruins of an old hermitage. In 1550, this same
person contributed to the improvements of the parish church of
San Blás. Finally, in 1555, Martín de Figueroa died in the same
hospital of San Bernardino which he had had built twenty years
earlier.[15]

Could this Martín de Figueroa have been the traveler and
author Martín Fernández de Figueroa? Circumstantial evidence
makes it possible. First of all, there is the close similarity in
names. The traveler Figueroa could well have lived until 1555;
had he gone out to the Indies while in his twentieis, he would
have been a man of seventy in 1555. His collaborator Juan
Agüero is reported active as late as 1550.[16] More encouraging
are the indications to be found in the pages of the *Conquista*
wherein Figueroa most definitely reveals himself as a deeply
religious and pious man. It would have been very much in
keeping with his character to take up the religious life and contribute to charitable works. For the present these remarks must
remain conjectural, but they are nonetheless intriguing possi-
bilities.

If Martín Fernández de Figueroa did enter the religious life,
such a decision would scarcely have distinguished him from
countless numbers of his contemporaries. That he did compose
and have published an account of his adventure-filled years in
the East most emphatically does. Although Portugal and Castile

were in the vanguard of the search for the Indies, they were slow to give literary expression to this quest. When the number of Iberian books on the East is compared to the number produced in the rest of Europe, it becomes clear that the Iberians were travelers and discoverers first, and that they "participated to a minimal degree in the accompanying literary creation." [17] Within this context, Figueroa's volume becomes all the more significant.

The *Conquista* reflects Iberia's long-standing interest in the East, but it appeared at a moment when Castilian eyes were beginning to move away from "the Indies we nowadays call Portuguese" toward their own recent discoveries in the West. The publication of Columbus' letter in 1493 announced that Castilian ships had reached the fabled Indies of the East, but intellectuals were skeptical. Santaella's *Cosmographia* shows perfect awareness of the difference between Columbus' discoveries in the West and those of Portugal in the East. In 1511 the first of Peter Martyr's *Decades* appeared in Seville, another important step in the communication of the growing realization of the true nature of the new world.[18]

By 1512, however, the Castilian public had not yet seen tangible proof that the value of the Indies of the West would be comparable to the rich cargoes pouring into Lisbon from the Indies of the East. For a while to come the Castilian reader would still look eastward for tales of exotic lands and conquests. In these circumstances, the *Conquista* must have been avidly read, both in Castile and Portugal, and the immediate popularity of the tiny volume would help explain why only one exemplar appears to have survived.

As the second decade of the sixteenth century drew to a close, news from the West became more positive and exciting.

In 1519, Fernández de Enciso returned from the Indies to publish his *Suma de Geographia*. A year later a small band of adventurers would ascend the Central American plateau and conquer the vast riches of the Aztecs. Two years later, in 1522, Cortés' letters would begin to appear; and in 1526 Fernández de Oviedo would publish his *Natural historia de las Indias*.

With the Age of the Discoverer fast giving way to the Age of the Conquistador, the Castilian reader interested in overseas adventures looked west to his own nation's Indies. It is not surprising that Figueroa's modest narrative was soon forgotten amid the mass of material dealing with events in America. The *Conquista* was the product of an earlier historical moment; it was published just before developments in the East would be overshadowed by Castilian accomplishments in the West.

In the years following his return to Castile, Martín Fernández de Figueroa must have shared his countrymen's pride in the great successes of Castilian conquerors in America. At the same time, he would be rightfully proud of his own initiative, his desire "to see lands," which had led him to Portugal and thence to the Indies of the East. In a very vital sense, the *Conquista de las Indias de Persia e Arabia* represents his attempt to associate himself in a lasting manner with the epic campaigns in which he had participated as a Spaniard in the Portuguese Indies.

 Onqsta dlas indias d Persia ꞇ Ara
bia q̃ fizo la armada dl rey don Ma
nuel de Portugal ꞇ delas muchas ti
erras: diuersas gentes: extrañas riq̃
zas ꞇ grandes batallas que alla ouo.

Cum priuillegio.

da ultima raridade

Umma τ breue vtil auiſo τ Hyſtoria del via
je τ armada ãl rey dõ Manuel de portogal a
grã coſta ſuya mãdo fazer para los reynos τ
indias d̃ pſia τ arabia en q̃ fue poz capitã ma
yoz el muy nõbrado cauallo Pedro de añaya.

n el nõbre de dios τ d̃ ſu glo
rioſa madre guia delos vian-
dantes τ peregrinos ſin man
zilla ſiẽpre virgen ſeñora τ ad
uogada nr̃a principiaremos
a cõtar muchas tierras d̃las
indias de pſia τ arabia: diuer
ſidad de gentes:ſectas: coſtũ
bres:frutos:arbores: edifici
os: mares:rios. E otras coſas Marauilloſas de ver τ
mas de oyr.como animales τ peſces: aues fieras:τ ſier
pes:q̃ en aq̃llas partes habitã quanto larga tengamos
licẽcia. Lo q̃l muy copioſa τ verdaderamẽte trato ſcrip
to. Martin fernandez de figueroa gẽtil hõbre natural
τ pariẽte nr̃o q̃ en cõpañia del honrrado cauallo τ virtu
oſo capitã Pedro de añaya anduuo:las vio: τ cõquiſto
ſegũ d̃las ẽpreſas q̃ los vẽcidos le dexarõ dã teſtimõio.
El q̃l como caſeramente:mucho aprouecho τ ala larga
tuuieſſe recõpillado:me rogo porq̃ los letozes no ſe eno
jaſſen del cũplido pceſſo de ſu camino:lo ſũmaſſe:τ abre
uiaſſe como me peçieſſe al vſo moderno:q̃ toue por mu
cha dicha.lo vno poz me informar del llenamẽte delo q̃
yo ſiẽpre deſſee ſaber:τ lo otro poz el tã claro varõ Pe
dro d̃ añaya pues q̃ en vida no lo conoſcierõ:en muerte

no carcfca dela buena fama ḡ merefcio:ḡ en verdad ha/
uida la noticia delos poztuguefes.alas manos biē auen
turada fue la ftirpe ḡ lo pereo:la generaciō ḡ del viniere
z la ḡ de fu tronco falio.E poz tener mas ḡ entēder ene
llo fcribi efta breue fūma facada como dicho tēgo d fu li
bzo z informaciō verifimil:z cōcozdada cō la cofmogra
phia de pogio florentino:z Marcopaulo veneciano:z
otrofi con vna letra dlalto rico z poderofo rey dō.Ma
nuel ḡ en lengua poztoguefa oue alas manos delas ciu/
dades z batallas ḡ fu armada combatiēdo z crudamēte
peleādo feñaladas z imoztales fizo.z pa ḡ mis amigos
hayā plazer z fe deleytē en leer cofas nueuas:extrañas z
algo diferentes alas de efpaña.delo qual mucho bien fe
figue:cognofcimiēto de cofas claras:aca no pticipadas
alla domefticas z fabidas.poz lo ql en los poetas z cof/
mographos affaz fcripturas ftā fin puerto d luz poz yg
nozācia dlas tierras,ppziedades d cofas:tracto d gētes
z nauigaciō de mares ḡ agoza mas fin fcrupulo fe entē/
derā.fera vtil efte tractado pa faber pegrinar:fufrir tra/
bajos:faluarfe d peligros:cō ḡrir hōzas z ganar eneſta
miferable vida las mundanas mercedes z ftados fobze
ḡ todos z mas en efpaña nos fundamos. Para nŕa fee
otrofi no dañofo ante neceffario poz el ql conofceremof
diuerfas cofas ḡ d fus marauillas:poz fus pficiones lo
aremos a dios ḡ las crio: z repzehēderemos las malas
coftūbzes:tomādo exēplo enlas fantas o buenas obzas
ḡ tan idiota gente fin pdicaciō euāgelica aū ha ḡrido a/
ceptar.verfe han diuerfas fuertes de gētes:maneras de
matrimonios:buenas:tozpes o beftiales vidas ḡ enlaf
indias viuē:atauios:veftidos:armas:cafas: manjares:
tractos.z muertes : exequias:z ē poca gēte diuerfidad:
z multitud de fectas defde lifbona bafta ḡtro mil z mas

leguas q̃ enel dicho viaje fuerõ señozeadas ya descubier
tas. Podzian dezir lo del sabio marques los casos d̃ ad
miraciõ: no los cuentes: ca no saben todas gētes: como
son. Pero como esto sea notoria vdad mas quiero ser
reprehendido poz hablar la q̃ con temoz de reprehēsiõ
dar la a oluido o callarla. E poz q̃ dessearan saber los q̃
ignozarē la forma como las dichas indias se descubrie/
rõ ante todas cosas contar o narrar se ha lo tā sabzoso
vtil z necessario. z sabido esto proceder se ha poz el trac/
tado como adelāte se cõtiene aun q̃ pressurosamente no
tado de spacio bien visto z concozdado do si falta ouiere
enla descripriõ del notadoz seso: juyzio: saber z virtud su
pla del prudente lectoz.   Jo. augur transmiereñ. bac.

¶ Titulo.j.introductorio d̃ como por la grã d̃ dios ⁊ in
dustria d̃ vasco d̃la gama fuerõ d̃scubiertas ⁊ cõq̃stadas
por los xp̃ianos enel p̃mer viaje las indias de Persia ⁊
Arabia año de.M̃.cccxcvij.

A comũ sentẽcia delos porto
gueses sabios ⁊ castellanosq̃
enel p̃mero viaje se acertaron
acerca la inuẽciõ ⁊ conq̃sta de
las idias q̃ agora d̃ portogal
llamamos:do mucha riq̃za d̃
speceria se trae a spaña: ⁊ lo q̃
he visto d̃llo scripto sabido d̃
vn piloto q̃ enel dicho viaje se
fallo:⁊ d̃ algũos studiãtes ⁊ hõrradas p̃sonas q̃ cõ la ri
q̃za q̃ alli su trabajo ⁊ idustria alcãço.tratã ẽsta ciudad
en otra specie d̃ sabiduria cõmutando su auer en cosa do
mas ligeramẽte puedã sacar su caudal es. q̃ como el rey
dõ Johã de portogal fuesse inclinado a saber cosas nue
uas:lo q̃l d̃scubriẽdo ⁊ ganãdo trr̃as se podria acq̃rir.re
gido por algũos sabios astrologos:expos pilotos:⁊
marineros doctos ⁊ enseñados enel mouimiẽto d̃losci
elos ⁊ enla grãdeza ⁊ cõdiciõ delas trr̃as ⁊ aguas mari
nas muchas naos ⁊ carauelas ẽbio por sus mares.diziẽ
do:q̃ no auẽturãdo en su faz iẽda mal ganaria ẽla agena
assi q̃ llegauã al cabo d̃ buena espança q̃ de lisbona dista
dos mill leguas:el q̃l nũca hauiã osado passar por la bra
ueza ⁊ altura d̃las ondas:q̃ toda fuerça de naos ⁊ indu
stria d̃ marineros era vista exceder.E por la diuersidad
d̃ aues ⁊ suertes d̃ pesces q̃ llamã boladores:elo q̃l todos
cõcordã ⁊ dize q̃ buelã ⁊ caẽ assaz vezes ẽlos nauios ẽtre
los ganosos passajeros ⁊ d̃suergõçados fãbriẽtos mari
neros:ẽ q̃ o ẽplea la gula o amatã la fãbre:tã temerosos

a iij

ð q̃dar alli como ciertos ð voluer a sus trr̃as. Hay enel
mes ð julio τ agosto τ eñl mas caluroso tp̃o grãdes fri/
os:eladas:nieues:granizos τ muchas tẽpestad̃s ð agu
as τ viẽtos assi q̃ cõ recelo no ẽtrassen ẽla cuajada mar o
no muriesse poz fiãdo eñl viaje todosse voluiã fasta q̃ vn
escudero no muy rico fidalgo poztoguel q̃ se llamaua va
sco ðla gama τ ðspues fue almirãte no temiẽdo la muer
te:τ q̃riẽdo auẽturar la vida do como q̃er q̃ le sucediesse
cobzaria hõzra dizo al rey dõ johã:q̃l passaria el cabo ð
buena spança:o pderia la vida en cũplimiẽto ð su õsseo.
a q̃en el rey dio naos muy bastecidas ð armas τ mãteni
miẽtos cõueniẽtes todas rubzicadas τ señaladas ð sus
armas τ señales q̃nas:q̃ eñl cãpo de ozĩq̃ vẽciẽdo cinco
reyes mozosel pmero rey ð poztogal gano. El q̃l gama
camino fasta el dicho cabo ð buẽa spãça q̃ ãte fue dicho
finis tozmẽtoz dõde q̃ndo su gẽte viẽdo los dias chicos
los tp̃os aspos:los mãtenimiẽtos algo merescedozes ð
renouarse tẽtarõ ð icitar a vuelta al dõ Vasco ðla gama
q̃s agoza almirãte. τ el dizo q̃l no hauia de voluer ð alli
cõ la vida a poztogal sin traspassar el cabo q̃ q̃ndo ẽtro ẽ
la nao luego hauia dicho ẽtraua eñl atauo no ᵱ pposito
de voluer a tras sin ver lo q̃ adelãte le podria succeder. τ
pozq̃ refuyã aspamẽte les dizo al q̃ ðl alli murmurasse lo
colgaria ðlas ẽtenas o lo lãçaria eñla mar. ellos cercados
de dos muertes vna a tras τ otra delãte pseuerãdo enel
mayoz temoz fizierõ los pilotos'el nozte sul τ toznauã pa
poztogal. lo q̃l sentio el almirãte:τ cõ grãdes amenazas
les fizo seguir el ðterminado camino:τ ẽ veyte dias con
grãdes afruẽtas ðl mar caminarõ q̃niẽta ᵴo seyscĩetas le
guas τ se fallarõ eñl mar mas caliẽte τ tẽplado τ fuerõ a
vna trr̃a q̃ se llama melide dõde tomarõ puerto τ fu..rõ
pacificamẽte recebidos.

¶ Titu. ij. como el almirãte gama fue hõzrado ðl rey de

melinde z descubzierõ fasta la india q̃ dista.vccc.leguas.

Legados los xp̃ianos a melinde su rey q̃ era
mozo los recibio z mucho amoz z trato muy
coztesmẽte al almirãte z a su gẽte dãdo vn in-
terp̃te piloto mozo z gẽte pa passar ala india
ochocientas leguas distãte d̃ melinde ẽla q̃l india fallarõ
a vn gaspar agoza llamado q̃ d̃ seuilla hauia passado a a
lexãdzia judio cõ su muger z fijos se fue poz trr̃a fasta hie
rusalẽ d̃ dõde ala india hauia passado poz el estrecho de
meca.d̃l q̃l fuerõ conoscidas las naos de españa ẽlas se
ñales de q̃ puã autozizadas z arriba dixi. z allegãdose a
ellas fue p̃gũtado poz vn faraute d̃ dõ vasco dla gama q̃
trr̃a era aq̃lla si era la india o pobze o rica z si hauia ẽlla
el aljofar ozo o especieria o algũas cosas d̃ trato al q̃l el
judio resp̃õdio q̃ aq̃lla trr̃a no era la poz q̃ p̃guntaua z q̃
era muy pobze z d̃spreciada lo q̃l el fazia poz no d̃scobzir
tãtos bienes a gẽte xp̃iana spañola.po como no hay tra
ycion q̃ no sea ãte sentida q̃ cometida si ouiesse logar la pe
na ante dla culpa el buen Almirãte d̃ generacion noble
poz ãtiguedad. conocio ser cosa cõtraria no solo a razõ
po a toda cõjetura d̃ visimilitud z p̃gũto al piloto mozo
q̃l rey de Melinde conel embiara si aq̃lla respuesta era
assi tanto poz tentar si concozdaua enel mal como si acer
taua enel bien.El q̃l lealmente resp̃õdio como era falsa
la respuesta z cierta la mucha riqza aueres z specieria d̃
la india de dõde alexãdzia se puerã z toda la redõdez de
las trr̃as assi xp̃ianas como infieles lo q̃l oydo poz el al
mirãte z regradescido mucho como era razõ los leales
seruicios remunerarse.lo touo en mas estima. z ẽbio a de
zir a gaspar q̃ viniesse a comer z folgar cõel a su nao:asse
gurãdo poz p̃nder lo q̃ de otra fozma no pudiera auer z
venido le mãdo atar crudamẽte pies z manos z asp̃amẽ

a iiij

re açotar porq́ la vdad q́ cõ falagos hauia ẽcubierto cõ
morra les açotes z crueles p̃siones su lẽgua cõfessasse co
mo aq̃l p̃rinaz q́ mejor la sabia enel caso.po el endureſci
do p̃elando eſcaparſe cõ la vida q̃s ſombra de muchos
trabajos temiẽdo lo paſſado por biẽ ẽpleado q̃ſi era eũl
z enlos ſemejãtes.nũca q̃ſo cõfeſſar lo q́ aſſaz vezes con
las paſſiones q̃le dauã hauia ſu lẽgua q̃rido manifeſtar
viſto: el almirãte lo mãdaua colgar d̃ forma q́ viẽdo q̃l
muerto poco ꝓuecho le traya el tener en ſecreto las riq̃
zas delos otros cõ vnaspalabras claras aũ q́ forçoſas
z temeroſas deſcubrio las riq̃zas grãdes de aq̃lla india
de todas aq̃llas trr̃as:marcsvias z gentes ala larga:lo
q̃l ſabido del almirãte entro enla trr̃a:fizo ſus ricas ꝓ
ſiones. z tratos cõ los ſeñores della.E aſſi voluio muy
proſpo cõ ſu cõpañia aũ q́ harta muerta a ꝑortogal.

C Titulo.iiij.como llego a portogal cõ muchas riq̃zas
dõ Vaſco de gama:era muerto el rey dõ Johã z voluio
por el rey dõ Manuel a Calicut.

V ãdo el almirãte llego a ꝑortogal yacõ po
ca gẽte d̃la q́ lleuo ẽ cõpañia fallo ſer muerto
el rey dõ johã d̃ portogal q́ hauia q̃dado ſe/
ñorcãdo z folgãdo ẽ ſu trr̃a z el vio q́ ꝑ tãdo
blados trabajos la vida hauia aſſaz vezesd̃ vẽtura buſ
cada viſto peligroſa. z el rey dõ mãuel d̃ portogal q́ le ſu
cedio le fizo muchas dadiuas z mercedes:z lo fizo almi
rãte q́ faſta eſtõces no lo era:diole.riiij.naos ricas z grã
des ẽ q́ traxeſſe eſpeceria..el q̃l muy mas cũplidamẽte el
ſegũdo viaje q̃l p̃mero ſolicito z dexãdo gẽte ẽ Calicut
voluio a portogal ꝓſpo cõ tã buẽ exẽplo q̃l q̃dara ẽ aug
mẽto de mas hõrras a ſus deſcẽdiẽtes.ala gẽte q́ ẽ Cali
cut q̃do los indios mataarõ:por q̃l razõ el rey de ꝑorto
gal les fizo guerra ſegũ delãte ſe narrara.lo q̃l auido por
p̃ſupueſto p̃nciparſe ha a cõtar el viaje z armada q̃l buẽ

cauallo Pedro de añaya fizo de q̃ no es razõ q̃ lo q̃ los
estrangeros publican sus naturales calle.

℃ Titulo.iiij. Como se partio de Portogal el buñ caua
llero Pedro de añaya capitan mayor de seys naos.

S Jete años despues dl dscubrimiẽto p̃mero
año de.M.d.v. el rey dõ manuel de Porto
gal mãdo gridar por su corte todo hõbre de
armas q̃ q̃siesse recebir su sueldo pa yr a las idias d psia
z arabia le daria cada mes dos cruzados z dos q̃ntales
de pemiẽta cada año z de comer fasta la buelta en su rey
no. z a los q̃ fuesse a çofala tr̃a ẽcubierta z ẽscrina daria
xx. mill mr̃s z dos q̃ntales de pemiẽta z pa sus p̃uisiões
mill z doziẽtos z cincuẽta mr̃s z p̃te d los q̃ p̃ndiessen in
fieles z enemigos d ñra fee. d lo q̃l mucha alegria ouierõ
los q̃ alla q̃riã yr z los ricos coboiciosos q̃ cõ su buelta
sp̃aua p̃sp̃ar. en̄l q̃l viaje ẽbio por su capitã mayor d seys
naos grãdes la via d çofala a Pedro de añaya su muy a
mado cauallo que hauia d q̃dar en aq̃lla tr̃a por capitã
el rey dio luego sueldo d q̃tro meses a los q̃ cõel yuã cõ el
q̃l assẽto marti frẽz d figueroa d sseoso d v tr̃fas: z otros
muchos esforçados z valiẽtes castellanos q̃ asseguraua
las sp̃aldas a sus x̃pianõs z faziã cara a los enemigos. z
stãdo d ptida cego la vista a tristã d acuña capitã mayor
q̃ yua pa las idias lo q̃l visto por el rey fizo capitã ẽ su lu
gar a dõ fracisco d almeyda bisrey q̃ fue ẽla india z le dio
xx: naos gruessas z menudas. el q̃l luego ptio p̃ su flota:
z en̄l puerto d portugal vna d las naos viscaynas se ẽago
z el rey le pueyo d otra q̃ tardo ẽ aderesçarse dos meses
dõ fracisco ptio d lisbona a.xxv. d março. año dl.s. d mil
z.d.z.v. z pedro d añaya a.xviij. d mayo los q̃ les discurri
erõ por las brauas õdas dl mar como adelãte se p̃tiene.

℃ Titulo.v. como nauegarõ pedro d añaya z sus gẽtes
por rezios z tẽpestuosos mares z tomaron el puerto de

Bezeguiche τ delas códiciones d̓ sus pobladores.
　　　　Aliēdo d̓l puerto a.xviij.d̓ mayo d̓ M̃.d.v.
S　nauegarõ τcozrierõ ꝗ aſſaz tozmētaſd̓l mar
　　　bonanças d̓los viētos τ mudanças d̓ vida
ccc.leguas:ꝗ diſtā las yſlas Canarias.pozdo paſſando
no fizierõ d̓tenēcia faſta ētrar mas ē ſu d̓ſſeo Caminarõ
cc.leguas mas adelāte τ tomarõ puerto ē Bezeguiche:
poz ſe pueer d̓ viādas τ refreſco ꝗ biē neceſſario teniā.la
gēte d̓ aꝗlla trr̄a es negra:creſpa:la habitaciõ caliēte de
maſiadamēte:aſſi ꝗ los negros creſpos della ādā deſnu
dos tienē ē grã eſtima cuētas azules:vd̓es: o amarillas
o d̓ latõ manillas τ ſemejātes joꝛeles pa las piernas lo
ꝗl vſan en aſſaz pꝛtes los moꝛos trahē flechas τ arcos τ
azagayas todos poz armas offenſiuas τ d̓ſenſiuas τ vi
endo ala dicha gēte ꝗꝓiana ꝗ ē trr̄a ſalio ſe aſſentauā ēla
arena a fazer oꝛon τ echauā la arena poz ſobꝛe la cabeça
τ hõbꝛos a tras. ala noche la gente voluio alas naos τ
otro dia ēla alua ſe pꝛtio.d̓ꝛada bezeguiche ala mão ſinie
ſtra.ēſil ꝗl viaje fallauā peſces llamados tubaronesꝗ co
mē los hõbꝛes ꝗ puedē auer ēla agua τ los voladozeſꝗ
tienē alas d̓ murciegalos τ otros diuerſos peſcados ſa
bꝛoſos d̓ comer. τ ād̓uuierõ ſin v̓ trr̄a nauegādo ochēta
dias faſta llegar a vna yſla ꝗ eſtaua al traues d̓l cabo de
buēa ſpança dõde los viētos τ tēpeſtades coſas nueuaſ
τ temeroſos paſſoſ les moſtrarõ.el ꝗl mar caſi ādā euaja
do d̓ ballenas τ lobos marinos:ēſil ꝗl logar ſe pierde el
noꝛte d̓ viſta:ꝗ diſtara mill leguas d̓ poꝛtogal: τ eſtõces
ſe rige poz el ſul:o polo ātartico.paſſarõ el dicho mar en
eſpacio d̓ ꝗnze dias τ fuerõ ala mão ſinieſtra:τla trr̄a dõ
de apoꝛtarõ fue el Cabo d̓las coꝛriētes. Acerca la ꝗl an
d̓uuierõ ocho dias ſin poder ſē d̓er vna legua poz la mar
voluierõ ala mar poz ꝗtro dias:τ llegarõ a vna bayia:do
ſe pueꝛerõ d̓ aſſaz peſcado:τcaminarõ pa çoſala ſu viaje

¶ Titulo.vj. Como aportarõ Pedro de añaya ↄ su gẽ
te a Quiloain ↄ dela manera de sus moradores.ↄ como
fallaron doze christianos q̃ se hauiã poido enla mar.

Ndãdo pegrinãdo por tan estrañas trr̃as el
bue cauallo pedro d añaya ↄ los suyos llega/
rõ a vna llamada d sus pobladores q̃loain q̃
dista d çofala doze leguas: su gẽte es moros
caseres ricos los q̃les no se circũcida como faze los mo
ros o los judios.ala q̃l gẽte ẽbio el capitã vn batel o ga/
leõ cõ gẽte armada dla q̃l sue por capitã ↄ caudillo fracis
co d añaya su fijo.dino d ser loado por q̃en es ẽ cuyo aio
bie se mostro siẽpre la lipieza de sus armineos ↄ la forta/
leza dlas ferreas barras en q̃ el castillo cruzado nueuas
fazañas guerrierõ.ↄ como llego a trr̃a fallo doze xp̃iãos
d portogal: q̃ eñl cabo dlas corrietes ꝗ vn capitã dlos d
dõ frco de almeyda se hauia poido la nao secha pieça sẽ
trr̃a tocãdo cõel cruel viẽto se rõpio.ↄ escaparõ d aq̃llos
criij.p sonas:ↄ el capitã ↄ otros siete hõbres la cobdicia
asogo.cõ losq̃les solgo mucho frco d añaya conociẽdo
q̃ erã xp̃ianos ↄ suyos los lleuo pa el capitã pedro d aña
ya su padre alasnaos q̃ suerõ bie recibidos:yuã d snudol
negros ↄ ecanijados:q̃ pesciã ẽbalsamados:d spojados
por los caseres d todos sus atauios:d gẽte armada cer
cados:ↄ escarnecidos:no comiã sino yeruas:porq̃ lo no
hauiã.ↄ cãgrejos:ↄ por amor de dios les dauã alli algũ
puño d mijo:el q̃l crudo comiã como paxaros.ↄ ãte q̃ les
diessen limosna (cõtauã q̃ los faziã baylar vna ora fasta
q̃ cãsados mortales eñl suelo cayã.ẽ q̃ loscaseres se dley
tauã.ↄ como estauã ya espando a pedro d añaya q̃ ellos
bie sabiã ꝫia p̃sto ẽ çofala.los q̃les fueron cubiertos d al
gu. atauio que enlas naos les dieron ↄ bien tratados
ↄ recreados por mãdado del Capitan mayor ↄ otro dia
leuãtarõ sus ancoras ↄ fuerõ a tomar puerto en çofala.

Erisimile es τ õ creer el grã plazer q̃ la gẽte
ouo q̃ndo trr̃a tãto õsseada vio:porq̃ẽ rãtos
trauajos por las desamozadas aguas sufrie
rõ:dõde llegarõja.xjx.õ septiẽbze.τ el buẽ ca
uallo.Pedro õ añaya fizo o mãdo alos pilotos tẽrassen
si la agua õl rio podzia sufrir las naos pa ẽtrar conellas
fasta zofala:τ por la poca agua q̃ fallarõ dixerõ q̃ no.po
q̃ las chicas podziã ẽtrar.lo q̃l visto õl buẽ capitã mãdo
q̃ saliesse la gẽte delas naos mayozes τ se ẽtrasse ẽlas me
nozes.q̃ pstamẽte como mãdamiẽto desseado fue cõpli
do.τ al.iiij.dia eran llegados.do grãdes palmares τ fru
tos de diuersos mãtenimietos fallauã.ẽlos q̃les palma
res no datiles hauia:porq̃ no era su fruto.po cocos assi
nõbzados o nuezes õ india las q̃les dize Pogio florẽti
no q̃ son similes al figo.po como q̃en lasha visto enesto
le osare ptradezir.la q̃l fruta es sabzosa:cada nuez como
vna cabeça õ hõbze τ otras menozes:q̃tan le la casca q̃s
gruessa q̃nto vn õdo:õla q̃l como sea sebzas dize fazerse
cuerdas τ maromas q̃ es pa seco como espto.llamase co
cos õ india porq̃ tiene ojos τ narizes τ pesce q̃stã coq̃n
do.Yo la vi τ pescio cabeça õ muerto τ assi todas las se
ñales tiene τ cosas q̃ eũlla se fallarã.dẽtro ẽla casca tiene
fruto blãco gruesso como la casca:su sabor es õ almẽdza
lleno õ agua muy sabzosa τ en todo el año dã las palmaf
el dicho fruto:delos Zofaleses se llama la dicha nuez na
zi.del q̃l se faze vino:τ vinagre:azeyte: τ miel:madera:τ
reja τ aũ atamtos de miserables psonas.hauia otrosi bi
gueras de marauilloso fruto cuyos figos se vueluẽ ẽla
boca mãteca:cuyas fojas son tã grãdes como adargas:
τ otras cosas notables de ver q̃ adelãte se contarã.

CＴitu.viij.como pedro õ añaya mãdo apcebir su gẽte
pa se ẽ cõel rey õ zofala τ ɔcertar sobze lo q̃ era venido.

Omo la gēte staua ya ganofa ð falir ē trřa. el
buē capitā pedro ð añaya folgaua dello pa lo
ql era venido:fizo apcebir z armar fu gēte de
las armas q̃ affaz leuauā.z ēbio vn faraute al
rey ð çofala como el q̃ era capitā mayor ðl rey ð portogal
ē aqlla vādale q̃ria vz fablar fi fu alteza q̃ria ð q̃ el rey fol
go mucho diziēdo q̃ fi.z luego fi a el pluguieffe. pedro ð
añaya q̃ era hōbre tābiē ,pueydo como esforçado plaziē
dole la refpuefta:como mas valga feñorear por amor q̃
por temor mādo fu apcebida egnte entrar enlos bateles q̃vādo algūa gēte ēlas naos por guarda.ð las q̃les mu
chos tiros ð alegria fizierō. dize q̃ falia todos por ordē
cō fus vāderas z stādartes ēlos bateles z falierō ē trřa y
Pedro ð añaya fasta diez hōbres no ,pfintiēdo falir los
q̃ ēlos batele estauā:la cauſa q̃ daua:era.por q̃ fi el rey ð
Zofala no vinieffe ēla cōcordia ql fablaffe z gēte tuuieffe
cōtra ellos fecreta q̃ mas pfto fe podriā recojer ēlos bateles diez q̃ mill.E q̃ ēlas naos fe podriā aprouechar ð
la artilleria o falir apcebidos de riefgo a trřa cōtra fus
eñmigos:lo ql fe fizo como ordeno.la gēte ðlos negros
q̃ a ðlos falio era cofa marauillofa.z ðl rey ð Zofala fue
biē recebido:el ql dixo a Pedro de añaya q̃ fe affentaffe
cabo el fobre vn tapete de feda q̃ alla todos fe affiētā ēl
fuelo.z Pedro ð añaya mādo a fu faraute fablar fu ēba-
xada largamēte lo ql fizo:entre la ql fabla el rey de porto
gal le rogaua le dieffe cāpo pa edificar vna cafa en q̃ pu-
fieffe fus mercācias.enlo ql todo el rey de Zofala vino z
dio le vn palmar q̃ eftaua lleno ð cafas en q̃ fu gēte pudi
effe repofar.los xpianos las cercarō ð cauas:facarō mu
cho delo q̃ enlas naos teniā z apofentarōfe en tierra co
mo fu capitā mayor les mando.
Titulo.ix.dela tierra:gēte:z mercancias de Zofala z

A diſtãcia ꝗ ꝺ poztogal a zofala bay ſon ꝺos
mill ꝛ ꝗnĩetas leguas:ſu trr̃a caliẽte:ꝺ mucho
arroz ꝛ mijo.trigo no lo bay.los carneros ꝺ
aꝗlla trr̃a ſon grãdes no teniẽtes cuernos ni
lana el pelo es como ꝺ perro blãco:dize figueroa ꝗ ẽ aꝗl
rio bay cauallos marinos ꝗ ſalẽ a paſcer ẽ trr̃a ꝛ ſe vuel
uẽ ala mar las cola ꝛ ãcas como porros ꝗ en nigũa coſa
diffierẽ excepto eñl efecto ꝺl fin pa ꝗ ſu nõbze ſuena.bay
cañas ꝺ açucar.la gẽte ꝺ zofala es toda negra faſta el eſ
trecho ꝺ meca ꝗ diſta tres mill leguas.Los mozaꝺoꝛes
ꝺ zofala ſon caferes ꝗ aꝺozã al ſol ꝛ las eſtrellas. ãꝺã ve
ſtiꝺos cõ paños ꝺ algoꝺõ pintaꝺos.ꝛ otros cubiertas
ſolamẽte las ptes vergõçoſas:no bay lino.las mugeres
traen deſcubiertas las cabeças:manillas ꝺ latõ enlaſ pi
ernas traẽ los labzos fozaꝺados ſeys o ſiete agujeros.
lo ꝗl tienẽ poz fermoſa ꝛ apueſta coſa.bay ſandalo blãco
ozo:ambar ꝛ otras riꝗzas:vna gallina vale vn mitical ꝗ
ſon ꝗniẽtos mr̃is.el ꝗl apciã alla como aca medio real.ꝛ
ciẽt leguas dẽtro ẽla trr̃a en vn reyuo de caferes ꝗ ſe lla
ma Benamotapa ſe falla el ozo cõ ꝗ tratã en aꝗllas par
tes muy copioſamente.

C Titulo .x. Como cercarõ cõ maꝺera los xp̃iãos ſu a
poſento ꝛ como ẽpeçaron aꝺoleſcer de que peſo mucho
a Pedzo de añaya.

Dmo el rey ꝺ Zofala les ouo ꝺaꝺo ꝺo puꝺi
eſſen ediſicar la lõja ꝺl rey ꝺ Portogal:babi
tar ſu gẽte ꝛ tener ſus mercãcias ꝛ enel cãpo
caſas algunas deſpobladas.las ꝗles las gẽ
tes ꝺel buẽ cauallo Pedzo de añaya cercarõ de cauas ꝛ
barreras de maꝺera lo mejor ꝗ ſupierõ a grã pzieſſa ꝛ ſa
lierõſe alli apoſar lo ꝗl velauã noche ꝛ dia pueſta la arti

lleria en ozdē como hōbzes q̃ se recelã de guerra ⁊ se ape
jã pa fazerla.pzincipiarō los mas dellos a efermar ᵭ ca
lēturas ⁊ mozir q̃lq̃er ᵭia dos o tres pſonas con q̃ tēbla
uã ſus aios ⁊ ſe mudauā ſus pēſamiētos.q̃ſierā ãte yr cō
la vida poz trabajos q̃ eſperar la muerte ē trr̃a ᵭ ſus ene
migos.elo q̃l no cōſentio el esfozçado capitã mayoz q̃ ſu
vida o muerte daua el ſeguro q̃ pa ſi tenia alos ſuyos ⁊
dizo q̃ nūca dios tal pmitrieſſe q̃ faſta auer effecto ᵭe ſu
venida dieſſe vuelta ſu pſona.Eneſta trr̃a es yna mara
uilloſa coſa q̃ la madera ſe hunde en la agua.E la piedza
nada.Lo q̃l como haya muchos teſtigos ᵭ viſta no ter
neys poz difficultad creer.El capitã ēbio poz pziſiones
el rio arriba cincuēta leguas:do vieron en vnas ſierras
Carbūculos como perros:q̃ ē la frēte yna piedza trayā
q̃ ᵭ noche mucha luz daua como muy ēcēdido fuego:dō
de ãdaua a caça de ratones como ſi liebzes o coſa mas ᵭ
ſſeada fuerã ⁊ ſi el ratō ē alguna caſa ſe metia llegauã los
caçadozes a ᵭzrocar la caſa:ſus armas ᵭ caça ſon arcos
⁊ flechas:el pã fazelo de mijo ⁊ cuezē lo en ollas ⁊ no en
foznos ſegū mas largamēte muchos q̃ en aq̃llas ptes ſe
han hallado de viſta podzã contar.

CTitulo.rj.cōmo llegarō dos naos ᵭ dō frãciſco a Zo
fala ⁊ q̃tarō ᵭ la toma ᵭ Al̃oçãbiq̃:Quiloã: ⁊ mōbaça.

Neſte cōmedio dos naos ᵭ dō frãciſco poz
toguesas llegarō cō mercãcias a trocar poz
ozo ⁊ ſabido ᵭ Pedzo ᵭ añaya recibierō mu
cho plazer aſi los vnos como los otros ⁊ bi
en recebidos ᵭl capitã mayoz pgūto como ſe ganarō a
q̃llos logares ᵭ Al̃oçãbiq̃:Quiloã:⁊ mōbaça q̃ ya ſe
havia ſabido en zofala do eztōces erã ⁊ el Capitã ᵭlas
naos reſpōdio como dō frãciſco vino a tomar puerto ē
moçãbiq̃ q̃ es buē puerto.⁊ fue ᵭ alli ſobze q̃ loã ciudad

pncipal τ vifpa de fantiago apoftol la tomo τ defbarato
jueues.ττv.d julio d. M.d.v.do mãdo edificar vna for/
taleza τ fizo τ leuãto por rey dla mi fma ciudad vn merca
dr mozo muy rico como el rey mozo q̃ ãte hauia feido fu
efle ē fuyda llamado Habzaē:el fegũdo Mahometozco
ni.q̃do alli por capitã Pedzo d herrera cuyo generofo
ozigē d ferrara en efpaña ãtiguamēte vino τ trafpaffo a
ca fus calderas barradas τ ferpētales cabeças infignia
mifteriofa.q̃ por efte capitã no merefcio menof q̃ por fuf
mayozes. E el bifrey dõ frãcifco fue fobze la ciudad de
Mõbaça miercoles.τiij.d agofto alla llegando ordena
rõ dla cõbatir τ el viernes dia d nfa feñoza adelãte el ca
pitã mayoz cõ toda fu gēte falio en trra τ puefta a fuego
τ a fangre la ciudad τ gēte della q̃ crudamēte fe dfendia
robada toda fu riq̃za dõ frãcifco fe prio pa la Jndia.
¶ Tiło.τij.como ydas las dos naos d dõ frãcifco: τ en
fermando la gēte d Pedzo d añaya.el rey d zofala le co
metio trayció.

Dcho fue el plazer q̃ en oyr la vitoria de dõ
frãcifco.ouo el buē cauallo Pedzo d añaya
τ las naos dl defpedidas :q̃do cõ fu gēte q̃ ē
fermo tã grauemēte q̃ no fe podiã tener fino
en tres pies. y no hauia q̃ velaffe fu fortaleza τ apofen/
tos τ porq̃ efto no fe fentieffe dl rey de zofala ēbiaua dof
o tres negritos Pedzo d añaya pa q̃ velaffen:τ muchaf
vezes fe leuãtaua el mifmo capitã a tañer vna cãpanilla
que en medio dela fortaleza ftaua lo qual el hazia por di
fimular la falta que la fanidad en fu gēte hazia τ la enfer
medad q̃ los fupmia.po como nada fea oculto q̃ no fea
reuelado fue fabido o pfumido dl rey d zofala el q̃l ēbio
en fu trra porcaferes pa tomar la fortaleza a pedzo d aña
ya τ matar toda fu gēte:a vn lugar de fu habitació que fe

dezia Mangabe. delo ꝗl todo vn moɔo grāde amigo de
Pedɔo ð añaya hauia auiſado ꝗ ſe nōbꝛaua Ciojacori
el ꝗl era mal ꝗſto delos moros poꝛꝗ alos ꝗpianos ama
ua mucho dezia ꝗ era ꝗpiano ɀ poꝛ ello le hauiā ꝗrido
matar el rey ð Zofala ɀ los caferes llegarō alos ꝗpianoſ
dādo voɀes ɀ alaridos echādo tierra ɀ leuātādo arena
cō los pies tirando flechas. Lo ꝗl ſentido de Pedɔo ð
añaya mādo llamar ɀ armar ſu gēte a mucha pꝛieſſa ɀ al
gūos ſaliā en camiſa aū ꝗ flacos ꝗ a penas dos podiā ar
mar vna balleſta ſegū cuēta figueroa ꝗ ay eſtaua. E los
bōbardeɔos ꝗpianos puſieron fuego alas bōbardas ɀ
artilleria aſſi cō los tiros gran gēte mato de Caferes ɀ
ſe retraɔā a tras ꝗnto podiā. Quiē podꝛia cōtar la exce⸗
lēcia grāde animo ɀ oɔdē de Pedɔo de añaya fiero leon
a ſus enemigos armado ɀa pūto ꝗ dezia como vieſſe ve
nir infinidad de ſaetas ɀ flechas dardos ɀ azagayas de
los Caferes: a ellos cōpañeros ɀ hermanos mios ge⸗
neroſos ꝗpianos de eſpaña dad enellos ꝗ la guerra de
los Caferes mas pece juego ð cañas ꝗ gēte ð lid aꝗ po
deys ſalua r la vida acreſcētar la honrra ɀ hazer mucho
ſeruicio a dios exalcar la ſanta fee catholica ɀ hōrra dela
valiēte ɀ magnanima' eſpaña nᵃra patria. No ſe paſſaua
pues ſu tpō en razones que mas era tpō eſtōces de aco
rrer cō vēdas ꝑa las feridas ꝗ ð ꝓſejos ꝑa ganar hōꝛaſ
ɀ ſu tajante eſpada fieramēte ðſpedaçaua la' enemiga gē
te ꝗ en arroyos ð ſangre ſe ꝗrtia ɀ ſus cuerpos en pol
uos: ꝗ eſta es ſu coſtūbꝛe de ꝗnar los cuerpos muertoſ
ɀ algū fuego ꝗ puſierō en los apoſentos poꝛ defuera los
ꝗpianos amatarō cō agua ɀ paños mojados ɀ aſſi duro
el cerco tres dias ɀ deſque no pudierō vēcer antes ſu gē
te era aſſi muerta herida ɀ maltratada huyerō ɀ ſe ðſuia
rō delos apoſentos de Pedɔo de añaya ɀ ſu cōpañia ɀ

b

el rey se voluio donde hauia salido. esta gête anda desnu
da llamâse vnos a otros cô siluatosd cuerno sus armas
son arcos flechas z porras de madera.

¶ Titulo. xiij. Como el rey de çofala êbio a fazer pazes
cô Pedro de añaya z su respuesta.

Jen qsiera el rey de çofala si pudiera fazer lue
go pazes cô Pedro de añaya: al ql êbio dos
moros. z oyda su êbaxada el capitâ mayor le
respôdio: q lo q despues de fecho no hauia d
sprouechar por de mas era gastar tpo en lo concertar z
z por q sabia q ellos no hauiâ dla guardar no qria fazer
pazes mas q dexasse al rey de çofala su señor q en venien
do mas gente xpiana del rey de portogal por qen el alli
era venido el lo qria a buscar z le cortaria la cabeça porq
a el fuesse castigo z alos venideros exêplo. cô lo ql recô
tado por los moros el rey se asseguro pêsando q pedro
de añaya no hauia de fazer nada fasta q mas gête le vini
esse z esto haualo el fecho por lo tomar masdscuydado
z a su volûtad.como el rey fizo conel.

¶ Titulo. xiiij. Como los moros despoblâdolos loga
res cô miedo el buê cauallo Pedro de añaya fue sobre
el rey de çofala cô cincuêta hôbres de su côpañia.

Os caseres cô grâ temor q alas deffensiuas
armas teniâ despoblarô los logares cerca d
la fortaleza z Pedro de añaya fue auisado co
mo el rey de çofala estaua muy solo cô sus cri
ados enel palacio.mâdo aparejar muy biê cincuêta hô
bres dlos q mas rezios o esforçados se sentiâ dxâdo su
fortaleza a buê recaudo cô gête ala ql mâdo qtoda aqlla
noche ql salia no durmiessen z entro en vn vergâtin z p
te de su gête en vn batel alos qles mâdo so pena de muer
te ninguno d otro todos d vno ni vno d todos se dsinâ

dasse q̃ āsi fizierõ.rio arriba callada τ secretamēte d̃spuf
dela media noche saliero͂ en trr̃a ponie͂do fuego alas ca
fas q̃ enel camino hauia τ fazie͂do el daño posible hasta
el palacio del rey d̃ çofala.dõde matarõ muchos moros
q̃ ala puerta bie͂ d̃scuydados dormiã dãdo cõ la puerta
enel suelo q̃ pa todo lleuauã apejo.τ entro pedro d̃ aña/
ya cõ seys cauallos delãte.τ la otra gēte q̃do fuera matã
do moros.τ el rey se leuãto alborotado dela camara τ ā
daua de camara en camara tãto cõ temor como cõ pessa
por la subita muerte q̃ āte si tenia.al q̃l andãdo buscãdo
de celda ē celda pedro d̃ añaya ēcõtro d̃ tras la puerta d̃
la cozina.τ el rey cõ grã furia le dio por el pescueço a pe/
dro d̃ añaya con vna azagaya q̃ tenia τ no le lleuo sino el
cuero d̃la carne:po como pedro d̃ añaya se sintio ferido
llamo los suyos q̃ traxessen luz.siq̃ra pa buscar q̃en assi
lo tratara τ venidos q̃ vna ētorcha vierõ al rey d̃ çofala
moro estar en pie τ dierõ muchas feridas fasta q̃ lo d̃ra
rõ sin reyno τ sin vida cortãdole la cabeça puesta cũl fie
rro d̃ lãça se voluierõ ala fortaleza:do estouo ē memoria
d̃ su señalada vitoria d̃ auer robado toda la trr̃a τciudad
d̃l rey d̃ çofala tenia sus palacios.
CZ Titu.xv.como pedro d̃ añaya capitã mayor enfermo
τ murio:τ como en su logar eligierõ otro d̃ su cõpañia.

Omo todas las grãdes alegrias seã mēsaje
ras d̃ cercana tristeza porq̃ el hõbre la muda/
ble fortuna no d̃ra estar siẽpre triste ni alegre
xx.dias d̃spues q̃ assi gozoso el buen cauallo
pedro d̃ añaya voluio a su fortaleza como fuesse mortal
τ el rey d̃ portogal su señor no tuuo poder pa le dar segu
ro d̃la vida enfermo d̃ calēturas:d̃la q̃l dolēcia plugo a
nr̃o señor Jesu Christo redemptor nuestro leuarlo
para si como a catolico christiano que como tal fenescio

a su gloria ꝑa la qual todos desseādo yr eneste pelgroso
τ trabajoso mar de vida nauegamos: q̄ no menos puso
manzilla en su gente de lloros τ sentimiento: q̄ gloria en
su fama de valiente τ esforçado cauallero christiano per
siguidor de moros enemigos d̄ nr̄a fee. τ dichas sus mis
sas τ exeq̄as lo mas honrradamente q̄ alla pudo ser fue
sepultado: τ en su lugar elegido por la gēte xꝑiana Ma
nuel fernandez que conellos por mayordomo venia τde
hay adelante fue tenido por su capitan mayor.

℄Titulo.xv.como la gēte de pedro de añaya q̄ cō Ma
nuel fernādez q̄do. ordeno fazer la fortaleza d̄ piedra eūl
mes de Abril.

Vertos los dos principales delas huestes
ꝗPedro de añaya capitā mayor τ el rey de Zo
fala. los xꝑianos jūtamēte cōel capitā manu
el fernādez q̄sierā alçar por rey de çofala al si
jo mayor τ fazer pazes conel τ con los moros caseres al
q̄l ēbiarō sus mesajeros sobre ello, τ el respondio q̄ nūca
dios q̄siesse q̄l fuesse amigo delos enemigos τ homici
das crueles de su padre en q̄en se hauiā encarniçado τ q̄
faria grā trayciō a q̄en lo engēdro τ grā injuria alos hu
essos τ cabeça cortada de su padre: q̄l reyno era suyo τ q̄
si de mano dellos lo hauia, d̄ recebir no lo q̄ria τ lo q̄ no
fiziera en vida de su padre menoslo q̄ria fazer en muerte
pues ninguno mas q̄l q̄ era ꝑmogenito la hōrra d̄ su pa
dre hauia d̄ sublimar q̄ no sin causa los fijos mayores do
blado mātenimiēto τatauio suelē d̄ stauā ordenado rece
bir τ de su padre la bēdicion: ꝑa poderla dar a sus meno
res hermanos τ aun de derecho de xꝑianos las scriptu
ras τ munimētos de hōrras τ faziēda en poder del ꝑmo
genito q̄ dar duiā q̄ el guerra sangre τ enemistad q̄ria co
nellos como si su padre viuiera τ no paz. lo q̄l sabido por

los xpianos fizierõ rey a otro fijo menoz del rey de çofa
la que lo acepto z les oio efclauos pa fazer la foztaleza õ
picoza q pncipiarõ el ql rey fe llamaua Coltan gulema z
eftaua en vn logar q fe ozia Buani q no qfo habitar oo
fu padze poz moftrar la trifteza q la muerte paterna fue／
le caufar al fijo.

¶ Titulo.vj. Como poz mãdaoo del bifrey fue entrega
da la foztaleza a nuño vaz pereyra.

Al q la foztaleza fe edificaua z crefcia de pie／
oza vino alli Nuño vaz pereyra cõ mãdami
ento del bifrey z le fue poz manuel fernandez
el ql fe ptio pa la india z poz los õ fu cõpañia
la foztaleza z capitania mayoz de aqlla cofta: entregada
de bay a qtro mefes vino a v la gēte xpiana poz la fama
q olla oyera z poz fer blãcoſ vn grã feñoz q bauia nõbze
Al>ucõde q era cafer feñoz de grãdes trras z traya vn fi
jo q figo z mucha gēte armada. los xpianos apcebidoſ
los recibierõ biē z fablaronfe nuño vaz pereyra. z el poz
interceffion de feys interptes q yua la palabza en feys lē
guas vuelta ante q la entēoieffen. z qoarõ muy amigos
pa adelante: z a fu fijo poz cõtētar al mucõde dio el capi
tan dadiuas q ellos tuuierõ en mucha eftima. pozq poz
fu trra bauiã de paffar los tratantes cõ ozo a çofala z fu
effe a fu reyno muy cõtēto z obligado alos xpianos.

¶ Titu.xvij. como la foztaleza õ çofala õla xpiana gēte
fue ētregada poz nuño vaz peyra a vafco gomez õ abzeo

Dificada la foztaleza de picoza ala mayoz p
effa q pudierõ como ē la pſpidad nũca falta
cõpañia ni qen acepte lo feguro: vino a çofa
la vn capitã llamado Dafco gomez de abzeo
cõ qtro naos de armada z notifico a nuño vaz fu poder
q del rey dõ manuel traya de q poz los otros capitanes

b iij

de su cõpañia fue informado τ fuele entregada la fortale
za τ capitania de Zofala vn domingo dspues de oyr mis
fa en fin de Septiembre segun lo cuenta Figueroa. que
ay eſtaua el ꝗl buenos cauallos τ Capitanes en sus naos τ compañia traya τ mando apregonar so pena d mu
erte. roda la gente ꝗ cõ Pedro de añaya hauia ydo sale
ſſe dentro de tres dias dela fortaleza τ ꝗ nadie les cõpra
ſſe los esclauos de Zofala. eſto fue tenido a mucho mal
aũ ꝗ la partida tenian por buena: yo de ningũ hõbre de
malos pensamientos τ enemigo de virtud τ delos ꝗ la
gloria primero merescieron puede fazer obra virtuosa τ
aſſi salieron de Zofala τ ẽbarcarõ cõ diego de melo capi
tan τ Nuño vaz pereyra para la india.

℃ itulo. xviij. Como Nuño vaz pereyra τ los ꝗ cõ el
ẽbarcarõ llegarõ a Moçãbiꝗ. cxc. leguas d Zofala.

Espues ꝗ embarcarõ en las naos d Diego
de melo ouierõ rezio τ cõtrario viaje por las
corrientes dela mar τ tardarõ de çofala a moçãbiꝗ ꝗreta τ cinco dias en cierto τ veynte le
guas d camino o viaje do inuernarõ aꝗl año. Los habi
tadores de moçãbiꝗ son moros caferes mercadores ri
cos su lengua mas clara ꝗ algarauia no tienẽ trigo sino
arroz τ mijo de ꝗ fazẽ pan: gallinas: cabras: y acas τ car
neros aſſaz aꝗ fueron bien recibidos del alcayde ꝗ hay
eſtaua xpiano. τ aꝗl año edificarõ alli vna fortaleza d pi
edra los capitanes τ alcayde como la ꝗ dexarõ ẽ çofala.

℃ Titu. xix. Como vino vn bergantin cõ nueua ꝗ vasco
gomez ꝗ ꝗdo ẽ çofala era pdido por la mar ꝗ ꝗtro naos.

D ꝗso dios ꝗ vasco gomez ꝗ tã furioso ẽtro
en çofala gozaſſe del sudor τ trabajo dlos ꝗ
fizo salir della τ segũ conto al alcayde de mo
çãbiꝗ vn bergãtin ꝗ eñl puerto entro sin re
gozijo de tiros de poluora como se suele fazer. vasco go

mez era pdido en la mar el ql hauia partido de çofala vi
spera de nauidad cõ qtr o naos z cõ la mas dela gente q
en çofala qdara z venia a moçâbiq z de alli a sant loreço
qs vna ysla a dscubzir clauo. z como ê vna ysla d engoz
se qdarõ.xvij. xpianos dela cõpañia d Basco gomez q
hauia alli salido poz mâtenimietos. z dla forma q hauia
seydo anegado en lo ql ouierõ biê entêdido no auer pla
zido a dios la manera q touo en la entrada d aqlla trra.
¶Titulo.xx. Como Tristan de accuña apozto en Al3o
çambiq con siete naos de especieria.

Ristan d accuña q hauia d venir poz bisrey
si no cegara sano de su vista. despues de naui
dad llego a moçâbiq cõ siete naos q ya traya
cargadas de specieria: dõde el cõ su gête fue
biê recibido: z el capitâ tristâ de accuña cõto nueuas de
su viaje como adelâte largamête oyreys.
¶Titulo.xxj. Del razonamiêto q fizo delas nueuas co
sas z marauillosas q al bisrey z a el auinierã.

Espues de biê recebido Tristâ de acuña les
fizo vn cortes razonamiêto z pncipio a qtar
las nueuas q muy desseosos estauâ oyr êlas
qles dezia cananoz auer estado cercado poz
los enemigos: z el cõ su gête llego z se descercara z lo q
mas fazia al proposito era. q dõ frâcisco hauia tomado
a Quiloa z a mõbaça: saliêdo dl puerto d mõbaça q tar
darõ ocho dias z fuerõ a melinde. z a santa helena do to
marõ agua fresca z es cinco leguas de melinde: z de alli
yendo pa la india atrauessarõ el golfo de meca en q hay
seteciêtas leguas z llegarõ a vna trra q se dzia angediua
ê idia ysla pqña: do fizo su gête vn castillo z vna galera:
ê q tardarõ vn mes: êl ql qdo manuel paçaña capitâ: z
luego el bisrey se ptio: z apozto âte el rio d onoz ql dl rey

b iiij

de garçapa vaſſallo del rey ð narſinga z ſu gẽte puſo fue
go a.xx.caſas zmas zq̃riẽdoſe recoger alas naos comẽ
çarõ a tirar flecheros los q̃les firierõ algũos delos xp̃i
anos z a dõ frãciſco ẽ vn pie:z ſabido poz el rey de Gar
çapa vino cõ dõ frãciſco en toda cõcozdia z amiſtad.el
rey de narſinga es delos mayozes ſeñozes q̃ hay ẽla idia
z tiene.lx.reyes vaſſallos grãdeſ q̃ en ſu oſtal hay mas ð
mill z q̃nientos cauallos:q̃lq̃er rocin vale.lx.ducados z
ſi es bueno.ccc.o.cccc.z dõ frãciſco ptio ð alli pa Cana
noz dõde,llego a.xxij.ð otubze.luego otro dia ſe vio cõel
rey de cananoz z cõfirmarõ ſus pazes.do mãdo ſo coloz
de caſa llana fazer vn caſtillo,el biſrey:z q̃do lozẽço ð bzi
to poz capitã.vn nauio: nao grãde z vna galera.z el biſ/
rey ſe ptio pa el puerto de cochin do vino nueua como ẽ
coullã matarã los judios a ãtonio ð ſaa z q̃nta gẽte cõel
eſtaua.ð q̃ dõ frãciſco ouo grã peſar: z ẽbio luego ſobze
ellos a dõ lozẽço ſu fijo cõ ſiete naos:z llegarõ al puerto
q̃s.xxiij.leguas ð cochin z q̃marõ.xxvij.naos ð mozoſ
cõ grãde riq̃za ð eſpecieria z aſſi voluio vitozioſo a ſu pa
dze dõ frãciſco eñl q̃l tp̃o el rey ð calicut bizo armada de
ochẽta naos grueſſas.cxx.mas peq̃ñas z ciẽt bateles q̃
ellos llamã parãos.z alos doze dias ð março ð.M.b.d.
vj.ãte cananoz ſe ẽcõrrarõ las armadas ðl rey ð Pozto
gal:z del rey ð Calicut:en q̃ veniã diez mill mozos jura
mẽtados:z llamaſſe el rey çamozin eñl q̃l encuẽtro dõ lo
rẽço moſtro mucho ſer iouſtrioſo z esfozçado q̃ alferro
cinco naos z las ſozbio la mar:delas delos mozos: z ðſ
baratarõ z vẽcierõ todas las otras q̃ fuxerõ: z cõeſta
grãde vitozia ſe voluio dõ lozẽço pa el biſrey ſu padze q̃
eſtaua en cochin:de q̃en fue cõ grãdes fieſtas reſcebido
z del rey de cochin q̃s enemigo del de calicut z amigo ð
dõ manuel rey de poztogal rico z poderoſo pñcipe.ðl q̃l

ēcuētro q̃do muy hoſtigado el rey de calicut: ₹ēbio a de
māḍar pazes:las q̃les el biſrey no q̃ſo fazer poz aplazer
al rey de cochin ſu amigo ₹ paſſado el inuierno a. viij. di
as del mes d agoſto adelāte dō lozēço fijo ōl biſrey ptio
cō ſiete naos a deſcobzir las yſlas del traues d cochin ₹
cō tēpeſtades rezias ₹ cōtrarios viētos fue apoztar a ce
ylā yſla dela canela muy pciada d rubis:zafiros:₹ otras
pcioſas piedzas ₹ tratoſe paz conel rey de ceylā ₹ q̃do el
dicho rey poz vaſſallo del rey de poztogal.₹vino poz vn
puerto ōl rey d coulā el q̃l q̃mo ₹ ōſbarato muchas naoſ
₹ caſas pzincipales matādo ₹ deſcabeçādo muchas gen
tes aſſi mozos como gentiles ptioſe pa cochin. a donde
llego.rij.dias de nouiēbze ₹ deſpues en março viniero
ſobze Łananoz ciēto ₹ ochēta mill mozos d todo el ma
labar dela india:₹ vno delos cōbates q̃ ouierō fue dia d
ſantiago entre los mozos ₹ lozēço de bzito cō gente de
dos naos grueſſas q̃l biſrey le ēbio fueron los xp̃ianos
vencedozes ₹ matarō.cccc.jndios ₹ fecha paz cōtarō vn
grā̄d miraglo q̃ andaua entre los xp̃ianos ſeñoz ſantia
go anciano cō la barua larga ₹ vna pozra de madera en
la mano.al q̃l los xp̃ianos no veyā ₹ los mozos mas dl
q̃ de otro ſe q̃zauā:poz q̃en pguntauā ₹ no fallauan nue
uas en cananoz.₹ ſe hauia buelto triſtā̄ d acuña a cochin
q̃ hauia venido ayudar al de bzito ₹ llegarō fuerō todos
conel biſrey a q̃mar vnas naos q̃ eſtauā en panā puerto
pzincipal de calicut ₹ q̃marō veynte naos de mozos q̃ eſ
tauā pa yr a meca:tomarō diez ₹ ſiete bombardas grue
ſſas ſin mozir aun q̃ ferida gēte xp̃iana.₹ el biſrey ſe vol
uio a cananoz:ſu fijo dō lozēço fue a cozrer la coſta ₹ tri
ſtan de acuña ſe hauia ptido pzimero dia de deziēbze co
mo haueys oydo.
℄Titulo.rrij.Łomo Triſtan de acuña ſe partio.

Cabo õ doze dias q̃ ouo tomado algũ refre
sco z folgado có la gente española puey̆do õ
mātenimiētos:despedido otrosi muy̆ cortes
mēte:tristā de acuña se partio pa el rey̆no de
Portogal z determinarõ de se y̆r de alli a su vētura ps/
pera o aduersa diego de melo z martin coello capitanes
pa la india:o en busca de Alfonso de alburq̃rq̃ q̃ mucho
loauā z estaua enel estrecho de mecha có sey̆s naos z se/
y̆s ciētos hóbres enellas pa vedar el passo dela india a
babilonia:z tomarõ vna trr̃a q̃ se nóbra q̃loa la q̃l bisrey̆
ouiera ante ganado en la q̃l y̆sla hay̆ songo q̃s vna villa
cercada a dos leguas õ q̃loa. longo songo. a sey̆s leguas
Aldásia trr̃a viciosa z fresca aq̃nze leguas cótra el norte
dela y̆sla está tomagũda trr̃a de granadas: z calebejar q̃
es rey̆no q̃nze leguas dela y̆sla fazia el norte vna grā ciu
dad q̃ se dize Zēguibar y̆sla muy̆ fertil z habũdosa õ buē
puerto z mātenimiētos dõde hay̆ los mejores limones
z narájas q̃ ay̆a en q̃lq̃era pte. acerca della hay̆ otra y̆sla
muy̆ viciosa z en todas estas hay̆ paz en derecho delas
dos y̆slas esta vna tierra firme llamada Otrando desde
la q̃l empieça el rey̆no de móbaça del puerto de Quiloa
se partieron despues q̃ siete o ocho dias folgaron có pe
dro de ferrera capitan dela fortaleza: z fuerõ se para Alse
linde. do la gente de aquella tierra faze estrecha vida lla/
manse buzarates muy̆ retray̆dos z agenos de conuersa
cion: muchos dellos no comen cosa mortal: q̃ero dezir
que reciba muerte: z q̃ tenga sangre. Llamanse por otro
nombre Bramenes. en aquella y̆sla bien recebidos fue
ron los christianos. z de ay̆ a doze dias aporto vna nao
a Aldelinde de Alonso de Alburquerq̃ en la qual venia
por capitan francisco de tabora z desembarcando fue
a fazer sabidores los christianos delas cosas que a Alõ

so de Alburquerque acaescieron en la toma de vna ciu/
dad que se llamaua Baraua z en otra ysla de Zacatora
como hauia tomado el castillo de fortaque alos moros
z que quedaua enel cabo de Guardafuni.

CTitulo.rriij.En que se recuentan las vitorias de Al/
fonso de Alburquerque capitan del estrecho de meca.

Jto Diego de Tabora como bien sabian a
uer ydo Alonso de Alburquerque por capi/
tan mayor de seys naos para el estrecho de
Meca z les hazia saber auer llegado a vna
ciudad que esta en tierra firme Braua nombrada z la en
traron por fuerça de armas matando muchos moros
z robando grãdes riquezas las quales sus dueños no
quisieron saluar pensandolo defender: ni sus mugeres
que alli quedaron muy ricas z apuestas con siete rocho
manillas a cada braço z otras tantas alas piernas muy
gruessas z preciosas. Lo qual fue ocasion de mucha cru
eldad: porque la gente ciega dela auaricia mas que alũ
brada de misericordia por no se detener poco espacio les
cortauan los braços: z piernas: z orejas: en que trayan
joyeles sin memoria de piedad. Esto no lo fiziera la gen
te de bien solo por ser mugeres arcas de generació z ser
de blandas z delicadas carnes z molles condicion qui/
en no se mouiera a piedad contemplando la fermosura
que enellas era a quien no sele cayera la espada dela ma
no ante que ensangrentarla en muger: dinos son los cru
eles vitoriosos en latal crueldad de ser reprehendidos
Pero bien se cree que los que tal obraron no serian de
los mejores ni medianos. Andauan todas llorãdo por
las calles bañadas en sangre. E otras con los niños
en los braços huyendo sin hallar guarida: Algunas

τ fartas dellas defendiã τ ãparauan los virtuofos ᵭ aᵹ
fe fallarõ.la ᵭl ciudad fue mandada abzafar τ affi fe hizo
τ fuerõ fobze otra ciudad ᵭ fe dize Madagadaro ᵭ eftaua
acerca:en la ᵭl puefto que los enemigos temerofos fue
ffen la ferocidad delos viẽtos τ cõtrariedades fizo alos
rpianos no efpar o cõbatir la τ affi el tpc cõtrario eftoz
uo fu bueno τ deffeado propofito:de dõde partidos lle
garon a çacatoza cuᵹa gente es temida entre fi por rpia
na aᵹuna las ᵭzefmas τ auiẽtos fin comer carne ni pef
cado tiene yglefias τ altares cruzes enellas: τ la maᵹoz
parte delas fieftas principales τ affi delos apoftolos:τ
fe nõbzã por fus nõbzes:fazẽ limofnas oᵹen todos los
dias:maᵹtines:vifperas:τ cõpletas.tiene en tanta vene
raciõ la cruz ᵭ el cõfigo la trahe no teme daño de enemi
go ni de jufticia fegũ la carta ᵭ del rey de Poztogal ẽ fu
lengua oue a mis manos largamente recuenta aũ ᵭ ene
lla da la bourra a triftan de acuña. efta trfa efta bien cer
cada de agua:ancozaron acerca el Caftillo: τ como co
nofcieron que eran poztoguefes facaron bombardas τ
pufieronfe en gran defenfion no queriendo pazes ni aũ
dexar prouecrfe de agua de çacatoza: τ alli mataron los
rpianos vn capitan çacatozi. la batalla fue muᵹ cruda τ
enella fe moftro coftante τ esfozçado vn capitã cuᵹo nõ
bze era Leonel coutiño τ mucho alos dl caftillo apffura
ua cõ fieros golpes ᵭ de fus manos hazia τ los mozos
dfamparãdo el muro:τ el poniẽdo efcalas affi ᵭ los rpi
anos ᵭ primero entrarõ abzierõ la puerta dl caftillo τ ẽ
tro la gẽte rpiana τ tomarõ la foztaleza do ningũ mozo
efcapo porᵭ ante ᵭfieron mozir ᵭ rendirfe ni ᵭdar cõ la
vida perdiẽdo fu patrimonio τ luego los vẽcedozes affe
gurarõ la trfa:aᵭlla gẽte era de foztaᵭ trfa de Arauia
aũ que vẽcida muriẽdo esfozçada. τ paffado el inuierno

fuerõ los españoles sobre la ciudad de Ozmuz conel ca
pitan Alonso de albnrqrq de generaciõ castellano:la cõ
qstarõ z ganarõ.los mozos se leuãtarõ contra los xpia
nos z fuerõ otra vuelta a çacotora. z de alli al cabo d gu
ardasuni esperãdo las naos infieles. z de hay Alõso de
alburqrq ebio a Diego d taboza a trfa d Adelinde poz
mãtenimiẽtos a cuyo ruego los dichos capitanes Die
go de melo z Muño vaz z los q conellos andauã afilan
do sus espadas en las moziscas genteſe fuerõ al Cabo
de guardasuni pa el prospo capitã mayoz.

C Titulo.rriiij. Del viaje q los capitanes fizieron para
Alfonso de alburquerque.

Aminando su viaje los dichos capitanes lle
garon a Magadazo de q ya fablamos z vie
ron vna nao de mozos q a trfa enderescauan
z qndo a ella llegarõ:la gente fuera vierõ que
estaua z pusierõ fuego cõ qnta riqza dentro tenia a sus
mercãcias.sin parar fizierõ viaje pa alfonso de alburqr
que de qen fuerõ honozablemente recebidos:el cabo de
guardasuni llamaſſe cabo pozq alli la costa del mar senes
ce.z hay alli otro cabo q se dize sozaq entre los qles en
tra el mar q llamã estrecho de meca llamaſe Arabia felir
poz vna grã poblaciõ q alli feliz se nõbza estrfa doliente
el ayze calido:sus habitadozes son alarabes: criadozes
de ganados:la agua dulce esta lexos:q trahẽ a vẽder en
cueros.d alli se fuerõ a çacatoza a tener el inuierno.

C Titulo.rrv. Delas cosas q figueroa cuẽta dela ysla
çacatoza en q estouo quatro meses.

Stuuierõ los capitanes cõ los qles estaua
martin fernandez de figueroa todo el inuier
no q alla es desde el mes de abzil fasta media
do agosto en la ysla de çacatoza:en la qᴸ hay

hōbres biē dispuestos estas yglesias no tienē santos ni
santas excepto cruzes como dla ordē dla trinidad z su
clerigo se llama cacis:tañen a missa cō rablas: en la ygle
sia los varones entrā po vna puerta z las mugeres poz
otra sin qbrantar el tal vso. las cruzes vntā con manteca
en las solemnidades. Las mugeres amā mucho ala gē
te christiana españa. saben algunos Arauigo:tienen
lengua propria: Los hombres andan desnudos: excep
to las partes vergonçosas: Las mugeres traen cami
sas moriscas:los cabellos largos esparzidos poz las es
paldas: Las mugeres son comunes: ques vna abomi
nable costumbre:assi que el marido vos combidara que
durmays con su muger:z el padre z la madre con sus hi
jas: Es gente libidinosa: En aquella tierra muy pocas
vezes llueue excepto rocio:no nasce enella trigo : arroz:
mijo:ni ceuada: Hay mucho ganado z palmares:do cu
esta vn cantaro de Vino mill z seyscientos marauedis:
vna aguja veynte marauedis. z assi otras muchas cosas
necessarias.
℄ Titulo. xxvj. De como se conquisto Ozmuz z las cō
diciones de sus gentes.

VN cauallero dela compañia del capitan ma
yoz Alonso de alburqrq̄ cōto fidelissimamē
te alos capitanes dela otra costa la conqui
sta d Ormuz q̄ figueroa scribio en vn libro
delas cosas q̄ alla hauia cō lo q̄l concordaua la letra del
rey don Manuel portuguesa. z dixo como despues q̄ la
fortaleza tomarō alos forzaines q̄ a manera de suyços
o soldados peleā:la q̄l dexado hauiā proueyda de gente
yēdo a buscar mātenimiētos fuerō guiados poz la mar
ala pte de Arabia z fuerō a Calayate ciudad rica de pu
erto:de q̄ el capitā mayoz folgo poz se fallar en tierra de

buenos mantenimiẽtos do tomarõ puerto aũ q̃ dificul
toso por estar apoderado de fermosas naos z la tierra d
mas vellos edificios:dõde gran ruydo cõ la artilleria fi
zierõ por los atemorizar z tomaron mantenimientos d
q̃ los moros proueyeron z no les fizo daño el Capitan
porque les hauia dado seguro z en señal vn anillo suyo
Calayate q̃ fue despues quando Ormuz se leuanto des
truyda era mas poblada fuera q̃ dentro. Alõso de albur
q̃rq̃ se partio otro dia z llegarõ a vn puerto nombrado
Curiate q̃ es otrosi del rey de Ormuz es vna poblaciõ
en la ribera muy rica: bien guarnescida de bombardas
ala q̃l el capitan mayor rogo les dexassen tomar mante
nimientos: de q̃ los moros no se fizieron caso: z otro dia
Alõso de alburquerque apcebio su gente z capitanes de
reguarda z dioles batalla: destruyolos z los moros fu
yendo los christianos matando: fuerõ las naos bien p
ueydas de riquezas z mantenimientos q̃ en tierra falla
ron. conuiene saber abundancia d Trigo:farina:arroz:
datiles:pescado:manteca:z miel. donde reposaron tres
dias. En todo el dicho recuentro o hizo no matarõ de la
gente delos christianos excepto vn negro del Capitan
mayor que se hauia desmandado. La qual vitoria auida
entrarõ sus naos: q̃ marõ z abrasarõ la mesquita tierra
z nauios que nada q̃do: z fueron por la mar adelante a
Mascate q̃ s del rey de Ormuz mayor q̃ Curiate cuyo
puerto era muy bueno z bien apcebido a defenderse po
como los moros cõ seguro se vierõ cõ el capitã mayor: el
qual assaz temor z espãto les puso fizieron lo que les mã
do z quedaron por vasallos del rey de Portogal don
de los christianos ouieron muy frescas z ricas prouisio
nes. pero ante pescarõ con ellos brauamẽte z fue la batalla
cruel por q̃ los moros q̃ brantarõ la paz q̃ prometieron

la ciudad puesta a sacomano: el regidoz della muerto: τ
vn capitã xpiano serido: la ciudad naos τ riqzas della a
brasadas τ vueltas ceniza. cõ la ql vitozia se recogierõ a
las naos: domingo demañana tres hozas de batalla: τ
de alli êbarcarõ τ suerõ Alfonso de alburqrã τ su gente
costa a costa a vn logar q se dezia çohar do estaua foztaleza: capitã τ gente de guarniciõ poz el rey de Ozmuz τ
vistas las naos delos xpianos conel temoz q ouierõ el
capitã τ su gente los mozos τ çohar se fizierõ vassallos
del rey dõ Manuel de portogal τ fizierõ grãdes fiestas
qdando la vandera delas quinas enla fortaleza diziêdo
mozos τ xpianos Portogal τ España.

⨀ Titulo. xxvij. Como llegarõ a Orsacan los christianos τ qles sucedio.

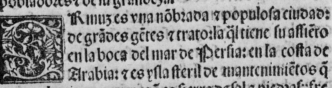

Legres con las passadas fazañas ensangrê-
tados los xpianos en aqlla camina τ perra gê
te q no osaua esperar: partidos de çohar pa
Orsacã qs muy mas rica τ poderosa. aporta
rõ sin cõtradiciõ poz las guerras comarcanas ya todos
los mozos absentes della ala ql pusierõ suego. y do efil
alcãce alos mozos sacados los ganados τ agua q roba
rõ τ desque se prouexerõ τ abrasada toda caminaron al
reyno de Ozmuz do aportarõ.

⨀ Titulo. xxviij. Dela ciudad d Ozmuz como viuê sus
pobladoze τ de su grandeza.

Rmuz es vna nõbzada τ populosa ciudad:
de grãdes gêtes τ trato: la ql tiene su assiêto
en la boca del mar de Persia: en la costa de
Arabia: τ es ysla steril de mantenimiêtos q
agua dulce tiene poca: porq es sierra de sol τ piedras: se
prouee se de agua de otra cercana ysla q Quexume se di
ze: la tierra firme de q se prouee es Persia: do hay ruas

melones τ figos τ otras cosas:es cabeça de reyno q̃ tie
ne muchas ciudades villas:τ logares:edificose en tal lo
gar porq̃ mas fuerte fuesse:τ tiene dos puertos de leuã
te τ poniente muy buenos:es cercada:sus edificios d̃ pi
edra altos:ala pte dela mar tiene vn castillo do el rey se a
posenta:en la otra pte sierras:en medio della esta la mes
clita muy grãde τ fermosa si mas puede ser:hay en la ciu
dad mercancias ricas de sedas:aljofar τ piedras precio
sas:el aljofar trahẽ de la ysta baharẽ:τ alli lo pesca̅:a cer
ca de ay hay vn rey q̃ se llama de lara q̃ es reyno su yo.
C Titulo.xxjx.Como fue cõq̃stada Ormuz por Alõso
de alburq̃rq̃ τ la gẽte q̃ lleuaua xp̃iana.

Llegados los capitanes xp̃ianos al reyno τ
ciudad de ormuz:vierõ estar enel puerto tres
cientas velas muy poderosas de moros q̃ en
aq̃lla trra tratauã:τ ellos yuã ẽ seys naues su
vãdera puesta ẽ la galuia q̃ acozarõ justo cõ las mas gru
essas naues:τ mãdo alõso de alburq̃rq̃ al capitã dla nao
del rey d̃ cãbaya q̃ ya temeroso estaua q̃ cõ dos moros
fuesse a lleuar vna ẽbaxada a Cojatar q̃ era moro τ go
uernador q̃l rey era moço.La q̃l era q̃ lo venia a sujetar
al rey de portogal su señor τ q̃ el era su capitã mayor alo
q̃l respõdio cojatar q̃ el era su capitã mayor.alo q̃l respõ
dio Cojatar q̃ el le pmetia fazer toda honesta paz τ cõci
erto no obstãte esso los moros τ sus naos τ gẽtes cõ as
saz armas venierõ a cercar a Alõso de alburq̃rq̃:τ alos
xp̃ianos el remedio fue poner fuego ala artilleria espa
ñola τ tirar bõbardas:τ luego la mar sorbio vna grãde
nao de moros de vn fijo del rey de cãbaya q̃ a cojatar fa
uorescia τ infinidad d̃ moros q̃ fuerõ muertas al menos
sin cuẽta τ los q̃ dellos qdarõ suyerõ cõ Cojatar ẽ calla
do sus naos τ otros a nado o como possible les fue q̃ pe

c

cia la mar yr̄to da cubierta dellos rodado. ¶Los nauios
de mozos fuerō cōbatidos ⁊ en breue señozeados dlos
xp̄ianos.biē se podria estōces llamar el mar bermejo q̄
ras̄ ĝua el cō la sangre delos mozos muertos.po la causa
porq̄ assi se dize es porq̄ las arenas son colozadas q̄la a
gua es como la dlos otros mares fenecierō estōces mas
de tres mill mozos ⁊ poz espacio d tres dias se adumierō
assi muertos folgādo sobze la agua en las marcas q̄ era
plazer delos ver dāçar a son.po aū despues no los dexa
uā menear a su sabor q̄ cō garfios agudos de fierro los
sacauā ga ver si lleuauā joyas ricas.algūos xp̄ianos fue
rō feridos ⁊ cō la vitozia ⁊ buena ādāça p̄sto fuerō ricos
⁊ sanos q̄ nūca poz mejoz ēpleadas.dierō llagas̄ q̄ aq̄llas̄
⁊ el capitā mayoz voluio a cozrer la ribera muy osado co
mo aq̄l a q̄ē biē suele dzir ⁊ q̄ino mas d.el.naos q̄ era fer
mosa cosa de ver ⁊ los arrabales dla ciudad lo q̄l viēdo
los mozos desampararō muchos a Ozmuz q̄ vn mozo
grā astrologo hauia dicho a cojatar q̄ en tal oza los xp̄i
anos alli hauiā llegado q̄ hauiā d cōplir su volūtad d co
mo s̄ fuyā no fue sabidoz alōso d albur q̄rq̄.⁊ cojatar ēbio
a pedir misericozdia ⁊ fazerse vassallo dl rey d poztogal
⁊ dio grādes riq̄zas al capitā mayoz lo q̄l fue cōcertado
como el capitā q̄ s̄o subjetādolo q̄nto ozdeno ⁊ la letra d
paz fue escripta en papel cō letras de ozo la lēgua d p̄sia
⁊ otra en arauigo cauada ē tablas de ozo cada vna meti
da en caza de plomo.el rey de Ozmuz poz quen cojatar
gouernaua se dezia çefadin auenadar.

¶Ti.xxx.dla solēnidad q̄ q̄ la vādra d poztogal se fizo.

Jen auēturada se pudo dezir la vādera d poz
togal ⁊ el cōde dō enriq̄ d costātinopla padze
de dō alōso enriq̄z p̄mero rey del.de q̄ē son
⁊ hā seydo descēdiētes reyes ⁊ vitoziosos p̄n

cipes de poztogal.qero q̃ sepaꝑs el parētesco q̃ los reꝑes
õ poztogal tienē cõ muchos cauallos õ salamāca cuꝑas
señales son las de aragõ cruzadas del cõde. dõ remõ:q̃
desciēdē de dos hermanos z assi de vn padze: pozq̃ don
enriq̃ de costãtinopla z dõ remõ de tolosa q̃ reedesico a
salamāca de q̃en vienē los remones de bastones o vari/
llas padze del ēpadoz dõ alõso z el papa Calisto grã põ
tisice en la ꝑglesia de dios fuerõ h̃ros. z el cõde dõ remõ
de san gil tuerto de vn ojo de q̃en desciēdē los remones
de ledesma z de dõ pedzo remõ su sijo z el cõde dõ remõ
õ tholosa z dõ enriq̃ fuerõ cuñados z p̃mos casados cõ
tres sijas del reꝑ dõ alõso. voluiēdo al p̃posito fuerõ cõ
certadas las pazes muꝑ sestejada la vãdera del reꝑ don
Manuel que poz mandado del capitan maꝑoz salierõ
a cauallo z de atauio poz las calles dela ciudad. cojatar
z los pzincipales della E tanta era la gente que mucho
los chzistianos se marauillauan de su vitozia z descaual/
garon alas puertas delos palacios reales aquien el reꝑ
salio a recebir z Bozge barreto que la vandera leuaua
se la entrego diziendo si recibia aquella Bandera como
de su reꝑ z señoz z tres vezes pzeguntado respondio que
si z fue puesta en la pzincipal tozre del castillo dõde esto/
uo la señal chzistiana poderosamente triumphando.

C Titulo.xxxj. Como ouo despues muchas rebueltas
z lides entre Alonso de Alburquerque z Cojatar.

Dchas discozdias ouo assegurado Ozmuz
entre los Capitanes españoles que causa/
ron quatro chzistianos passar se a Cojatar
E q̃l pēsasse fazer traꝑciõ a alõso õ alburq̃r
q̃ z pozq̃ las guerras fuerõ muchas grãdes z diuersas

. c ij

no me deterne en ello po q̃ero q̃ sepays q̃ en las differen
cias destano la p̃ncipal ciudad d̃ q̃rumé τ grãdo logaré
de Dzmuz a fuego τ a sangre. Cojatar τ su gẽte fuerõ si
empze muy maltratados: tomãdo otra vez cõ cuatro na
uios a calayate los xpianos q̃ cozrierõ τ psiguierõ tan
cruda τ ensangrẽtadamẽte la trr̃a de ozmuz q̃ cojatar τ
el rey çesadin ẽbiarõ a dõ fráciſco biſrey d̃las indias poz
seguro el q̃l moſtrarõ a Alõſo de alburq̃rq̃ q̃ ya enel pu
erto eſtaua pa los cõbatir τ como vio las pazes τ que el
rey Cesadin τ Cojatar erã vaſſallos del rey de Porto
gal ceſſo su guerra q̃ eſpaua fazer cõ grande τ eſforçado
animo q̃ cõtra infieles τ mozos ſiẽpze touo. τ aũ d̃ſpues
porq̃ cojatar no le q̃so dar los q̃tro xpianos q̃ a el ſe pa
ſſarõ le deſbarato τ deſtruyo a Mahã q̃ era cerca la yſla
delara: q̃ diſta q̃tro leguas de Dzmuz: dõde fazia la pte
de q̃rumé fue deſbaratado vn galeõ de Diego de melo
τ el muerto q̃ como yua todo armado no pareſcio en ci
má dela agua de q̃ los xpianos ouierõ mucho peſſar po
el murio poz la ſe de xpo τ como buẽ cauallo τ enel cielo
τ en la trr̃a terna p̃petua glozia. de ay ſe p̃io Alõſo de al
burq̃rq̃ pa la india τ fallarõ el τ su gẽte al biſrey d̃ grãde
armada en cananoz y los q̃les ouierõ vnos τ otros grã
plazer τ alegria τ cõtarõſe las coſas q̃ les acaeſcierã lar
gamẽte como era razõ.

**C Titulo .xxxij. Como cõtarõ los d̃l biſrey la muerte d̃
dõ Lozéço de almeyda τ lo q̃ les hauia acaeſcido.**

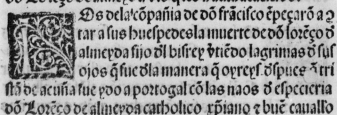

Os dela cõpañia de dõ fráciſco ẽpeçarõ a ꝯ
tar a sus hueſpedes la muerte de dõ lozéço d̃
almeyda ſijo d̃l biſrey ỽtiẽdo lagrimas d̃ ſuſ
ojos q̃ fue d̃la manera q̃ oyreys. d̃ſpues q̃ tri
ſtã de acuña fue ydo a portogal cõ las naos d̃ eſpecieria
dõ Lozéço de almeyda catholico xpiano τ buẽ cauallo

como su muerte da testimonio se prioð cananoza a cozrer
la costa fasta caul: llego a vn puerto q̃ se llama o nombza
dabul lleno de muchas naos aũ q̃ no apcebidas: Et los
mozos con temoz q̃ hauiã delos xp̃ianos acometieron
pazes sin las q̃les como no fazĩ cierras z se aparejauan
de guerra los xp̃ianos dieron enellos z desbararaõ los
q̃mãdo diez naos q̃ despojaõ z hauiã dado en seco: los
xp̃ianos có po barrueco z diego perez capitães salierõ
é trr̃a tomaõ el valuarte z toda la artilleria ð dabul vol
uiédose alas naos sin peligro. z pticerõ de alli pa caul sin
lleuar ningun ferido ni muerto. en la q̃l ciudad de caul a
poztarõ: q̃s el puerto muy bueno z dista poz veynte legu
as ð dabul: z fuerõ pacificamẽte recibidos porq̃ sus ha
bitadozes teniã paz con los xp̃ianos q̃ se proueyeron de
agua z de palomas q̃ muchas hay alli z caminarõ su vi
aje pa augediua do dõ francisco de almeyda bisrey esta
ua: del q̃l bien recibidos: fuerõ ẽbiados otro viaje có ve
ynte cinco naos de cochin q̃l bisrey ẽcomẽdo a su fijo dõ
lozẽço defendiesse z guardasse porq̃ el rey de cochin era
ðl rey de poztogal q̃ yuan a cargar de trigo a caul. dõde
en llegando estouo dõ lozẽço todo el mes de febzero fa
sta doze de março. z q̃riendose partir para caul vierõ ve
nir poz la costa dela mar cinco naos de manera delas ð
españa có gauias z siete galeras q̃ parecian ser delas de
alõso de alburq̃rq̃ a prima facie có todo se recogierõ los
xp̃ianos a sus naos porq̃ temã nueuas q̃ en la ciudad ð
Dio estauã naues ð rumes o ð turcos alla assi dichos z
llegãdo al puerto fuerõ muchos los tirosde artilleria z
grãde la lid q̃ ouierõ z firierõ veynte z cinco hõbzes có
flechas en la cõpañia del capitan mayoz delos quales so
lo vno murio. Et otro dia poz la mañana grãde fue el cõ
bate que otrosi ouo porque afferraron las naos delos

chriſtianos alas delos rumes τ las deſbarataron quaſi
todas τ metieron muchos dellos ſangrietos en la mar
que era marauilla quan colorada eſtaua: τ fue muerto eſ
tonces Mamaly el mayor armador del rey de Calicut:
duro aquella batalla haſta hora de viſperas: ſolas dos
naos delos rumes quedaron: las quales eſtando pueſ
tas en la agonia dela muerte vieron delas naos del rey
de Cambaya grande armada venir por la mar cuyo ca
pitan era malicayaz ſeñor de vna ciudad ques dicha de
Dio en ayuda delos rumes con quarenta τ nueue naui
os de remos τ llegaronſe al puerto. Lo qual viſto por
los chriſtianos ordenaron de ſe ſalir del puerto por po
der mas a ſu ſaluo pelear E la nao en que yua la capita
nia de don Lorenço τ el quedo traſera τ fue tã deſdicha
do que fue a caer en vnas eſtoças Do nunca pudo ſalir
yendo muy delanteras las de ſu compañia. alli los Ru
mes ſin ninguna piadad con ſus naos τ gentes ocurrie
ron τ forçada la defenſion delos chriſtianos la metierõ
debaxo dela agua donde murio de dos bombardadas
don Lorenço de almeyda delante los ſuyos como exce
lente Capitan: buen chriſtiano por la fe de Xpo τ ſeñala
do cauallero de portogal que en ſu linaje ſera alos pari
entes eterna corona. De alli Malicayaz lleuo viuos di
ez τ ocho chriſtianos los quales embio a campanel qs
vna villa muy fuerte τ victioſa Donde eſta quaſi ſiempre
el rey de Cambaya el qual es criado τ ſuele ſer con pon
çoña quando niños en poca quantidad τ aſſi ge la acreci
entan creſciendo τ ſi algun grande de ſu reyno le ha eno
jado fazele veſtir vna camiſa ſuya τ ſudando con ella mu
ere: o mandales comer betel maſcado en ſu boca τ luego
inchado dela ponçoñoſa ſaliua muere, τ el rey de Cam
baya folgo mucho de ver aquellos chriſtianos que nun

ca los hauia visto. τ de alli los lleuarõ ala ciudad de dio
donde era señor Abdalicayaz τ los rumes se fueron para
alla que hay buen puerto. E de alli se querian yr a forta／
lescer en Calicut. Los christianos quando acordaron
de poner remedio en la nao de don Lorenço que atras
quedara viendola so el agua τ mueria la gente no podie
ron remediar que ya para ello estauan en sus bateles a／
parejados. E assi muy tristes se partieron a Cochin do
el bisrey estaua τ con las nueuas ninguno oso yr excep／
to francisco de añaya Capitan en vna carauela de ve
la latina porque entendio ser don Francisco tan cuerdo
que no se offenderia de aquello en que ellos no hauian
seydo culpantes. Oyda la triste relacion con el mayor es
fuerço de coraçon que pudo dissimulo diziendo que grã
gloria le quedaua por la muerte de su hijo en auer muer
to como bueno τ catholico christiano τ leal caualler o τ
que Dios lo dio τ dios lo tomo que se hiziesse su volun
tad. E despues que algun tiempo se aderesçaron el bis／
rey don francisco que lastimado traya su coraçon en el
secreto de sus entrañas se partio con su gente para Ca／
nanor adonde se juntaron con la de Alonso de Albur／
querque τ de ay caminaron con deziocho velas en bus
ca delos rumes.

C Titulo.xxxiij. Como el Bisrey se partio de cananor
en busca delos rumes llego a honor mergeo: τ ãgediua.

On frãcisco bisrey con deziocho velas a.ix.
dias dõziẽbre dõ Al. d. viij. años ptio dõ Ca
nanor en busca dlos rumes e q̃ yua mill τ tre
ziẽtos hõbres biẽ aparejados de todas ár／
mas a guerra necessarias: τ fue la batalla en vna muy cla
ra τ quieta noche: salio la luna que era estonces el lleno
della sin dar tanta claridad como vna estrella E estouo

c iiij

affi efpacio ve vos horas:Lo ál tomaron eftos poz bue
na feñal.Antiguamente mirauã muchos en las buenas
feñales z fuerõ caufa ve acometer zvécer muchos reyes
grãdes hueftes batallas z capitanes aq de otra fozma
podierã fallar eftozuo:como la pmera feñal q enel mun/
do fe pufo fue aálla aguila q en la vãdera ve jupiter con/
tra fu paoze el rey faturno fe affento en véga dela fangre
de fus hermanos lo ál touo poz bué aguero pufola ẽ fu
vandera:z qdo vitoziofiffimo feñoz: z en la romana mo
narchia oy dia hay en roma la pzincipal cafa o la della q
fe nõbzã de bonis augurijs:lo ál eftando alla note z pze
gunte la caufa ve fu excelente apellido: z les dixe como
la pzincipal cafa z folar velas generofas montañas õ ca
ftilla era nõbzada de aguero defcendiéte vel cõde fernã/
gõçalez: ve fangre real como alos leydos z chzoniftas
es manifiefto.pues el bifrey de poztogal partido.õ cana
noz grãde amigo ve xpianos z del rey ve poztogal z ade
refcarõfe dos naos enel puerto de mergio cercano ve a/
lli ál rey ve garçapa hauia dado al rey dõ manuel la gen
te vefta tierra es bien difpuefta:adozã losydolos:qñdo
el marido muere la muger de fu gana fe lança eñl fuego
q dizen van a fazer bodas conel al otro mundo.z de alli
fe fuerõ a angeduia q ay eftaua el bifrey tomãdo agua z
de ay fe carteauã malicayaz z el bifrey en q el malicayaz
fe efcufaua dela muerte de fu fijo del bifrey pozq el no lo
conociera z el lo hauia fecho en fu defenfiõ pozq los xpi
anos le hauiã acometido a el:z aũ tratado muy mal a fu
gente z de ay fablarõ fobze paz z fue en bufca delos Ru
mes q mataron a fu fijo.

CTitulo.xxxiiij.Como don francifco llego a Davul
z la deftruyo.

On francisco visrey se partio para Dabul
z primero dia de Enero ancozaron en su pu
erto z leuantaron con vn viento para se lle
gar mas ala ciudad. fue tanta la artilleria d
los mozos que era muy gran espanto z quiso dios que
ningun christiano fue muerto: Ante muchas naos Da
bulesas desbaratadas: E a pesar delos mozos los chri
stianos salieron en tierra matando enellos: Do perdio
la vida el Capitan mozisco: E otro gran señor que en
vnas muy ricas andas venia como dueña que mas ri/
co que esforçado deuia ser pues no se preciando de Ca
uallero andaua como muger cosa effeminada z que mal
parescia a todos: z parescera do quiera que se vsare tan
abominable z fea cosa aquello de andar en Andas z ju
gar poz estilo: justas: torneos: o cañas: o esgrima. Es
cosa muy reprobada en los Caualleros: que ser ama
dozes honestos curialmente se permitte. Assi que que
dando enel campo z andando vencedozes no supieron
quien puso fuego ala ciudad que ardia cõ infinita rique/
za que era el mayoz plazer del mundo. Alli se ahogo vn
esforçado christiano hermano de Martin coello Ca/
pitan que poz salir en tierra cayo en la Mar cobrando
muerte de doblada vida. E enel puerto quemaron diez
naos Dabulesas varadas z seys naos grandes enca/
denadas z veynte no tan grandes llenas de arroz. Si
racal que el mejoz dela india dizen ser. Dabul esta en vn
valle puesta z sube poz vnas cuestas: o sierras o hasta v/
na cerca vieja que alli esta que ante fue alli muy noblemẽ
te edificada z poblada. Luego los christianos cozrierõ
toda la costa quemando logares z haziendo grande es
trago. hay alli oztaliza assaz: cañas d açucar: vacas: gal
linas muchas fuentes de sabzosas aguas z en la ciudad

de Guoa vieron tantos faltigallos que apenas se pare
cia el sol τ el cielo los quales destruyen aquella tierra τ
es manjar que los moros vsan:τ tienen tinajas:τ otras
vasijas llenas dellos en côserua por aquella ribera grâ
dissimo estrago hizieron los españoles τ en les pozos
do hauiã de beber los moros les dexauã assaz cuerpos
muertos:aquella ciudad era del reyno de Guoa que es
taua lexos dela mar.E despues de siete dias partieron
se del puerto τ vieron vn batel en que yuã Vn rume prin
cipal con treze hombres τ dos mugeres los quales aco
metidos delos christianos pelearon reziamente birien
do mas de veynte christianos τ fuerõ todos los rumes
muertos que no quedo sino vna muger porque la otra
mas principal murio abraçada conel Rume su marido
que touo por consolosa muerte.

C Titulo.xxxv.De como camino de die en busca delos
rumes fuerõ el bisrey τ su gente τ delo ã fizierõ.

Partidos fueron los xpianos dela ciudad de
caul por la costa τ viaje d câbaya:do en ãtor
ze leguas con las muchas marcas tardarõ
ocho dias:que dista el puerto de caul del rey
no de cani ã se pte conel de câbaya:τ es alli vn rio:do es
ta vna poblaciõ de mayn al ãl llegarõ:τ la hondura del
agua era ocho o nueue braças:τ son las marcas tã grã.
des τ tantas ã en espacio de dos horas ãdarõ las naos
en dos braças sino ã se aptarõ de alli:τ el bisrey êbio su
mêsaje a tierra:ã le dexasse por sus dineros tomar mãte
nimiêtos τ agua fresca pues no les fazian daño por ser
del rey de câbaya d ã ellos poco se curarõ:tõ francisco
mãdo armar toda su gente τ salierõ a tierra ã despobla
da estaua matando vacas:bufalos:de ã habûda ciacin
dad de main:fue antiguamête muy populosa:tiene vn

castillo cabo la agua de canteria z ôtro esquinas con cu
bos z bermosas almenas:los muros fortissimos de di
ez piés en ancho:dentro bay vna rica mezclita la atigua
z otras mezclitas cô ados que duran media legua grá
des z fermosos de ymagineria las sepulturas.Esto vie
ron el capitan z su gente en aquel logar noche z dia:To
mando mantenjmientos los que pudieron auer agua z
arroz:destrozarô quatro mill palmares z mas z no fizie
ron daño ala ciudad por no enojar a malicaraz z al rey
de Cambay porque alos rumes echasse de sus puertos
de ay se partieron para la ciudad de Dio por vn terrible
golpho espacio andando de quinze diasque no sabian
donde erâ.po quiso dios que vino vn necessario viento
de noche que en amanesciendo los puso a vista de Dio
z llegando al puerto las naos delos Rumes salian que
las daño mucho porque como el puerto se cierra con ca
dena no les pudieran entrar:dentro del qual hauia mas
de treziêtas velas z para llegar las naos de christianos
hauian de yr junto ala ciudad que por alli va la canal de
la'cozriente dia era de santa maria de febrero de quinien
tos z ocho años dos dias del mes.ordenarô entrar dô
de los rumes estauan.

CTitulo.xxxvj.Como fueron desbaratados los Ru
mes z las armadas de Malicaraz z del rey de Calicut
por los xpianos.

Tro dia por la mañana los xpiâos se atauia
rô de todas las armas q̃ lleuauâ z adereçar
a sus naos cô sacas de algodô z colchones
̃̃ z âparo delos tiros ð bôbardas tomãdo
sobze las naues redes por cubierta pa ofensiô delas pe
dradas ôlas gauias lo q̃l era assaz vtil z necessario.tres

dia de febzero fiesta de sant blas entraró dētro poz la ca
nal a afferrar las naos dlos rumesq̃ biē apcebidos esta
uã: ꜩ el delātero fue nuño vaz pereyra do fuerō muchos
los tiros de poluoza de ābas ptes los xpianos llamādo
a nr̄a señoza: santiago: ꜩ a san blas cuya fiesta celebzauā:
delos q̃les los mozos matarō nueue psonas de Pozto
gal q̃ como catholi cos ꜩ leales dierō las vidas aq̃l dia
ꜩ cobzarō otra inmoztal ꜩ mayoz d̃ q̃ gozarã in eternũ ꜩ
cō vn tiro de bōbarda fue sozbida dela mar vna gruessa
nao de rumes dādoles luego los xpianos grã grita que
tābiē si no lleuarã cubierta de cierto recibieran grã detri
mento dlas piedzas ꜩ saetas q̃ estauā a fazes encima las
xpianas naos ꜩ afferraron otra nao de rumes en q̃ pue
sto q̃ bien defendida matando muchos entrarō ꜩ algu
nos mozos saltauā en los bateles ꜩ otros se lāçauā ē la
ma r po los leales defendiã poz dentro o poz defuera su
nao. los albazis q̃ son de trr̄a del p̄ste juan cautinos he
rrados en la fruēte en tres logares a manera d̃ cruz fuy
ō q̃ dela muerte delos rumes no les pesaua mucho. dō
de nuño vaz pereyra fizo tan señaladas ꜩ vitoziosas faza
ñas ꜩ su espada era tan çeuada en las carnes delos ene
migos q̃ merescio eterna cozona ꜩ biē poz señal la Cruz
ꜩ bzaço q̃l defiende en campo sangriento cō las ozladas
quinas de sangre de reyes de poztogal de q̃ el claro ꜩ es
fozçado descendiente alli lo firicrō a el poz mas vitozia
le dar cō vna flecha enel pescueço q̃l con alegre cara reci
bio sintiendola mas poz plazer q̃ poz enojo yendo sintiē
do la llaga dando gracias a nr̄o señoz q̃ lo crio de ay a
tres dias como catholico christiano balēte ꜩ muy esfoz
çado cauallero murio: quedando su nomb... inmoztal ꜩ
La fama de gentes en gentes eternalmente publicando
con lagrimas las claras fazañas ꜩ muerte de tal perso

na q̃ cubꝛio de luto q̃ fizo lloꝛofos los de fu cõpañia ⁊ ꝯ
la eſtima q̃ del hauia a fus cõtrarios los q̃ algũ conofci/
miẽto de caualleria o de virtud teniã. biẽ auẽturado fue
el dia ẽ q̃ nafcio pues en tal hoꝛa ⁊ tp̃o fenefcio dichofos
fe terniã muchos delos viuiẽtes fer muertos q̃ndo d
fi tan inmoꝛtal memoꝛia como d el ⁊ poꝛq̃ hõbꝛe hũano
no es fuficiẽte loarlo callo ⁊ fabꝛeys q̃ ay jarretarõ vna
pierna a vn xp̃iano ⁊ caỹẽdo enel fuelo los rimes lo ma/
tarõ crudamẽte cõ la muerte delos buenos ⁊ vida dlos
eſfoꝛçados mas ꝓfpos eſtauã los xp̃ianos q̃ ofauã en/
trar en las naos delosenemigos. eſfe dia vn caualło poꝛ
togues cuyo nõbꝛe era figueredo ꝓbo a fubir a la tolda
delos rimes ⁊ poꝛ vn foꝛado q̃ eſtaua jũto conel maſtel
dela nao le dierõ cõ vna pica poꝛ ẽtre las piernas ⁊ falio
la pũta della al pefcueço q̃do efperado ⁊ cõ vn garfio cru
el lo derrocarõ abaxo poꝛ lo q̃l no merefce menos q̃ tan
to q̃nto fue cruda la muerte tãto es mas excelẽte fu glo/
ria q̃ otro tãto fizierã al mejoꝛ de efpaña fu enemigo q̃ri
ẽdo los deſtruyrã alli tomarã quanto fue grãde el marti
rio merefcio coꝛona d buẽ caualło ⁊ ylluſtro las cinco fo
jas de figuera cercados conel coꝛdõ q̃ poꝛ la batalla de/
las dõzellas leonefas q̃ delos móꝛos los ꝓncipales her
manos libertarõ el efclarefcido gallego folar merefcio:
Matarõ los rimes otrofi a pero can q̃ fubir q̃ria: ⁊ de/
rrocarõ al fijo de manuel paçaña finalmẽte q̃ la tolda ⁊
nao poꝛ los xp̃ianos cõ la artilleria fue fola agua en glo
ria de efpaña ⁊ vituperio delos rimes ⁊ yẽdo fe al hon
dõ vna delas naos de poꝛtogal en q̃ nuño vaz ỹua o fue
ra poꝛ capitã en vn maſtel dela nao fe faluo martin fernã
de figuer... al q̃l dierõ vna lançada en vna pierna q̃ ato
cõ vn paño de algodõ como pudo ⁊ fe fue ala nao fancti
efpiritus ello fizo tan eſfoꝛçadamẽte aq̃l dia q̃ poꝛ fer vi

no aũ atocarlo no me atreuere τ como yo escriuo looꝛes
de otros no faltara ꝗen alla o aca los escriba del ꝗ tãbiẽ
los meresce como losꝗ alla se fallarõ aũ ꝗ tuuiesse mayo
res encomiẽdas ꝗ el.despues desto affeꝛrarõ las naos
otras cõ la artilleria metiẽdo so el agua sangriẽta cruda
damẽte peleãdo los rumes descayẽdo los ꝗpianos veni
endo en la nao de malicayaz mõꝛerõ tres ciẽtos τ cincu
enta hõbꝛes duro la pelea dsde hoꝛa dtercia fasta la no
che delos ꝗpianos murierõ ꝗreta τ cinco feridos ꝗuie/
tos τ mas:τ dela gẽte rumesa no se libꝛo excepto Albilia
cẽ capitã cõ veynte rumes ꝗ en vna barꝗta se salierõ.los
barcos de calicut τ carauelas viẽdo el desbarato fuyerõ
pa calicut.Albeliacẽ fue ferido de vna saeta en la pierna
de foꝛma ꝗ ꝗdarõ poꝛ vẽcedoꝛes los ꝗpianos enel puer
to τ los rumes muertos τ vẽcidos de ꝗen estaua la mar
cuajada.assi ꝗdo el puerto poꝛ el bisrey τ su gente el ꝗl ce
rrarõ luego cõ la cadena.

℃Titulo.xxxvij.℃omo el bisrey fizo pazes cõ Albalica
yaz τ se dierõ vno a otro los cautiuos ꝗ teniã.

Vida la dicha vitoꝛia ꝗ cree ꝗ no le tẽblasse
la cõtera a malicayaz poꝛ los passados trãces
cõtẽplãdo los ꝗ le podꝛiã auenir entẽdierou
sus farautes'ẽ ꝗcertar las pazes assi ꝗ le ẽbio
los ꝗpianos ꝗ cautiuos tenia τ arriba deximos ẽ la mu
erte de dõ loꝛẽço lo ꝗl poꝛꝗ es larga cosa de contar abꝛe
uio.τ el bisrey dio a malicayaz ꝗtro moꝛos ꝗ solamente
ꝗdarõ dela batalla τ oꝛdeno de se partir dela ciudad de
Dio pa inuernar en cochin biẽ pueydo de todos mãte
nimiẽtos τ cosas necessarias τ la muerte de su fijo cõ la
salsa ꝗl pudo fazer de ay ẽbio a alõso de no...ña a dõ alõ
so ꝗ estaua en çacatoꝛa poꝛ capitã ꝗ vituallas a nueue di
as defebꝛero alçarõ ancoꝛas τ fuerõ pa la india es razõ

q̃ se pays q̃l se llama india τ es desde el reyno de cãbaya
fasta el cabo de Comarin. τ la otra tierra de cambaya es
guzarates τ de psia al estrecho de ormuz es Arabia se
lix los mãteni mientos como españa la seta q̃ tienẽ õ ma
homa en persia τ arabia que enguoa Cambaya: Caul
τ dabul adorã los ydolos τ son los mas negros. estonces embia ua el rey don Manuel cõ Diego de sequera
en quatro naos a descubrir Clauo porque dela pimiẽta
assaz hay en Malabar: Calicut: Cananor: Cochin: co
ylan Caliculan reynos suyos. τ dela ysla Zamatora: la
canela viene dela ysla Euylan donde las puentes, casas
τ edificios son de madera τ arboles dela canela que no
hay otra en aquella tierra: τ alli hay piedras preciosas:
Rubis: Zafiros: τ otras de rico valor. El clauo nasce
en la ysla Maluco que dista de Melaca dozientas τ cin
quenta leguas. El birey ordeno partirse de cochin con
quatro naos de especieria a Portugal E que quedasse
su poder τ fuesse gouernador dela india Alonso de Alburquerque que estaua en Cananor τ luego vino el ma
rischal sobrino de Alonso de Alburquerque con diez τ
seys velas τ fizo que luego el birey le dexasse toda la go-
uernacion dela india delo qual el holgo que se queria ya
venir a su tierra τ priose de Cananor con tres naos pa
Portogal quedando Alburquerque gran señor τ muy
psp̃ero que luego determino yr sobre calicut τ destruyr
la ciudad rey τ gentes della.

C Titulo.xxxviij. Como Alonso de alburq̃rque se par
tio para calicut a destruyrla.

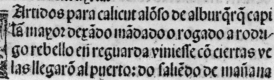

Artidos para calicut alõso de alburq̃rq̃ capi
tã mayor dexãdo mãdado o rogado a rodri
go rebello en reguarda viniesse cõ ciertas ve
las llegarõ al puerto: do saliẽdo de mañana

fuerõ sentidos los xpianos:alos ãles grã grita los mo
ros dierõ.po cõel grã temoz dla artilleria d xpianos ẽuã
fuyẽdo pozlos palmares los indios.τ los españoles se
guros ẽ trra salir osarõ ãmãdo muchos edificios τ ma
tãdo cruelmẽte muchos delos enemigos ã no en capita
nia mas de diez en diez o veynte ẽ veynte adauã faziẽdo
certeros tiros cõ sus arcos de ã mucho se atauiã en lid:
son gẽte ligera adã en carnes excepto las ptes vergõço
sas ã cõ vna toca ciñe.τ fuerõ dõ ãtonio sobrino dl capi
tã mayoz τ rodrigo rebello a ãmar ciertas naos ã stauã
en la costa ã erã ãtozze poz todas. E alõso de alburãrã
el marischal τ manuel paçaña:τotros capitanes caualle
ros τ hõbzes de biẽ xpianos entrarõ poz las callesd ca
licut triũphãdo vitoziosamẽte cõ la vadera dela cruz an
te si τ tras ella las de poztogal.la poblaciõ dla calicut no
esta cercada de muros. po dura su habitaciõ cinco legu
as los palacios del rey distã vna legua ã son de rico mu
ro τ piedza cercados τ foztalecidos:ãte los ãles esta vna
plaça ã mucha fermosura causa ala foztaleza dõde staua
enella vn coymal:ãs como en españa cõde cõ grã multi
tud de nayres.ã assi dizẽ alla alos cauallos. pozlos ãles
ãso el marischal ẽtrar auez tomar los palacios:cuya vi
sta cõpzo poz la vida ã fue alli vna grãdissima batalla la
mas esquiua alos xpianos ã en las indias ouo muy cru
da en ã la gẽte poztoguesa fue desbaratada:mucha se re
cogio alas naos. Matarõ ẽde al excelẽte τ magnanimo
marischal ã su sangre vertiendo poz la se de xpo τ hõzra
de su trra fazañosas cosas faziẽdo oluidãdo su ppzia vi
da poz el honoz de todos dio la amina a dios ã lo crio:
firierõ otrosi enel pescueço cõ vna flecha a Alõso de al
burãrã capitã mayoz pozã no ãdasse dela cõpañia ãzo
so Matarõ al bueno τ esforçado cauallo vasco d siluey

ra q̃ ãte ſi cõ vna laça tenia poz ſu mano muertos ſiete in
dios Digno q̃ no ſeneſca ſu fama pues puſo la vida poz
nſa ſe z ſu muerte dio poz buẽ exẽplo.no ſe q̃do en la po
ſada manuel paçaña digniſſimo capitãq̃ marauilloſamẽ
te peleaua traçãdo cabeças alos pſidos indios poz ga/
nar la hõzra q̃ mereſcio ẽbuelta en la ſangre d̃ ſu muerte
z otros capitanes z eſſozçadas gẽtes trocarõ el mal d̃l
cuerpo poz el biẽ d̃l a alma:la crueldad fue grãde q̃ cõel
mari ſcbal vſarõ pozq̃ le decceparõ las piernas pro la glo
ria la excede poz el martirio mereſcida.hauia e calicut.ir.
mill hõbzes de pelea de alli el capitã mayoz ẽbio ſus deſ
culpas d̃ aq̃l deſcõcierto al rey d̃ poztogal los cargadas
naos fuerõ a cananoz z de ay a liſbona z alõſo de Albur
querque ſe fue a cochin.

CTitulo.xxxix.Dela ciudad de calicut z ſus gẽtes.

Alicut es aſſi dicha de cal z piedza z cardar q̃
aca ſe dize cutiz o tocar aſſi q̃ ſe interpta roq̃
de piedza.era ãtiguamẽte imperio aũ q̃ ſolo
vno deuia ſer enel mũdo como vn põtifice.A
goza es reyno ſu puerto el mas celebze d̃ india dõde na
os de canela:pimiẽta:gẽgibze:z otras mercãcias ſe car/
gauã pa toda la redõdez delas trras lo q̃l deſpues dela
moztãdad enella ouierõ los poztogueſes magnanimos
ceſſo:q̃ no tã cõplidamẽte es viſitado hay e calicut z ſus
trras multitud de pemiẽta.la q̃l como dize ſe falla en co/
chin z cananoz aſſaz es frutice como yedza in arboz ri
yerua q̃ ſe retuerce o enlaza en cadena en los arbozes la
pimiẽta es en razimos verdes cogida q̃ al ſol ſeca ſe ru/
elue negra q̃l a eſtas ptes viene.La canela naſce en la in
ſula de ceylan q̃ tiene la foja q̃l de laurel la caſca de ſus ar
bozes es la canela q̃ a ca ſe dize.el clauo naſce en la yſla q̃
naluco ſe nõbza en arbozes peq̃ños cuya flor es clauo d̃

o

cabeça τ las nuezes moscadas es el fruto ðl arbor el cue
rezico ðelas nuezes se dize maça:en calicuτ en muchos
reynos ðe india son gētiles q̃ adorā ydolos:aiales τ sus
figuras criā en casa bueyes τ vacas el matador õllas tie
ne pena ðe muerte eneſſa trra no hay jodios las gentes
negras las tetas ðelas mugeres chicas por lo q̃l peſcē
mejor.los varones traē oro pēdiēte ðelas orejas:las eſ
padas sin vaynas τ adargas mayores q̃ rodelas:ay mu
chas suertes ðe estados τ gētes.los principales son nay
res q̃ son cauallos alos q̃les no llegā los otros estados
saluo seyēdo xp̃iano:moro:o judio:aſſi q̃ no sea ðe su se
ta τ aſſi no q̃rriā tractar con muchos ðlos xp̃ianos τ ðe
ziā q̃ biē conoscīā ellos ser los xp̃ianos que alli estauan
ser tan buenos τ mejores q̃ ellos po por q̃ tratauā cō la
gēte mas baxa q̃ ðe aq̃lla trra no q̃riā q̃ llegaſſen a ellos
mayormente quando veniā lauados : no eſcupē dētro
en casa q̃ lo tienen por suzia cosa:comē cō la mano dere
cha q̃ cō la siniestra se lauan:burlauā ðelos xp̃ianos por
q̃ comiā con ambas manos.adoran los indios ðe Cali
cut al diablo con el q̃l fablā τ se aconsejan dizen que creē
auer vn Dios mouedor ðelos cielos criador ðelas cria
turas bueno τ q̃ no faze mal. po por q̃ el diablo es malo
τ peruerso que les puede dañar lo honrrā τ adorā:po
el diablo es mal amigo τ aſſi pierden el seruicio comuni
cansele mas pa acreſcentarles ðe pena lo q̃ les muestra
ðe amor.

¶ Titulo.xl.Dela forma q̃ llegarō a boa τ ð sus habita
dores.

 Ano ðela serida el capitā Alōso ðe albur q̃r q̃
se partio pa el estrecho ðe meca luego q̃ llega
ſſe junto al reyno ðe honor tinogi q̃ era gran
hōbre ðe armada o gran costario por la mar

de seta gentil fizo entender al capitan mayor como Za/
bayo rey de guoa era muerto z cerca la sucession por te/
ner muchos herederos z hauia grādes rebueltas enel
reyno que podria ligeramente tomarlo: lo ql determina
ron fazer los xpianos z Timogi en su ayuda. Guoa q̄
ro q̄ se pays como es vna fuerte z fermosa ciudad assen/
tada ē vna breue ysla inexpugnable: passan a ella por pa
ssos en los quales torres almenadas cō capitanes z gē/
tes estan los q̄ entrā o salē enella vā en barcos: es de mu
cho arroz ganados: māteniuientos z aguas sabrosas
dulces z sanas: La fortaleza es fortissima cō cauas muy
fondas llenas de agua, intra muros hay dos fermosos
castillos sobre el rio vno z otro cara ala ciudad: adorā
sus habitadores al sol z ala luna z animales: cuyo abo/
minable vso q̄ ellos por santo tiene es q̄ muriendo el ma
rido la muger se ha de yr luego a q̄mar ō volūtad gano/
sa z espacio de tres dias la traen por las calles principa
les con muy dulces musicas z cāciones muy vestida z ri
camente apuesta se van ala hoguera: la qual en vn hoyo
esta bien inflamada z grande donde como llegada al re
dedor del fuego tres vueltas z apartada del fuego corri
endo se mete enel muy crudamente a donde sus parien/
tes con ollas de manteca z azeyte le ayudan por la con/
solar entre las viuas llamas: los hombres en aquella ti
erra andan desnudos por los grandes calores que hay
Las mugeres traē en las narizes pēdiētes joyas ō oro
Llegados pues alōso de alburq̄rq̄ z timogi a guoa āco
rarō āte su rio z ōspues ētrarō por el cōtra los q̄les los
infieles tirarō mucha artilleria q̄ en los almenados va
luartes teniā: lo q̄l como ōlos xpianos fue visto soltarō
sus bōbardas ō forma q̄ ōbarataro la mas gēte delos
valuartes ētrādo por las bōbardheras q̄ biē se defendiā:

D ij

po poco les aprouecho:porq̃ sin temor dllos fuerõ ētra
das:d q̃ se marauillarõ diziēdo: aq̃llos no hõbres sino
diablos ouiã f̃:pues tã sin temor dla muerte por los mas
peligrosos logares faziã su ꝓspo aũ q̃ fatigoso viaje.los
moros como ia gēte xꝑiana vierõ ē trr̃a fuyerõ alas q̃les
los españoles fuerõ enel alcãce z voluierõ por la artille/
ria dlos valuaris q̃ en sus bateles alas españolas naos
llegarõ. Otro dia ancorarõ ãte la ciudad sus naos q̃ di/
stauã dos leguas donde los infieles muy brauos se mo
strado cõ su espessa z ꝑssurosa artilleria en defensiõ se pu
sierõ:po dios nr̃o señor defensor z ãparo delos xꝑianos
mostro aq̃ por ellos vn grã misterio q̃ en la ribera estauã
diez z seys naos grãdes entre las q̃les hauia vna la ma
yor q̃ dizē jamas se fizot ãdãdo la cruda batalla vn jouē
puso fuego ala nao principal q̃ enel medio staua z como
los infieles lo vierõ toda su gēte fue a amatar el fuego d
samparãdo el mas necessario passo: z vã por matar el jo
uē el q̃l pēsando q̃ en las manos temã dspareslio:esto cõ
tauã los d guoa aũ q̃ otros por no cõfessar el misterio q̃
sabiã deziã vno q̃ capitã della q̃siera ser por no gela auer
dado la q̃mara:lo q̃l no era asi segũ despues biē luego se
descubrio.hauia dlos rumes.cccc. carpinteros faziēdo
las naos q̃ hauiã de yr en busca delos xꝑianos z en su so
corro veniã del soldã q̃torze mill rumes si necessarios fu
essen assi aq̃l dia fue grãde la liça q̃ ētre ellos ouo tasta q̃
la obscura noche cerro otro dia q̃l sol descubriesse las ca
ras alos enemigos.

℃ Titulo.xlj. Como fizierõ los de guoa pazes cõ Alon
so de alburquerque z fue entrada la ciudad.
Ds de goa visto el daño q̃ declaradamiēte re
cibia otro dia dos delos mas hõrrados mo/
ros o infieles vinierõ a pedir pazes al capitã

mayor alos q̃les relpõdio no ser su volũtad:si el reyno
z ciudad de Buoa no le era entregado qual lo hauia ça
bayo rey della possydo:z le hauia de dar las naos que
los rumes hauian fecho para yr contra ellos z dozien/
tos rumes que en la ciudad estauan:donde no que a nin
guno dellos daria vida z mandaria abrasar toda la ciu
dad:casas gentes z tierra sin misericordia. En lo qual
vinieron los moros dandole las llaues dela fortaleza
E el capitan Alõso de alburq̃rq̃ salio en tierra podero/
samente con las vanderas z estandartes de Portogal
cõ sonidos regozijados de atanales z trompetas vierõ
las fortalezas z castillos en las quales dexaron gente: z
otra fortaleza edifico Alõso de alburq̃rque en aq̃lla ciu
dad:z dela mudança delos manjares morieron quarẽ
ta hõbres delos xpianos:tomaron delos rumes caua/
llos muchos:artilleria:armas de malla z de sierro:vna
casa de flechas:z poluora:azeyte:pescado: cobre:z pla
ta z otras cosas de rico valor. Sabido por el çoltan ça/
bayn sijo del rey çabayo ayunto grandes gentes de gue
rra z vino cõtra los xpianos:z este rey de goa hauian se
ydo del rey de aquen z çabayo su vassallo se hauia leuan
tado cõtra el. E viendo todas las cosas como passauan
en goa:sue auisado el rey d aquen z embio luego vn grã
capitã q̃ se dezia Camalcã z al fijo d el rey çabayo cõ grã
exercito q̃ serian sesenta mill hõbres de pelea: mas de di
ez mill de cauallo:z ochocientos espingarderos:Assen
taron pues sus tiendas fronteras de vn passo en q̃ esta/
uan por capitã garcia de sosa q̃ con su industria z essuer/
ço los sizo leuantar de alli z passarse a otra parte por mi
edo q̃ auia ã dela artilleria z del logar.biẽ mostro z dio
a entender los de sosa venir dela real casta de portogal
como es verdad z sus armas que son las quinas z cru/

çadas lunas de ſcubzen con la ql vitozia ſin detenimiēto
ſalieron en tierra faſta nueue o diez delos xpianos tras
los infieles:z los otros de Garcia de ſoſa veniā époſõ
llos q̃ poz los cozrientes no deſembarcaron tan pzeſto
como era razon para ſocozrer alos delanteros delos q̃
les diez fue Martin fernandez de figueroa que esfozça
da z animoſamēte peleando:matando z firiendo en los
contrarios le dieron cõ vna flecha que le rompio el boz
de del capacete z le traſpaſſo el roſtro de parte a parte la
qual tomo poz el fierro z la ſaco del roſtro .Acabada de
ſacar le dierõ vna pedzada en la pierna z otra enel capa
cete muy cruel que ayna arrodillara ſi el grande z valiẽ
te eſfuerço que leuaua poz eſcudo no le ſocozriera haſta
que alos bateles llegaron z ſocozridos fueron. Mata
rõ alli vn xpiano z firierõ a todos aq̃llos q̃ aſſi acometi
eron tan gran fazaña de animo a q̃ no diez po ciento no
fizierā cara. z aſſi de aq̃lla vez ſe voluierõ ala fortaleza cũ
los vateles z los feridos fuerõ bien curados.

¶Titulo.xlij.Como ouo Grãdes batallas lides z rezi
as pelcas entre los xpianos z infieles.

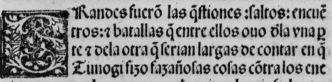

Randes fuerõ las q̃ſtiones :ſaltos: encuẽ
tros:z batallas q̃ entre ellos ouo õla vna p
te z dela otra q̃ ſerian largas de contar en q̃
Timogi fizo fazañoſas coſas cõtra los ene
migos aun que los mozos quel capitan bauia fecho de
gente le fueron traydozes z ſe paſſaron alos contrarios
del capitan mayoz z aun muchos delos de Timogi fue
rõ contra ſu ſeñoz:enel qual comedio los muchoseñemi
gos quiſieron entrar en tierra do fueron deſbaratados
z muchos muertos aſſi que ſe lançauan fuyẽdo enl mar

do se asogauan otros muertos. Los christianos queda
o con gloriosa vitoria. Jorge de acuña al qual matarõ
alguna gente: garcia de sosa z Timogi fizieron maraui/
llosos vencimientos en que fueran bien empleados los
ringlones d amadis que ocupã loozes que muchos me
rescieron. Despues delo qual ydo garcia de sosa a bene
steri desendiendo z amparando el passo esforçadamen
te le fue mucha de su gente muerta z dsbaratada el fue se
rido z vn hermano suyo muerto digno de no ser puesto
en oluido segun desendia alos insieles la entrada Gar
cia de sosa ouo de perescer en vn peligroso vatel que las
aguas leuaron a puerto de sus enemigos: po como di/
os remedia en las necessidades prestamente: remando
con la mas fuerça que los christianos pudieron se salua
ron por el passo que francisco pereyra guardaua. Dize
figueroa que parescia el dia del juyzio segun las cosas q̃
auenieron. E alas casas de benesteri abrasaron los insi
eles. por lo qual dõ antonio q̃ en las galeras estaua fue
forçado recogerse ala fortaleza z vna nao suya q̃ se llama
ua la espera metio so la agua cõ toda la artilleria q̃ dspu
es sacaron los moros. E el capitã mayor embio vna na
ue por mantenimientos la qual al salir dela barra se per
dio.

C Titulo. xliij. Como los moros embiauan los christ
anos renegados alos christianos por les hazer enojo

A causa delas tã rezias batallas fue q̃ hauia
fecho el Capitan mayor seys mill moros de
pelea soldados de Goa: E hizieron trayciõ
por lo qual todos daños q̃ alli se recrescierõ
hauidos muchos encuentros se cansarõ: assaz vezes los
moros en sus vateles venian ala orilla del rio faziẽdo se/

ñ ales de paz a las vezes por rescatar moros τ otras por
que viessen los Christianos alos renegados como los
trayan a cauallo con pajes τ moços despuelas τ atauia/
dos De que gran pesar hauia Alonso de Alburqrque
τ su gente Vn dia los moros vinieron ala orilla del rio
con camisas blancas faziendo señales que los christia/
nos viniessen conellos seguramente a fablar τ el capitã
mayor embio alla vn vatel de que yua por capitan Johã
Muñez E estando quasi juntos hablo vn renegado a/
los christianos preguntando como estauan τ les hauia
sucedido en aquellos trances Johan Muñez le interro
go que quien era El renegado replico que se llamaua ju
an deras fisico del capitan mayor Al qual Johan nuñez
haziendo de ojo que armassen vn tiro de espingarda di/
ro que porque se hauia ydo alos infieles τ hauia renega
do Estando en palabras diole por meytad del coraçon
la espingarda que cayo renegadamente muerto τ duro
aun tres dias po acabo dellos malauenturadamente fe
nescio E vuelto Johan nuñez buen capitã τ catholico
varon lo couto al capitan mayor el qual fizo dar al espin
gardero cinquenta cruzados.

¶ Titulo. rliiij. Como los moros quisieron combatir
las naos christianas τ mataron a dõ Antonio sobrino
dl capitan.

Os infieles sabiendo la mucha flaqueza q̃
christianos hauia de gente τ socorro excep/
to el del cielo. mando Abdalcã cõbatir las na
os christianas de q̃ Alonso d alburq̃rq̃ fue
auisado fue contra las galeras τ vateles q̃ el capitã ma
yor embio por tentarlos τ los q̃ en su amparo vinieron
gran lisa τ pelea. assi de artilleria como de personas. Si
mõ de andrada. τ fernan perez su hermano cõ ocho ca

uallos en vna galera delos enemigos saltarõ do essuer·
ço z sangrientas espadas era restigos de sus virtuosas
obras z claras fazañas aql dia fue serido el bué cauallo
dõ Antonio sobrino del capitan mayor muy essorçador
catholico q seys dias despues murio siedo causa d assaz
tristeza|porq entre las muchas virtudes q tenia era bié
qsto|Murio gran gente delos contrarios entre los q
les vn sobrino de melcan desesperadamente ouo z dos
capitanes los mejores de su hueste,

C Titulo.xlv.Como se partio de Guoa a cananor z d
los capitanes z gente de portogal z de sus mudãças.

Nel mes d agosto era qndo el capitã mayor
viendo la triste vida q en guoa faziã salio dl
rio pa cananor a puecrse de viãdas q no te
niã z aũ q los moros o infieles:aũ q diga al
gũas vezes moros entiendése gentiles|o infieles|do es
ta ya declarado.qsierõ resistir z dsbaratar los xpianos
en la salida no pudierõ|dõde solo vn xpiano murio|fue
rõ camino la via d ãgeduia|vierõ venir a ellos doze na
os qtro yuã a melaca|ocho yuã ala india| z vn nauio dl
marischal|capitã dlas ocho era gõçalo d seqra las qles
hauiã d voluer en portogal cõ especieria.assi q conosci
dos ouierõ mucho plazer z fuerõ a cananor ay vinierõ
gõçalo de seqra z duarte de lemos con otras qtro naos
el ql venia de ormuz|las qles sabiédo q hauia guerra cõ
tra el rey de cochin fuerõ alo sauorescer cõtra el principe
sijo de su hermana|que alla hereda|z porq el se hauia de
entrar en la cueua do el rey su antecessor hauia muerto z
el no qria qs vna costũbre q alla teniã q no reyna mas el
rey de qnto viue el otro rey q esta é la cueua z muerto ha
de entrar el sucessor enella z el sobrino heredar. alli fue d
sbaratado el pncipe z le tomarõ el galeon en q yua z aun

otro tãto fizierã a el si no eſtuuiera pſto en trřa de alli de
termino Aloſo de alburãrq̃ yr pa Goa z mãdo q̃ todo
bõbze ſe rccogieſſe alas naos dado caſo q̃ tuuieſſen licẽ/
cia de ſe yr pa poztogal ya en aq̃l año:determinarõ algu
nos õ ſe aſconder z no yr maſen ſu cõpañia pues hauiã
viſto a guoa z eſtauayan ſartos della mayozmẽte q̃ s no
fuerõ conel poz eſpacio mas de tres años hauiã ydo ya
ſiete z algũos õllos nueue q̃ eſtauã en las indias pueſta
ar tablero la vida cada rato z momẽto como baueys vi/
ſto .vno delos q̃ cõ mucha cauſa ſe q̃darõ fue martin fer
nandez figueroa q̃ marauilloſo exẽplo õ bõdad dzo en
aq̃llas ptes z trazo a eſtas. de alli fue prido el capitã ma
yoz pa guoa:a dõde llegando algũos fuerõ mal feridos
z cõ valietes z magnanimas fuerças de diego mẽdez de
vaſtõcelos capitã mayoz pa melaca:z de manuel õla cer
da del linaje delos reyes de frãcia:z de Simõ de ãdzada
z ferñaperez ſu hřo juntamẽte cõ la venturoſa muerte
del caualſo dõ hieronimo capitã de veynte z cinco xpia/
nos ſe tomo z triũpho goa poderoſamente.en los infie
les fue tal el eſtrago q̃ no hay papel al pſente prõpto pa
tã largamẽte eſcrebir:delo q̃l todo auiſo poz vna caraue
la q̃ ẽbio a cananoz a duarte de lemos,q̃ tenia ſiete naos
cargadas pa poztogal en q̃ trazo faſta liſbona a figue
roa z a otros cauallos zhõbzes de biẽ.pueſto q̃ otra co
ſa le ẽbiara rogar el capitã mayoz.

CTitu.xlvj.Delas coſas que en Melaca hauia.

Datro naos hauia el rey de poztogal ẽbia
do a deſcobzir clauo:ruybarbo zotra eſpeci
eria en las q̃les poz capitã yua diego de ſeq̃
ra z llego do el biſrey eſtaua quedo Gar
cia de ſoſa capitã en vn buen nauio ẽbio fuerõ a melaca
poz el cabo de comerin biẽ edificado de tẽplos z muros

d marmoz cõ hystozias õ bulto muy ricas. figueroa di
ze q̃ son mejozes q̃ en roma. po como los romanos yo
aya ystio creo no las excedera las õ comarin.hay alli vn
tẽplo enel q̃l tal costũbze guardã q̃ el q̃ enel entra no ha
de comer poz tres dias q̃ del saliere:es muy rico tẽplo õ
grãdes rẽtas q̃ da de comer a masõ cinco mill virgines
q̃ seyendo de hedad casan z las q̃ no q̃rẽ ser casadas pu
eden alli estar pa siempze como beatas. en aq̃lla trr̃a sõ
ydolatras:hay bzamenes q̃ duermẽ cõ las reynas aũ q̃
no q̃era su marido el rey. poz lo q̃l el rey seluio bzamene
pozq̃ cõ muger de vno otro no puede yazer:es tierra de
muchos mantenimientos.excepto de trigo que no se da
alli. yendo pues a melaca passarõ poz ceylan do nasce la
canela como assaz dixi:z poz çamatoza:do nasce la pimiẽ
ta:los dineros de cuya trr̃a son pimiẽta z medidas õlla
es õ muchas riq̃zas z piedzas pciosas:en la q̃l ysla ouo
pazes entre el rey della z los xpianos.z de alli ptierõ pa
melaca dexãdo ala mano siniestra cõtra el noote ciertas
yslas en las q̃les vnos a otros se comẽ:su mãjar no es si
no carne humana :apoztarõ a melaca distãte de cochin
q̃trocientas leguas poco mas o menos ysla muy rica z
habundosa assaz do cõtratarõ pazes.el clauo viene alli
de Maluco que lo traen los Chines gente cercana de
Melaca:Cuyo calçado son botas de cuero:Blancos
como chzistianos:Alo que comen no llegan con las ma
nos:Excepto con vnos palos de muy olozosa madera
Beben poz escudillas muy limpias que ellos dizen poz
mas lindas que de Cristal:Las quales son dozadas z
de diuersas colozes.En la ysla de Melaca hay gentes
de diuersas tierras poz las muchas mercancias cõ que
tratan:sus faciones anchas:blancas:como las de An
tilla del xpianissimo z mas que poderoso rey de castilla:

sus armas son de fierro:los fierros delas lãças ondea/
dos z en forma de lenguas tiran flechas cõ zebratanas.
los xpianos estouierõ alli algunos dias puexdos d suf
mercacias cõfiado en la paz dlos enemigos:la ql no gu
ardarõ:ante matarõ muchos z fuerõ los portuguefes
desbaratados z a sus bateles recogidos se pticron al ca
bo de camarin en la ql cargaua diego de seçra llegando
av cõ tres naos q otras dos pescierõ:vna q metierõ fo
la agua z otra en vna obscura noche e la ysla poluozeda
se robzo:delas qles la gẽte se saluo.d alli fuerõ dos capi
tanes e dos naos a cochin:Garcia d sofa z hieronimo
de texeda:q del capitã mayor fuerõ biẽ recibidos z trata
dos fasta q voluierõ en portogal. E diego de fequera fe
partio para Lisbona.

℄Titulo.xlvij.Delos elephantes indios z sus differẽ
cias z propriedades.

Oenta figueroa testigo de vista las cõdicio
nes pcios z estima delos elephãtes dlas indi
as q qero sepays en las indias d persia z ara
bin hay muchos dellos domesticos mãsos z
tratables z de mucho trabajo cuyo pcio es dos mill du
cados son muchos dellos tan prudẽtes animales q no
les falta de mas de aia racional sino la fabla:pa tener en
tẽdimiẽto de fabios varones:entiẽdẽ la légua z voz in/
dia z lo q les mãdã fazer el q va en cima el pone en execu
ciõ cõ su trõpa z faze tã cuerdamẽte qnto otro aiai pudi
efse echar z leuãtar facilmẽte:tiene coyunturas como o/
tros animales z fuerça de ochenta hõbzes:facã bateles
del mar bõbardas:o masteles mejor q cient hõbzes po/
niendo todas sus mayores fuerças enello. en guerras
arman sobze ellos castillos en q guan seys o siete ╌╌ de
ros:dos espadas le atan en los cuernos cõ que fazẽ cru

damête ado le mandan. aun que cient cuchilladas enlas
piernas vn elephante resciba no cae ni se jarreta por te
ner grâdes carnes enellas: es el mayor animal del mun/
do para sobir enel mandandogelo inclina las piernas
traseras: su color es d ceniza: tiene poco pelo: las orejas
como adargas: los ojos chicos como de vn puerco: po
co pescueço: sus dientes son cuernos aun q salen por la
boca nascientes dela cabeça son huecos hasta el medio
delos quales es el marfil. La cola del elephante como d
puerco los pies anchos z redôdos como de buey: son
pesados z no ligeros: su mantenimiêto es arroz cozido
con mâteca hojas de palmas z yeruos: su ayuntamien
to como de varon a muger: tienê gran acuerdo o memo
ria delo q se faze muestra gozo o tristeza. En goa hay ti
gres: puercos môteses. leones: ûças: venados: z otras
animales q españa ôssea criar. En cochin hay culebras
z tienê vn capillo delantelos ojos z quando alçan el ca
pillo muestran gesto como de muger en la ql figura affir
man auer tentado el diablo enemigo de natura humina
a Eua. tienê en muchos reynos delas indias tal costû/
bre si alguno acreedor encuêtra el deudor lleua vn ramo
en la mano verde z fazele vn circulo al rededor enel qual
pone el ramo verde z assi so grandes penas no puede el
deudor salir de alli sin le pagar lo q le deue o concertarse
conel acreedor. en otras partes z prouincias: las muge
res tienen quantos maridos quieren: z en otras cosen
las naturas alas niñas en nasciendo fasta ser para casar
vna delas quales traxo Tristan de acuña ala Reyna de
Portogal lo qual se deuia guardar en todas partes si a
ellas no les fiziesse agrauio porque estuuiessen mas se
guras sus honrras.

C Titu. xlviij. dla venida d duarte d lemos en portogal.

Espues q̃ Duarte d'lemos cargo síte naos
que leuauan vn martes onze de Deziembze
de mill z quinientos z onze años del nasci/
miẽto de nṙo saluadoz Jesu xp̃o: partierõ
de Cananoz z poz la costa a Angediua z otros logares
en los quales z su venida ouo muchos encuentros z re
zios passos: fuerõ poz la ysla dlos açozes: z poz otra lla
mada de las flozes: fuerõ ala tercera que della dista cin/
quenta leguas alli ancozando vieron las otras naos q̃
de india venian los quales fueron bien recibidos z con
taron como hauiendo salido a proueerse de agua junto
al cabo de buena esperança en la agua de saldaña vierõ
muchas cabeças de muertos sepolturas pedaços d' ve
stidos z conoscieron ser gente del Visrey cuya cabeça z
cuerpo fallaron cauando en vna sepultura o foya q̃ poz
almoada vna piedza tenia lo que no hauia en otras que
bien conoscieron en los dientes z faciones z recogiẽdo
se a sus naos supieron o hauiã sabido como los negros
de aqlla tierra hauiã muerto al Visrey: a Gorge barre
to: z Pero barrero: Manuel telles: Antonio de ocãpo
Martin coello: z Lorenço de bzito: z otros muchos q̃
fuerõ. lx. psonas las mas catholicas: valiẽtes generosos
z esforçadas de portogal que cõ muerte de sus cuerpos
martyres. Inmortales fiziero sus animas. Desto fuerõ
los xp̃ianos muy pesantes z marauillados sabiẽdo los
muertos z pocos q̃ q̃daron con las naos d'aquellos q̃
eran ydos a portugal. E luego vierõ venir las naos de
duarte de lemos que se quedaran a tras delas de su cõ
pañia con las tempestades del cabo de buena esperan/
ça de que todos fueron muy cõtentos z alegres conui/
nando ya juntos bieron tierra de portogal a: xxiiij: dias
de janio vispera de sant Juan. año del señoz de mill z qui

nientos τ onze entrando en Lißbona a tres dias de Ju
lio miercoles salieron en tierra con harto desseo della:
La nao de gonçalo de sequera deziã auerse perdido en
la tormenta del cabo de buena esperança que otro año
ante en aquel viaje perescieron tres naos cuyos nõbres
erã sant Gabriel: τ sant Raphael: τ la india curo Capi
tan fue el honrrado varõ fernan suarech.

Titulo.ji.Del plazer que ouieron en Portogal con
la venida delas naos delas Indias.

Rande fue el plazer que enel puerto τ ẽ la
tierra τ corte del rey de portogal ouo por la
venida delas naos a cuyos capitanes τ gen
tes el rey don Manuel remunero sus traba
jos τ cuytas passadas enel viaje delas indias τ de lißbo
na figueroa se partio para Salamanca su patria τ na
tural habitaciõ a ruego ð Luys godinez esposo ð doña
Catalina de cardenas su hermana que le escribio.trazo
vn libro excelente como enel prohẽnio dize τ eu forma
delo que enesta hystoria haueys conoscido por theorica
quel vio por experiencia:lo qual todo aprueuan los mu
chos testigos que de vista hay assi en Portogal como
en toda españa.

Deo gracias.

fue impressa la presente obra en la muy no
ble τ leal ciudad de Salamãca en casa de
micer Lorẽço de leõ de dei. Acauose
primero dia de Setiempre ð
M.ð.xij. años.

Appendix

Portuguese Historians and the *Conquista*

Titles of the *Conquista*	Castanheda, *Historia*	Barros, *Asia*	Góis, *Chronica*	Correia, *Lendas*
I-III	Book I	Década I, books i-vii	Part I	Book I (through 1504)
IV*	II, 1	I, viii, 3; ix, 6	II, 1-2	I, Almeida, 1505, 1
V	II, 10	I, ix, 6	II, 9	I, Almeida, 1505, 1, 5
VI	II, 10	I, ix, 6	II, 9	I, Almeida, 1505, 5
VII	II, 10	I, ix, 6	II, 9	I, Almeida, 1505, 5
VIII	II, 10, 11	I, ix, 6	II, 9	I, Almeida, 1505, 5
IX	II, 11	I, x, 1	II, 9	I, Almeida, 1505, 5
X	II, 11	I, x, 2	II, 9	I, Almeida, 1505, 5

*Each entry indicates the chapters of the histories which deal with matters discussed in the corresponding title of the *Conquista*. In Castanheda, *read* book II, chapter 1; Barros, first decade, book eight, chapter 3; Góis, part II, chapters 1 and 2; and Correia, book I, Armada de Francisco de Almeida, anno 1505, chapter 1.

Titles of the *Conquista*	Castanheda, *Historia*	Barros, *Asia*	Góis, *Chronica*	Correia, *Lendas*
XI	II, 1-9	I, viii, 1-8	II, 2-3	I, Almeida, 1505, 2, 4
XII	II, 29	I, x, 3	II, 9	I, Almeida, 1505, 5
XIII	II, 29	I, x, 3	II, 9	I, Almeida, 1505, 5
XIV	II, 29	I, x, 3	II, 9	I, Almeida, 1505, 5
XV	II, 29	II, i, 6	II, 9	I, Armada sem Capitão-Mor, 1507, 1
XVI	II, 29	II, i, 6	II, 14	I, Armada sem Capitão-Mor, 1507, 1
XVII	II, 29	II, i, 6	II, 14	I, Armada sem Capitão-Mor, 1507, 1
XVIII	II, 29, 44, 71	II, i, 6	II, 14	I, Armada sem Capitão-Mor, 1507, 1
XIX	II, 71, 84	II, i, 6	II, 14, 21	I, Armada sem Capitão-Mor, 1507, 1
XX	II, 90	II, i, 6	II, 14, 21	I, Armada sem Capitão-Mor, 1507, 1
XXI	II, 84	II, i, 6	II, 21	I, Armada sem Capitão-Mor, 1507, 1
XXII	II, 8-9, 12-26, 42-52, 65	I, viii, 9-10; ix, 4-5; x, 4-6; II, i, 4-6	II, 4-8, 11-12, 15-17, 24	I, Almeida, 1505, 6-19; I, Tristão da Cunha, 1506, 6-7
XXIII	II, 84-85	II, iii, 2	II, 24, 36	I, Armada sem Capitão-Mor, 1507, 9

Titles of the *Conquista*	Castanheda, *Historia*	Barros, *Asia*	Góis, *Chronica*	Correia, *Lendas*
XXIV	II, 37-38	II, i, 2	II, 22	I, Tristão da Cunha, 1506, 1-3
XXV	II, 84-85	II, iii, 2	II, 36	I, Armada sem Capitão-Mor, 1507, 9
XXVI	II, 39	II, i, 3	II, 22	I, Tristão da Cunha, 1506, 3
XXVII	II, 53-57	II, iii, 1	II, 31	I, Armada sem Capitão-Mor, 1507, 2-9
XXVIII	II, 53-57	II, ii, 1-2	II, 31	I, Armada sem Capitão-Mor, 1507, 2-9
XXIX	II, 58	II, ii, 1-2	II, 32	I, Armada sem Capitão-Mor, 1507, 2-9
XXX	II, 59-61	II, ii, 3	II, 33	I, Armada sem Capitão-Mor, 1507, 2-9
XXXI	II, 62-74, 85-89	II, ii, 4-5; iii, 1-2	II, 33-36	I, Armada sem Capitão-Mor, 1507, 2-9
XXXII	II, 62-74, 85-89	II, ii, 4-5; iii, 1-2	II, 33-36	I, Armada sem Capitão-Mor, 1507, 2-10
XXXIII	II, 75-82	II, ii, 6-9; iii, 1	II, 25-26	I, Tristão da Cunha, 1507, 8-17
XXXIV	II, 95	II, iii, 3-4	II, 37-39	I, D. Francisco Visorey, 1508, 3-4
XXXV	II, 96	II, iii, 3-4	II, 37-39	I, D. Francisco Visorey, 1508, 3-4
XXXVI	II, 97	II, iii, 4	II, 40	I, D. Francisco Visorey, 1508, 3-4
XXXVII	II, 98-100	II, iii, 5-6	II, 40	I, D. Francisco Visorey, 1508, 3-4

Titles of the *Conquista*	Castanheda, *Historia*	Barros, *Asia*	Góis, *Chronica*	Correia, *Lendas*
XXXVIII	II, 101-121	II, iii, 7-9	II, 41	I, D. Francisco Visorey, 1508, 3-7
XXXIX	III, 1-4	II, iv, 1	II, 41, 43	II, A. Albuquerque, 1-3
XL	III, 1-4	II, iv, 1	II, 41, 43	II, A. Albuquerque, 1-3
XLI	III, 7-30	II, iv, 5; v, 1-7	III, 3-7	II, A. Albuquerque, 6-17
XLII	III, 7-30	II, v, 1-7	III, 3-7	II, A. Albuquerque, 6-17
XLIII	III, 7-30	II, v, 1-7	III, 3-7	II, A. Albuquerque, 6-17
XLIV	III, 31-32	II, v, 1-7	III, 3-7	II, A. Albuquerque, 6-17
XLV	III, 32	II, v, 1-7	III, 3-7	II, A. Albuquerque, 6-17
XLVI	III, 33-35	II, v, 8	III, 10-11	II, Gonçalo Sequeira, 1510, 18-20
XLVII	II, 110-116	II, iv, 2-4	III, 1-2	II, A. Albuquerque, 2-5
XLVIII	.... Elephant description, and so on			
XLIX	II, 122; III, 45	II, iii, 9	II, 44; III, 15	I, Armada de Jorge Aguiar, 1508, 7; II, Gonçalo Sequeira, 1510, 18
L	.... No mention of Figueroa's return			

Selected Bibliography

Acuña, Hernando de. *Varias Poesías,* ed. Antonio Vilanova. Barcelona: Clásicos Castellanos, 1954.

Agnew, S. *See* Pollock, N. C.

Aguado Bleye, Pedro. *Manual de historia de España.* 3 vols. Madrid: Espasa-Calpe, 1954.

Ajo G., Carlos María, y Sainz de Zúñiga. *Historia de las universidades hispánicas.* 3 vols. Madrid: Centro de estudios e investigaciones "Alonso de Madrigal," 1957.

Albuquerque, Afonso de. *Cartas de Affonso de Albuquerque.* 6 vols. Lisbon, 1884-1915.

Albuquerque, Braz de. *The Commentaries of the Great Afonso Dalboquerque.* 4 vols. London, 1875-1884.

Álvares, Father Francisco. *The Prester John of the Indies . . . The Translation of Lord Stanley of Alderley (1881) revised and edited with additional material by C. F. Beckingham and G. W. B. Huntingford.* 2 vols., paged continuously. Cambridge: Hakluyt Society, 1961.

Amadís de Gaula, ed. E. B. Place. 2 vols. Madrid: Consejo Superior de Investigaciones Científicas, 1959-1962.

Amador de los Ríos, Rodrigo. *España, sus monumentos y artes, su naturaleza e historia: Murcia y Albacete.* Barcelona, 1889.

Anghiera, Pietro Martire D'. *P. Martyris ab angleria Mediolanensi. Opera. Legatio babilonica* [.] *Occeanea decas. Poemata.* Seville: Jacobo Cromberger, April 1511.

———*De orbe nouo Decades,* ed. Antonio de Nebrija. Alcalá: Arnaldo Guillelmo, November 1516.

———*De Orbe Novo. The Eight Decades of Peter Martyr D'Anghera,* tr. F. A. MacNutt. 2 vols. New York, 1912.

Antonio, Nicolás. *Bibliotheca Hispana sive Hispanorum.* 2 vols. Rome, 1672.

———*Bibliotheca Hispana Nova.* 2 vols. Madrid, 1788.

Arbolí y Faraudo, Servando, Simón de la Rosa y López, *et al. Biblioteca*

Colombina: Catálogo de sus libros impresos. 7 vols. Seville and Madrid, 1888-1948.

Axelson, Eric. *South-East Africa 1488-1530.* London, 1940.

Barbosa, Duarte. *The Book of Duarte Barbosa,* ed. M. L. Dames. 2 vols. London, 1918-1921.

Barros, João de. *Asia de Ioam de Barros. dos feitos que os Portugueses fizeram no descobrimento & conquista dos mares & terras do Oriente.* Lisbon, 1552-1553.

————*Crónica do emperador Clarimundo donde os Reys de Portugal descendem . . . ,* ed. M. Braga. 3 vols. Lisbon, 1953.

Bell, Aubrey F. G. *Gaspar Corrêa.* Oxford, 1924.

Benítez Claros, Rafael, ed. *Libro de las cosas maravillosas de Marco Polo.* Madrid: Sociedad de Bibliófilos Españoles, 1947.

Boléo, Oliveira. *Apontamentos para uma geografia física de Goa.* Lisbon: Agênica Geral do Ultramar, 1955.

Boxer, Charles R. *Four Centuries of Portuguese Expansion, 1415-1825: A Succinct Survey.* Johannesburg: Witwatersrand University Press, 1961.

————*Race Relations in the Portuguese Colonial Empire, 1415-1825.* Oxford: Clarendon Press, 1963.

————ed. *The Tragic History of the Sea, 1589-1622.* Cambridge: Hakluyt Society, 1959.

————"Three Historians of Portuguese Asia (Barros, Couto and Bocarro)," *Boletim do Instituto Português de Hong Kong,* I (1948), 15-44.

Brunet, Jacques-Charles. *Manuel du libraire et de l'amateur de livres,* 5th ed. 8 vols. Paris, 1860-1880.

Burger, Konrad. *Die Drucker und Verleger in Spanien und Portugal von 1501-1536.* Leipzig, 1913.

Cadalso, José. *Cartas marruecas.* Madrid, 1935.

Camões, Luis de. *Os Lusiadas.* "Ee edition," Lisbon, 1572.

————*The Lusiads of Luiz de Camões,* tr. L. Bacon. New York: Hispanic Society of America, 1950.

Cardozo, Manoel. "The Idea of History in the Portuguese Chronicles of the Age of Discovery," *Catholic Historical Review,* XLIX (1963), 1-19.

Caro Baroja, Julio. *Los judíos en la España moderna y contemporánea.* 3 vols. Madrid: Ed. Arión, 1961.

Castañeda, Vicente, y Amalio Huarte. *Nueva colección de pliegos sueltos.* Madrid, 1933.

Castanheda. *See* Lopes de Castanheda, Fernão.

Catalogue de la bibliothèque de M. Fernando Palha. 4 vols. Lisbon, 1896.

Catalogue of the Library of Ferdinand Columbus: Reproduced in facsimile from the Unique Manuscript in the Columbine Library of Seville by Archer M. Huntington . . . New York, 1905.

The Catholic Encyclopedia. 16 vols. New York, 1907-1912.

Clavijo, Ruy González de. *Embajada a Tamorlán,* ed. F. López Estrada. Madrid: Consejo Superior de Investigaciones Científicas, 1943.

Collingwood, Robin G. *The Idea of History.* Oxford: Oxford University Press, 1962.

Correia, Gaspar. *Lendas da India.* 4 vols. Lisbon, 1858-1866.

Cortesão, Armando. *Portugaliae monvmenta cartographica.* 6 vols. Lisbon, 1960.

Couto, Diogo do. *O Soldado Prático,* ed. M. Rodrigues Lapa. Lisbon, 1937.

Croce, Benedetto. *History, its Theory and Practice,* tr. D. Ainslie. New York: Russell and Russell, 1960.

Crone, G. R., tr. and ed. *The Voyages of Cadamosto and Other Documents on Western Africa in the Second Half of the Fifteenth Century.* London, 1937.

Davenport, Frances G., ed. *European Treaties Bearing on the History of the United States and its Dependencies to 1648.* Washington, 1917.

Díaz del Castillo, Bernal. *Historia verdadera de la conquista de la Nueva España.* Mexico: Ed. Porrúa, 1964.

Díez de Games, Gutierre. *El Victorial. Crónica de Don Pero Niño, Conde de Buelna, por su alférez Gutierre Díez de Games,* ed. J. de la Mata Carriazo, Madrid, 1940.

Documentos referentes a las relaciones con Portugal durante el reinado de los Reyes Católicos, ed. A. de la Torre y L. Suárez Fernández. 3 vols. Valladolid: Biblioteca "Reyes Católicos," 1958-1963.

Documents on the Portuguese in Mozambique and Central Africa, 1497-1840, ed. National Archives of Rhodesia and Nyasaland, and Centro

de Estudos Históricos Ultramarinos Lisboa. 2 vols. Lisbon, 1962-1963.

Duffy, James. *Shipwreck and Empire: Being an Account of Portuguese Maritime Disasters in a Century of Decline.* Cambridge, Mass.: Harvard University Press, 1955.

Enciclopedia Universal Ilustrada Europeo Americana, i.e. "Espasa-Calpe." 70 vols. Madrid, 1907-1930.

Esperabé Arteaga, Enrique. *Historia de la Universidad de Salamanca.* 2 vols. Salamanca, 1914.

Esteves Pereira, Francisco Maria, ed. *Marco Paulo . . . conforme a impressão de Valentim Fernandes, feita em Lisboa em 1502.* Lisbon, 1922.

Faria e Sousa, Manuel. *Asia Portuguesa.* 3 vols. Lisbon, 1666-1675.

Ferguson, D. *The Discovery of Ceylon by the Portuguese in 1506.* Colombo, 1908.

Fernandes, Valentim, ed. *Marco paulo. Ho liuro de Nycolao veneto. O trallado da carta de huum genoues das ditas terras.* Lisbon: Valentim Fernandes, 1502.

Fernández de Enciso, Martín. *Suma de geographia que trata de todas las partidas & prouincias del mundo: en especial delas indias . . .* Seville: Jacobo Cromberger, 1519.

Fernández de Navarrete, Martín. *Colección de los viages y descubrimientos que hicieron por mar los españoles desde fines del siglo XV . . .* 5 vols. Madrid, 1825-1837.

Fernández de Santaella, Rodrigo, ed. *Cosmographia breue introductoria enel libro de Marco paulo. El libro del famoso Marco paulo veneciano . . . Con otro tratado de micer Pogio florentino.* Seville: Stanislaus Polonus and Jacobo Cromberger, May 28, 1503.

Ferrand, Gabriel. "Le pilote arabe de Vasco da Gama et les instructions nautiques des arabes au xvᵉ siècle," *Anales de Geographie,* XXXI (1922), 289-307.

Freeman-Grenville, G. S. P., ed. *The East African Coast: Select Documents from the first to the earlier nineteenth century.* Oxford: Clarendon Press, 1962.

Gallardo, Bartolomé José. *Ensayo de una Biblioteca Española de libros raros y curiosos.* 4 vols. Madrid, 1863-1889.

Galvão. Antonio. *Tratado dos descobrimentos,* ed. Visconde de Lagoa

and E. Sanceau. 3rd ed., Porto: Biblioteca histórica de Portugal e Brasil, 1944.

García Carraffa, Alberto y Arturo. *Diccionario heráldico y genealógico de apellidos españoles y americanos.* 88 vols. Madrid, 1920-1963.

Góis, Damião de. *Chronica del rei don Manuel.* Lisbon, 1556.

Gómez de Santisteban. *Libro del Infante Don Pedro de Portugal. Publicado segundo as mais antigas edições por Francis M. Rogers.* Lisbon: Fundação Calouste Gulbenkian, 1962.

Hammond, Lincoln D., ed. *Travelers in Disguise: Narratives of Eastern Travel by Poggio Bracciolini and Ludovico de Varthema.* Cambridge, Mass.: Harvard University Press, 1963.

Hart, Henry H. *Luis de Camöens and the Epic of the Lusiads.* Norman: University of Oklahoma Press, 1962.

———*Sea Road to the Indies.* New York: Macmillan, 1950.

———*Venetian Adventurer. The Life and Times of Marco Polo.* Stanford: Stanford University Press, 1942.

Hay, Rupert. *The Persian Gulf States.* Washington: Middle East Institute, 1959.

Hazañas y la Rua, Joaquín. *Maese Rodrigo, 1444-1509.* Seville, 1909.

Hennings, Johann C. *Bibliotheca seu Notitia librorum rariorum.* Kiel, 1766.

Heyd, Wilhelm von. *Histoire du commerce du Levant au moyen-âge.* 2 vols. Leipzig, 1885-1886.

Huarte, Amalio. *See* Castañeda, Vicente.

Hunter, William W. *The Imperial Gazetteer of India.* 26 vols. London, 1907-1909.

Koenig, W. F. "Ernesto and Eugenio do Canto, A Contribution to Azorean Bio-bibliography," *Library Quarterly of Chicago,* IV (1934), 253-264.

Lach, Donald F. *Asia in the Making of Europe. Volume I: The Century of Discovery.* 2 books, numbered consecutively. Chicago: University of Chicago Press, 1965.

La Fuente, Vicente de. *Historia de las Universidades, Colegios y Demas Establecimientos de Enseñanza en España.* 4 vols. Madrid, 1884.

Lagoa, J. A. de Mascarenhas Judice. *Grandes e humildes na epopeia portuguesa do Oriente (séculos XV, XVI e XVII) pelo visconde de Lagôa.* Lisbon, 1942-1947.

Lapesa, Rafael. *La obra literaria del Marqués de Santillana*. Madrid: Insula, 1957.

———"Los *Proverbios* de Santillana: Contribución al estudio de sus fuentes," *Hispanófila*, No. 1 (Sept. 1957), 5-19.

León Pinelo, Antonio de. *Epitome de la Biblioteca Oriental i Occidental Nautica i Geografica*. Madrid, 1629. 2d ed. 3 vols. whose columns are numbered continuously. Madrid, 1737-1738.

Leonard, Irving A. *Books of the Brave: Being an Account of Books and of Men in the Spanish Conquest and Settlement of the Sixteenth Century New World*. Cambridge, Mass.: Harvard University Press, 1949.

Lida de Malkiel, María Rosa. *La idea de la fama en la Edad Media castellana*. Mexico: Fondo de Cultura Económica, 1952.

Lopes de Castanheda, Fernão. *Historia do descobrimento & conquista da India pelos Portugueses*. Coimbra, 1551-1561.

López de Mendoza, Iñigo. *Obras de Don Iñigo López de Mendoza, Marqués de Santillana,* ed. J. Amador de los Ríos. Madrid, 1852.

Manrique, Jorge. *Cancionero,* ed. Clásicos Castellanos. Madrid, 1929.

Manuel I [King of Portugal]. *Carta de el-Rei D. Manoel para o juiz, vereadores . . . ,* ed. E. do Canto. Lisbon, 1907.

Marichal, Juan. *La voluntad de estilo: Teoría e historia del ensayismo hispánico*. Barcelona: Seix Barral, 1957.

Martyr, Peter. *See* Anghiera, Pietro Martire D'.

Mendes Pinto, Fernão. *Historia Oriental de las Peregrinaciones de Fernán Mendez Pinto . . . ,* tr. Francisco de Herrera Maldonado. Madrid, 1620.

Menéndez Pidal, Ramón. *Los españoles en la historia y en la literatura*. Buenos Aires: Espasa-Calpe, 1951.

———*Historia de España: Tomo I: España Protohistórica*. 3 vols. Madrid: Espasa-Calpe, 1952-1954.

Morison, Samuel Eliot. *Christopher Columbus, Mariner*. Boston: Little, Brown, 1955.

Morris, H. T., and F. W. Penchley. "The Historical Development of Aden's Defenses," *The Geographical Journal,* CXXI (1955), 11-20.

Neves, Álvaro. "Eugénio do Canto, Notícia Biobibliográfica," *Academia das Sciências de Lisboa,* 1st ser. II (1916), fasc. 1.

Newton, Arthur P., ed. *Travel and Travelers of the Middle Ages*. New York, 1926.

O'Gorman, Edmundo. *La invención de América. El universalismo de la cultura de occidente*. Mexico: Fondo de Cultura Económica, 1958.

——*The Invention of America. An Inquiry into the Historical Nature of the New World and the Meaning of its History*. Bloomington: Indiana University Press, 1961.

——*La idea del descubrimiento de América*. Mexico: Centro de Estudios Filosóficos, 1951.

Olschki, Leonardo. *Marco Polo's Asia. An Introduction to his "Description of the World" called "Il Milione,"* tr. J. A. Scott. Berkeley and Los Angeles: University of California Press, 1960.

Pacheco Pereira, Duarte. *Esmeraldo de Situ Orbis,* tr. and ed. G. H. T. Kimble. London, 1937.

Palau y Dulcet, Antonio. *Manual del librero hispanoamericano*. 7 vols. Barcelona, 1923-1927. 2d ed. 15 vols. Barcelona: A. Palau, 1948-1963.

Panzer, Georg W. *Annales Typographici*. 11 vols. Nuremberg, 1793-1803.

Parks, George B. *Richard Hakluyt and the British Voyages,* 2d ed. New York: Ungar, 1961.

Parmlee, Katharine W. "The Flag of Portugal in History and Legend," Romanic Review, IX (1918), 291-303.

Parr, Charles McKew. *Jan van Linschoten: The Dutch Marco Polo*. New York: Crowell, 1964.

——*So Noble a Captain. The Life and Times of Ferdinand Magellan*. New York: Crowell, 1953.

Parry, John H. *The Age of Reconnaissance*. London: World Publishing Company, 1963.

——*The Establishment of European Hegemony 1415-1715. Trade and Exploration in the Age of the Renaissance*. New York: Harper, 1961.

Penchley, F. W. *See* Morris, H. T.

Penrose, Boies. *Travel and Discovery in the Renaissance, 1420-1620*. Cambridge, Mass.: Harvard University Press, 1955.

Peres, Damião, ed. *História de Portugal*. 7 vols. Lisbon, 1922-1935.

Pérez Embid, Florentino. *Los descubrimientos en el Atlántico y la*

rivalidad castellano-portuguesa hasta el Tratado de Tordesillas. Seville: Escuela de estudios hispanoamericanos, 1948.

Pérez Pastor, Cristóbal. *La imprenta en Toledo.* Madrid, 1887.

Philips, C. H., ed. *Historians of India, Pakistan, and Ceylon.* London: Oxford University Press, 1961.

Pieris, Paulus E. *Ceylon: The Portuguese Era.* 2 vols. Colombo, 1913-1914.

Pina, Rui de. *Crónica de el-rei D. João II.* Coimbra: Atlántida, 1950.

Pollock, N. C., and S. Agnew. *An Historical Geography of South Africa.* London: Intl. Pub. Services, 1963.

Polo, Marco. *The Book of Ser Marco Polo,* ed. Henry Yule. 3rd ed. 2 vols. London, 1903.

Pritchett, Victor S. "The Writer as Traveler," *The New Statesman and Nation* (London), LI (June 16, 1956), 693-694.

Pulgar, Hernando del. *Crónica de los Reyes Católicos.* 2 vols. Valencia, 1780.

Ramusio, Giovanni Battista. *Navigationi et Viaggi.* 3 vols. Venice, 1550, 1559, 1556.

Renault, Gilbert [pseud. "Remy"]. *Goa, Rome of the Orient.* London: A. Barker, 1957.

Resende, Garcia de. *Miscellanea & variedade de historias, costumes, casos & causas que em seu tempo accontesceram.* Evora, 1554.

Riant, Comte. "Inventaire des matériaux rassemblés par les Bénédictins au XVIIIᵉ siècle pour la publication des Histoire des Croisades," *Archives de L'Orient Latin,* II (1884), 105-204.

Roa y Erostarbe, Joaquín. *Crónica de la Provincia de Albacete.* 2 vols. Albacete, 1892.

Rogers, Francis M. "The Attraction of the East and Early Portuguese Discoveries," *Luso-Brazilian Review,* I (1964), 43-59.

——*The Obedience of a King of Portugal.* Minneapolis: University of Minnesota Press, 1958.

——*The Quest for Eastern Christians. Travels and Rumor in the Age of Discovery.* Minneapolis: University of Minnesota Press, 1962.

——*Of Travels and Travelers. A Series of Television Scripts.* Cambridge, Mass., 1963.

——*The Travels of the Infante Dom Pedro of Portugal.* Cambridge, Mass.: Harvard University Press, 1961.

————"Valentim Fernandes, Rodrigo de Santaella, and the Recognition of the Antilles as 'Opposite-India,' " *Boletim da Sociedade de Geografia de Lisboa,* LXXV (1957), 279-309.

Rosa y López, Simón de la. *See* Arbolí y Faraudo, Servando.

Rose, Herbert J. *A Handbook of Greek Mythology, Including its Extension to Rome.* London, 1928.

Sanceau, Elaine. *The Perfect Prince: A Biography of King Dom João II.* Porto: Livraria Civilização, 1959.

————*Indies Adventure. The Amazing Career of Afonso de Albuquerque Captain-General and Governor of India (1509-1515).* London, 1936.

Santaella. *See* Fernández de Santaella, Rodrigo.

Santisteban. *See* Gómez de Santisteban.

Sanz, Carlos. *Bibliografía general de la carta de Colón.* Madrid: V. Suárez, 1958.

————*La carta de Colón, 15 febrero-14 marzo 1493.* Madrid: Ed. Maestre, 1956.

Schurhammer, Georg. *Die zeitgenossischen quellen zur geschichte Portugiesisch-Asiens und seiner nachbarländer (Ostafrika, Abessinien, Arabien, Persien, Vorder- und Hinterindien, Malaiischen archipel, Phillipinen, China und Japan).* Leipzig, 1932.

Sixth International Colloquium on Luso-Brazilian Studies. *Europe Informed: An Exhibition of Early Books which Acquainted Europe with the East.* Cambridge, Mass. and New York, 1966.

Sojo y Lomba, Fermín de. *Ilustraciones a la historia de la M. N. y S. L. Merindad de Trasmiera.* 2 vols. Madrid, 1930-1931.

Streit, Robert. *Bibliotheca Missionum.* 21 vols. Munster, 1924-1963.

Tafur, Pero. *Andanças e viajes de Pero Tafur por diversas partes del mundo avidos,* ed. M. Jiménez de la Espada. Madrid, 1874.

Tamayo de Vargas, Tomás. *IUNTA DE LIBROS La maior que España ha visto en su lengua Hasta el año de CI.IC.XXIV. Por Don Thomas Tamaio de Vargas Cronista de su Mag. Al Exmo. Sor. Almirante de Castilla, etc.* Madrid, 1624.

Thomas, Henry. *Spanish and Portuguese Romances of Chivalry.* Cambridge, 1920.

Varthema, Ludovico de. *Itinerario de Ludouico de Varthema Bolognese nello Egypto / nella Surria / nella Arabia deserta & felice /*

nella Persia / nella India & nella Ethiopia. Rome: Stephano Guille-
reti de Loreno and Hercule de Nani Bolognese, 1510.

————]*tinerario del venerable varon micer Luis patricio romano: enel
qual cuenta mucha parte dela ethiopia Egipto: y entrambas Arabias:
Siria y la India . . .* , tr. Cristobal de Arcos. Seville: Jacobo Cromberger, 1520.

Vicens Vives, Jaime. *Historia social y económica de España y América.*
4 vols. Barcelona: Teide, 1957-1959.

Villar y Macías, Manuel. *Historia de Salamanca.* 3 vols. Salamanca, 1887.

Washburn, Wilcomb E. "The Meaning of 'Discovery' in the Fifteenth
and Sixteenth Centuries," *American Historical Review,* LXVIII
(1962), 1-21.

Welch, Sidney R. *South Africa under King Manuel, 1495-1521.* Johannesburg: Cape Town . . . Juta & Co., 1946.

Whiteway, R. S. *The Rise of Portuguese Power in India, 1497-1550.*
Westminster, 1899.

Wilson, Arnold T. *The Persian Gulf. An Historical Sketch from the
Earliest Times to the Beginning of the Twentieth Century.* Oxford,
1928.

Zabel, Morton D. *The Art of Travel. Scenes and Journeys in America,
England, France and Italy from the Travel Writings of Henry
James.* New York: Doubleday, 1958.

Zúñiga, Sainz de. *See* Ajo G., Carlos María.

Notes

CHAPTER I. SETTING

1. For a comprehensive study of the role of printed books in the European explorations during the Age of Discovery, see Francis M. Rogers, *The Quest for Eastern Christians: Travels and Rumor in the Age of Discovery* (Minneapolis, 1962). This work contains an extremely valuable list of early printed books, covering the years 1467-1546.

2. The only remaining copy of the first edition of Columbus' letter on his first voyage is one of the treasures of the New York Public Library. For a recent reproduction of this letter, see Carlos Sanz, *La carta de Colón, 15 febrero – 14 marzo 1493* (Madrid, 1956). A study of the dissemination and influence of the letter has been made by the same author in, *Bibliografía general de la carta de Colón* (Madrid, 1958). An English translation is available in many editions, most notably Samuel E. Morison, *Christopher Columbus, Mariner* (Boston, 1955).

3. For a study of this oration, see Francis M. Rogers, *The Obedience of a King of Portugal* (Minneapolis, 1958).

4. In 1906 the dedicated bibliographer Eugénio do Canto began publishing the King Manuel letters, those written in Latin as well as in Portuguese. A set of the letters was furnished to the Smithsonian Institution and may now be consulted at the Library of Congress. For information on Canto and his work, see Álvaro Neves, "Eugénio do Canto, Notícia Bio-bibliográfica," *Academia das Sciências de Lisboa,* 1st ser., II (1916), fasc. 1. See also W. F. Koenig, "Ernesto and Eugenio do Canto, A Contribution to Azorean Bio-bibliography," *Library Quarterly of Chicago,* IV (1934), 253-264.

5. Printed in Milan in 1492, *India Recognita* was originally book IV of Poggio Bracciolini's larger treatise *De Varietate Fortunae,* composed some fifty years earlier. For an analysis of the *India Recognita,* which the Papal Secretary based largely on the travels of the Venetian Nicolò de' Conti, see Rogers, *Quest for Eastern Christians,* pp. 46-49. For a recent English edition and commentary on Nicolò's travels, see Lincoln D. Hammond, ed., *Travelers in Disguise: Narratives of Eastern Travel by Poggio Bracciolini and Ludovico de Varthema* (Cambridge, Mass., 1963).

6. Rodrigo Fernández de Santaella, ed., *Cosmographia breue introductoria enel libro de Marco paulo. El libro del famoso Marco paulo veneciano . . . Con otro tratado de micer pogio florentino . . .* Seville: Stanislaus Polonus and Jacobo Cromberger, May 28, 1503. An exemplar of the 1503 edition is in the Hispanic Society of America in New York City. The quotations used herein are taken from the 1947 edition of Rafael Benítez Claros, who based his work on the second (1518) edition; see R. Benítez Claros, ed., *Libro de las cosas maravillosas de Marco Polo* (Madrid, 1947). For a study of the life and works of Santaella, see Joaquín Hazañas y la Rua, *Maese Rodrigo, 1444-1509* (Seville, 1909). Valentim Fernandes prepared his edition early in 1502; see Valentim Fernandes, ed., *Marco paulo. Ho liuro de Nycolao veneto. O trallado da carta de huum genoues das ditas terras.* Lisbon: Valentim Fernandes, February 4, 1502. A beautifully bound exemplar is in the Harvard College Library. For a modern edition, see Francisco Maria Esteves Pereira, *Marco Paulo . . .* (Lisbon, 1922). Santaella's debt to Fernandes is studied in Francis M. Rogers, "Valentim Fernandes, Rodrigo de Santaella, and the Recognition of the Antilles as 'Opposite-India,' " *Boletim da Sociedade de Geografia de Lisboa,* LXXV (1957), 279-309.

7. For a discussion of this term, see Rogers, *Quest for Eastern Christians,* particularly pp. 89, 91-92.

8. The February 1506 pay list for the fort of Sofala, under the heading Pedro de Añaya's "Captain's men," has the following entry: "Item a Figueroa seu homen hum miticall." Since there is no other Figueroa mentioned, nor any Martín Fernández among several Fernandes, it is most probable that this listing refers to Martín Fernández de Figueroa. I am indebted to Charles R. Boxer for pointing this information out to me. It may be seen in the following important collection of documents published jointly by the National Archives of Rhodesia and Nyasaland and Centro de Estudos Históricos Ultramarinos, *Documents on the Portuguese in Mozambique and Central Africa, 1479-1840* (3 vols., Lisbon, 1962-1964), I, 425-426.

9. For a study of the district of Trasmiera and the Agüero family, see Fermín de Sojo y Lomba, *Ilustraciones a la historia de la M. N. y S. L. Merindad de Trasmiera* (2 vols., Madrid, 1930-31). Though not explained in the text, I take "M. N. y S. L." to represent "Muy Noble y Siempre Leal," the honorary designation of the area.

10. For a reproduction and description of this chapbook, which is in turn a re-edition of an earlier work, see Vicente Castañeda y Amalio Huarte, *Nueva colección de pliegos sueltos* (Madrid, 1933), pp. 79-98. For the notice that this edition was probably published in Valencia at the press of Christofol Cofman around 1510 and the suggestion that the original Spanish edition was printed in Salamanca, I am indebted to a letter from F. J. Norton, of the University Library, Cambridge, England. Mr. Norton, who is in the process of preparing a history of Spanish printing between 1501 and 1520, has been unable to trace the Italian original. A copy of the *pliego suelto* may be seen in the Biblioteca Nacional, Madrid, no. R/4122. The Spencer Collection of The New York Public Library has a 1545 edition, with a somewhat different title page: *Flores Romanas prouadas de famosos e doctos varones*

compuestos para salud & reparo de los cuerpos humanos: gentilezas & burlas de hombres de palacio & de criança . . .

11. This book is listed in Bartolomé José Gallardo, *Ensayo de una Biblioteca Española de libros raros y curiosos* (4 vols., Madrid, 1863-1889), I (1863), clm. 971 (no. 982). Gallardo makes no mention of Agüero's verses; for this information and the indication that a copy of this book may be found in the Osterr. Natl. Bibl. Vienna, C. P. 2C 7, I am again indebted to F. J. Norton.

12. Gallardo, *Biblioteca Española*, IV (1889), clms. 796-797 (no. 4088). No date is given for this work, of which many editions were printed.

13. F. J. Norton has kindly provided the indication that this work was published by Juan de Porras around 1512, and that a copy is located in the Bibliothèque Nationale de Paris, Res. Y². 858. It appears in the Register of the original library of Hernando Colón; see *Catalogue of the Library of Ferdinand Columbus: Reproduced in facsimile from the Unique Manuscript in the Columbine Library of Seville by Archer M. Huntington* . . . (New York, 1905), no. 3975. It was not present when the multivolumed inventory was prepared: Servando Arbolí y Faraudo, Simón de la Rosa y López, *et al., Biblioteca Colombina: Catálogo de sus libros impresos* (7 vols., Seville and Madrid, 1888-1948). A relatively modern edition of the *Triunfo Raimundino* may be consulted in Manuel Villar y Macías, *Historia de Salamanca* (3 vols., Salamanca, 1887), II, 158-175.

14. Cristóbal Pérez Pastor, *La imprenta en Toledo* (Madrid, 1887), no. 216.

15. I have not been able to verify these claims, which may be found in the *Enciclopedia Universal Ilustrada*, L (1928), p. 759, REMON y Trasmiera (Juan de): "Escritor español del que sólo se sabe fue corregidor de la ciudad de Alcaráz (Albacete) desde

1547 hasta 1550." The article cites Nicolás Antonio and Pérez Pastor.

16. F. J. Norton considers the book the first certain production of this printer. A listing of the other works printed by León de Dei may be found in Konrad Burger, *Die Drucker und Verleger in Spanien und Portugal von 1501-1536* (Leipzig, 1913).

17. *Catalogue of the Library of Ferdinand Columbus* . . . , no. 3972. The *Triunfo Raimundino* entry is on the same page.

18. S. Arbolí y Faraudo, S. Rosa y López, *et al., Biblioteca Colombina: Catálogo de sus libros impresos.*

19. The first list appeared in Valladolid in 1603, as part of a book written by Fray Antonio de San Román, *Historia General de la Yndia Oriental. Los descubrimientos, y Conquistas, que han hecho las Armas de Portugal, enel Brasil, y en Otras partes de Africa, y de la Asia* . . . Melchior Estácio do Amaral compiled the second list in Lisbon in 1604, as part of a book entitled *Tratado Das Batalhas, E Sucessos Do Galeam Santiago Com os Olandezes na Ilha de Santa Elena* . . . In 1618, Francisco de Herrera Maldonado prepared his translation of Fernão Mendes Pinto's *Peregrinaçam,* and to show that Pinto was indeed veracious and not mendacious, he invited the reader to compare Pinto's narrative with the works included in his list; see *Historia Oriental de las Peregrinaciones de Fernán Mendez Pinto* . . . (Madrid, 1620). Herrera Maldonado expanded his list in another work, also published in Madrid in 1620, entitled *Epitome Historial Del Reyno de la China* . . . These lists have been studied in detail, the various entries identified and discussed in the volume prepared by the Sixth International Colloquium on Luso-Brazilian Studies, *Europe Informed. An Exhibition of Early Books which Acquainted Europe with the East* (Cambridge, Mass., and New York, 1966).

20. A copy of this manuscript may be consulted in the Biblio-

teca Nacional de Madrid, *IUNTA DE LIBROS La maior que España ha visto en su lengua Hasta el año de CI.IC.XXIV. Por Don Thomas Tamaio de Vargas Cronista de su Mag. Al Exmo. S^{or}. Almirante de Castilla etc.* In two parts, the catalogue is listed as MSS 9752 and 9753. In the second part, at the bottom of folio 60^{v} is the reference to Figueroa, and at the top of folio 61^{r} is the listing of Figueroa's work.

21. Antonio de León Pinelo, *Epitome de la Biblioteca Oriental i Occidental Nautica i Geografica* (Madrid, 1629), pp. 40 and 41. Under the Augur listing the editor mistook "Islas" for the correct "Indias." Incidentally, Tamayo de Vargas gave the royal Imprimatur to this volume. The second edition of the *Epitome* (3 vols. whose columns are numbered continuously, Madrid, 1737-38), clm. 242, repeats the Juan Augur entry. On clm. 243, after four intervening items, it repeats the Figueroa item, adding: "por mandado del Rei, Don Manuel de Portugal, M. S. segun *D. Nicolás Antonio.*"

22. Nicolás Antonio, *Bibliotheca Hispana sive Hispanorum* (2 vols., Rome, 1672), I, 484, and II, 82. These descriptions are repeated in the second edition of Antonio, *Bibliotheca Hispana Nova* (2 vols., Madrid, 1738), I, 639, and II, 101.

23. Johann Christoph Hennings, *Bibliotheca seu Notitia librorum rariorum* (Kiel, 1766), part I (A-Contardi), p. 157.

24. Georg Wolfgang Panzer, *Annales Typographici* (11 vols., Nuremberg, 1793-1803), VIII (1800), 288. The book is described as follows: "Jo. AUGUR de la conquista de las islas de Persia y Arabia, de las muchas tierras, div. gentes y estrannas y grandes batallas que vio. *Salmanticae apud Laur. de Leon de Rey.* MDXII. 4.

25. Jacques-Charles Brunet, *Manuel du libraire et de l'amateur de livres,* 5th ed. (8 vols., Paris, 1860-1880), I, clm. 556 (no. 27974). Brunet attributes the *Triunfo Raymundino* to Juan de Trasmiera,

IV, clm. 1212 (no. 15111), not perceiving that Juan Augur and Juan Remón are one and the same person.

26. See note 12.

27. Antonio Palau y Dulcet, *Manual del librero hispano-americano* (7 vols., Barcelona, 1923-1927), III (1925), 206. Palau does, however, record Juan de Trasmiera's *Pleyto de los judios,* VII (1927), 64.

28. Palau y Dulcet, 2nd ed., V (1951), 314 (no. 88471). In this edition he expands his reference to the Colón Register, but with one error: "Julio 1518" for the correct "Julio 1514." For the Augur reference, see I (1948), 556 (no. 19506).

29. *Catalogue de la bibliothèque de M. Fernando Palha* (4 vols., Lisbon, 1896), IV, 49 (no. 4139), *s.v.* "AUGUR DE TRANS-MIERA (Juan)." The cataloguer cites Antonio. For Rogers' description of the *Conquista,* see *The Travels of the Infante Dom Pedro of Portugal* (Cambridge, Mass., 1961), p. 350, note 39. This account is expanded in his *Quest for Eastern Christians,* pp. 126-127.

30. As far as can be determined, the only extant copy of the *Conquista* is in the Harvard College Library. The distinguished bibliographer and historian Antonio Rodríguez-Moñino suspects that distinctive markings on the upper right-hand corner of the title page may indicate that this was the personal copy of Hernando Colón.

CHAPTER III. COMMENTARY

1. Luis de Camões, *Os Lusiadas* (Lisbon, 1572). The quotations which I have used are taken from the "Ee edition." The English translations used are from Leonard Bacon, *The Lusiads of Luiz de Camões* (New York, 1950). Katharine Ward Parmlee in her

article "The Flag of Portugal in History and Legend," *Romanic Review*, IX (1918), 291-303, notes the tradition that on the night before the battle of Ourique, the crucified Christ appeared to Afonso Henriques in a vision. The future king is said to have been commanded to place the five shields on his arms in memory of the five wounds of Christ.

2. See Chapter I, note 20.

3. See Chapter I, note 17.

4. For a detailed discussion of the commercial aspects of the Indies voyages, see Wilhelm von Heyd, *Histoire du commerce du Levant au moyen-âge* (2 vols., Leipzig, 1885-1886), I, 493-530. A more concise summary is available in John H. Parry's *The Age of Reconnaissance* (London, 1963), ch. 2.

5. Hernando del Pulgar, *Crónica de los Reyes Católicos* (2 vols., Valencia, 1780), I, 152-154.

6. Antonio de la Torre y Luís Suárez Fernández, ed., *Documentos referentes a las relaciones con Portugal durante el reinado de los Reyes Católicos* (3 vols., Valladolid, 1958-1963), I, 207. Documents in the collection show that Pedro de Añaya made repeated attempts to recoup monies lost as a result of his emigration. He was unsuccessful; see I, 217-230.

7. For an analysis of the King Manuel letters covering the decade beginning in 1505, including the June 12 Latin letter, see Rogers, *Quest for Eastern Christians*, pp. 122-132. The June 19 letter is part of the series published by Canto, *Carta de el-Rei D. Manoel para o juiz, vereadores, . . .* (Lisbon, 1907).

8. There are many instances in the text where *España* cannot be read as "Spain." In Title II, for example, Gaspar recognized the *naos de España* by their coat of arms, which are the *quinas* of

Portugal; "Spain" is obviously inappropriate here. Gómez de San-tisteban's *Libro del infante don Pedro de portugal: el qual anduuo las quatro partidas del mundo* was published around 1515, prob-ably in Seville by Jacobo Cromberger. Rogers discusses Santiste-ban's use of *España* in *The Travels of the Infante Dom Pedro of Portugal*, p. 160.

9. This proverb, listed as number LXII, and the entire col-lection may be consulted in José Amador de los Ríos, ed., *Obras de Don Iñigo López de Mendoza, Marqués de Santillana* (Madrid, 1852), p. 52. For an extensive study of Santillana, see Rafael La-pesa, *La obra literaria del Marqués de Santillana* (Madrid, 1957), and, by the same author, "Los *Proverbios* de Santillana: Contri-bución al estudio de sus fuentes," *Hispanófila* No. 1 (Sept. 1957), 5-19.

10. The Latin text of the second *Inter Caetera* as well as that of other bulls relating to Portuguese and Spanish discoveries may be seen in Frances Gardiner Davenport's valuable edition of *European Treaties Bearing on the History of the United States and its Dependencies to 1648* (Washington, 1917), pp. 71-75. A search for the precise meaning of the terms *descubrir* and *invención* has engendered a lengthy dialogue among scholars. Edmundo O'Gor-man claims that Columbus did not "discover" America, since he never knew what he had seen; Vespucci instead "invented," that is consciously perceived America; see *La idea del descubrimiento de América* (Mexico, 1951). O'Gorman expanded and refined his thesis in the 1961 Patten Foundation Lectures delivered at Indiana University and published as *The Invention of America. An Inquiry into the Historical Nature of the New World and the Meaning of its History* (Bloomington, 1961). W. E. Washburn, claiming that O'Gorman defines too rigidly the terms *invención* and *des-cubrir,* points out that their meaning was not clearly delimited during the period of the discoveries; see "The Meaning of 'Dis-covery' in the Fifteenth and Sixteenth Centuries," *American His-*

torical Review, LXVIII (1962), 1-21. The use of these terms in the *Conquista* lends significant support to Washburn's position.

11. For a recent edition of Pina, see *Crónica de el-rei D. João II* (Coimbra, 1950). A modern biography has been prepared by Elaine Sanceau, *The Perfect Prince: A Biography of King Dom João II* (Porto, 1959).

12. For an account of *Romanus Pontifex,* see Rogers, *Quest for Eastern Christians,* pp. 64-65. The text of the bull, in Latin and in English translation, may be read in Davenport, *European Treaties Bearing on the History of the United States and its Dependencies to 1648,* pp. 13-26. Florentino Pérez Embid's study of Portuguese and Castilian claims and litigations relating to overseas discoveries is quite valuable; see *Los descubrimientos en el Atlántico y la rivalidad castellano-portuguesa hasta el Tratado de Tordesillas* (Seville, 1948). A new edition of Father Francisco Álvares' 1540 narrative of the Lima expedition has recently been published by the Hakluyt Society, *The Prester John of the Indies . . . The Translation of Lord Stanley of Alderley (1881) revised and edited with additional material by C. F. Beckingham and G. W. B. Huntingford* (2 vols., paged continuously, Cambridge, 1961).

13. For a discussion of the extent to which Manuel's title corresponded to political reality, see Rogers, *Quest for Eastern Christians,* p. 167.

14. Duarte Pacheco Pereira's account may be seen in *Esmeraldo de Situ Orbis,* tr. G. H. T. Kimble (London: Hakluyt Society, 1937), pp. 153-154. For Barros' description, see *Asia,* I, iii, 4. For acceptance of Duarte Pacheco's statement and Columbus' corroboration, see Ernest G. Ravenstein, "The Voyages of Diogo Cão and Bartholomeu Dias, 1482-88," *Geographical Journal,* XVI (1900), 625-655. Ravenstein rejects Barros' account as "one of those pretty legends frequently associated with great events."

15. An identification of the Moorish navigator and an explanation of his many talents may be found in Gabriel Ferrand, "Le pilote arabe de Vasco da Gama et les instructions nautiques des arabes au xvᵉ siècle," *Annales de Geographie,* XXXI (1922), 289-307.

16. For a geographical description of Sofala and the surrounding area, see N. C. Pollock and S. Agnew, *An Historical Geography of South Africa* (London, 1963). The specific instructions issued to Pedro de Añaya may be consulted in Academia Real das Sciências de Lisboa, *Cartas de Afonso de Albuquerque* (6 vols., Lisbon, 1888-1915), II, 282-283.

17. Diogo Gomes' "De prima inventione Guineae" was published by J. A. Schmeller (Munich, 1847). It may be read in translation in G. R. Crone, tr. and ed., *The Voyages of Cadamosto and other Documents on Western Africa in the Second Half of the Fifteenth Century* (London: Hakluyt Society, 1937). Both Gomes and Cadamosto place Bezeguiche and his kingdom in the vicinity of Cape Verde.

18. One of the most tragic aspects of Portuguese activities in India was the great frequency of shipwrecks, especially on the homeward voyage. James Duffy has studied this theme; see *Shipwreck and Empire: Being an Account of Portuguese Maritime Disasters in a Century of Decline* (Cambridge, Mass., 1955). Camões deals with the shipwreck experience in canto V, stanzas 46-48. Especially valuable is Charles R. Boxer's recent edition of *The Tragic History of the Sea, 1589-1622* (Cambridge, 1959).

19. As noted, the *Triunfo Raimundino* has been published in M. Villar y Macías, *Historia de Salamanca,* II, 158-175. The reference to the Añaya device is on page 161. The Añaya coat of arms depicts diagonal blue bars on a white field; see A. y A. García Carraffa, *Diccionario heráldico y genealógico de apellidos españoles y americanos* (88 vols., Madrid, 1920-1963), VIII (1922), 124-129.

20. Duarte Barbosa's book, written around 1518, was first published in 1550 in volume one of Ramusio's great collection; see Giovanni Battista Ramusio, *Navigationi et Viaggi* (3 vols., Venice, 1550, 1559, 1556). The Hakluyt Society has made it available in English translation, *The Book of Duarte Barbosa,* ed. M. L. Dames (2 vols., London, 1918-1921).

21. The legend of the Monomotapa is succinctly presented in Boies Penrose, *Travel and Discovery in the Renaissance, 1420-1620* (Cambridge, Mass., 1955), pp. 133-138. According to Eric Axelson, the amount of gold which the Portuguese eventually obtained at Sofala fell far below original expectations; see *South East Africa, 1448-1530* (London, 1940).

22. Rogers, *The Travels of the Infante Dom Pedro of Portugal,* pp. 138, 185. Rogers notes that a very similar passage appears in Martín Fernández de Enciso's *Suma de geographia* (Seville, 1519). Enciso clearly did not know of the *Conquista.* If he had, he would not have reported that the Portuguese had been driven out of Sofala and the fort destroyed by the natives.

23. For a detailed history of Kilwa drawn from native sources, see João de Barros, *Asia,* I, viii, 6. One of the Arabic histories that Barros appears to have used may be read in an English translation in a very interesting and helpful collection; see G. S. P. Freeman-Grenville, ed., *The East African Coast: Select Documents from the first to the earlier nineteenth century* (Oxford, 1962), pp. 34-49.

24. The *Triunfo Raimundino* description of the Herrera coat of arms has no mention of it being an *insignia misteriosa,* but the term is used to characterize the insignia of another family, the Arauzo Sosa; see Villar y Macías, *Historia de Salamanca,* II, 172; both references are on the same page.

25. National Archives of Rhodesia and Nyasaland and Centro

de Estudos Históricos Ultramarinos, *Documents on the Portuguese in Mozambique and Central Africa*, I, 509.

26. *Ibid.*, p. 551.

27. For a summary of Abreu's activtities in the Indies, see João Antonio de Mascarenhas Judice Lagoa, *Grandes e humildes na epopeia portuguesa do Oriente (séculos XV, XVI, e XVII)* (Lisbon, 1942-1947), no. 6 (1942).

28. Ludovico de Varthema, *Itinerario de Ludouico de Varthema Bolognese nello Egypto/nella Surria/nella Arabia deserta & felice/nella Persia/nella India & nella Ethiopia* (Rome: Stephano Guillireti de Loreno and Hercule de Nani Bolognese, Dec. 6, 1510). The *Itinerario* was translated into Spanish in 1520: *Itinerario del venerable varon micer Luis patricio romano: enel qual cuenta mucha parte dela ethiopia Egipto: y entrambas Arabias: Siria y la India . . . ,* tr. Cristóbal de Arcos (Seville: Jacobo Cromberger, 1520). The passages cited are taken from the latest English edition of the *Itinerario,* in Hammond, *Travelers in Disguise.*

29. *Ibid.*, p. 127.

30. *Ibid.*, pp. 211-214.

31. *Ibid.*, p. 214.

32. *Ibid.*, pp. 214-220.

33. *Ibid.*, p. 220.

34. D. Ferguson places the date of the discovery in 1506; see, *The Discovery of Ceylon by the Portuguese in 1506* (Colombo, 1908). P. E. Pieris disputes this affirmation in his *Ceylon: The Portuguese Era* (2 vols., Colombo, 1913-1914). Pieris bases his argument in favor of the 1505 date upon Castanheda. The *Conquista* thus verifies Ferguson's position.

35. Hammond, *Travelers in Disguise,* pp. 220-223.

36. *Ibid.*, pp. 222-223. Castanheda's remarks are in II, xlix.

37. *Ibid.*, p. 116.

38. Benítez Carlos, *Libro de las cosas maravillosas de Marco Polo*, p. 179. Santaella's verdict differs from that of Valentim Fernandes, who was more tolerant; see F. M. Rogers' article, "Valentim Fernandes, Rodrigo de Santaella, and the Recognition of the Antilles as 'Opposite-India.'" *Boletim da Sociedade de Geografia de Lisboa*, LXXV (1957), 279-309. The same author's *Quest for Eastern Christians* provides a broader study of the contact between Eastern and Western Christendom and specifically discusses Socotra on p. 26.

39. For a brief discussion of the Trinitarians, see *The Catholic Encyclopedia* (16 vols., New York, 1907-1912), XV (1912), 45-47.

40. For more recent descriptions of Hormuz and the surrounding areas, see Arnold T. Wilson, *The Persian Gulf. An Historical Sketch from the Earliest Times to the Beginning of the Twentieth Century* (Oxford, 1928), and Rupert Hay, *The Persian Gulf States* (Washington, 1959).

41. *Book of Duarte Barbosa*, ed. Dames, I, 122-125. For Varthema's account, see Hammond, *Travelers in Disguise*, p. 117.

42. Herbert J. Rose, *A Handbook of Greek Mythology, Including its Extension to Rome* (London, 1928), pp. 43-49.

43. Sojo y Lomba, *Ilustraciones a la historia de la M.N. y S.L. Merindad de Trasmiera*, II, 83-135. Agüero makes his claim to being a González in his account of their coat of arms; see Villar y Macías, *Historia de Salamanca*, II, 170. Cadalso's astute remarks are in Letter XXVI of the *Cartas Marruecas*.

44. *Book of Duarte Barbosa*, ed. Dames, I, 192-193, note 3.

45. Villar y Macías, *Historia de Salamanca*, I, 162.

46. *Ibid.*

47. For the explanation of the etymology of Calicut and the corresponding tradition, see William W. Hunter, *The Imperial Gazetteer of India* (26 vols., London, 1907-1909), IX (1908), 289-290. For Agüero's derivation of Salamanca, see Villar y Macías, *Historia de Salamanca*, II, 158. According to Menéndez Pidal, the place name Salamanca derives from a settlement of the Vaccaei, a pre-Roman tribe, by the name of Helmantiké; see *Historia de España, dirigida por Ramón Menéndez Pidal, Tomo I: España Protohistórica* (3 vols., Madrid, 1952-1954) II (1952), 372.

48. Hammond, *Travelers in Disguise*, pp. 134-136.

49. Of the many descriptions of Goa, one of the more interesting is Gilbert Renault's *Goa, Rome of the Orient* (London, 1957).

50. Hammond, *Travelers in Disguise*, pp. 173-174.

51. For Sousa's heraldry, see Villar y Macías, *Historia de Salamanca*, I, 168-169. The expedition against Aden has been analyzed by H. T. Morris and F. W. Penchley, "The Historical Development of Aden's Defenses," *The Geographical Journal*, CXXI (1955), 11-20. They show that Sousa played a prominent part in the assault.

52. Irving A. Leonard, in his *Books of the Brave* (Cambridge, Mass., 1949), studies the effects that the romances of chivalry had upon the Spanish fighting man who went forth to conquer the Castilian Indies. He concludes that books such as the *Amadís* stimulated, encouraged, and inspired young men eager for fame and fortune. Leonard's discussion of the intense criticism leveled at this genre concentrates on the rebukes of moralizing writers such as Vives and Guevara. He laments that there are so few references to the romances of chivalry in the accounts written by Spanish soldiers who fought and traveled in America. He evidently did not know of the *Conquista,* for he makes no mention of it. Thus, Figueroa's narrative sheds new light on the complex relation be-

tween the books of chivalry and the actions of sixteenth-century Spaniards. It criticizes certain aspects of the world of chivalry, at the same time celebrating the history of an enterprise significantly influenced by the chivalric ideals of fame and fortune. For a recent edition and study of the *Amadís,* based upon Garcí Rodríguez de Montalvo's 1508 Zaragoza edition, see Edwin B. Place, ed., *Amadís de Gaula* (2 vols., Madrid, 1959-1962).

53. Villar y Macías, *Historia de Salamanca,* II, 161-162.

54. *The Book of Ser Marco Polo,* ed. Henry Yule, 3rd ed. (2 vols., London, 1903), II, 309.

55. Sequeira's instructions, dated February 13, 1508, may be found in the National Archives of Rhodesia and Nyasaland and Centro de Estudos Históricos Ultramarinos, *Documents on the Portuguese in Mozambique and Central Africa,* II, 269.

56. Hammond, *Travelers in Disguise,* pp. 142-143.

57. Written in Portuguese and addressed to the Bishop of Segovia, this letter may be consulted in the collection of A. de la Torre and L. Suárez Fernández, *Documentos referentes a las relaciones con Portugal durante el reinado de los Reyes Católicos,* III (1963), 193-194.

58. Villar y Macías, *Historia de Salamanca,* II, 159.

59. Villar y Macías' history of Salamanca mentions the Cárdenas family frequently, but no Catalina in the early sixteenth century.

CHAPTER IV. THE NARRATIVE IN HISTORY AND LITERATURE

1. Hernando de Acuña, *Varias poesías,* ed. Clásicos Castellanos (Barcelona, 1954). One is reminded here of the *Conquista's* belief that *sólo uno debía ser en el mundo como un pontífice* (Title XL).

2. In accordance with literary convention, Barros claims that he was merely the translator of the book entitled, *Crónica do emperador Clarimundo donde os Reys de Portugal descendem . . . ,* published in Lisbon around 1520. For a recent edition, see Marques Braga, ed., *Crónica do Imperador Clarimundo* (3 vols., Lisbon, 1953).

3. According to Aubrey F. G. Bell, "the history at which he [Correia] had worked so persistently was considered too outspoken to be published in the sixteenth century"; see *Gaspar Corrêa* (Oxford, 1924). There are, of course, mistakes in the *Lendas,* as in the other histories; Correia for example, did not distinguish clearly between Dias' voyage and Gama's first expedition.

4. For an evaluation of the historical methods of the Portuguese historians, see Manoel Cardozo, "The Idea of History in the Portuguese Chroniclers of the Age of Discovery," *Catholic Historical Review,* XLIX (1963), 1-19. The historians are also discussed in J. B. Harrison's chapter "Five Portuguese Historians," part of *Historians of India, Pakistan, and Ceylon,* ed. C. H. Philips (London, 1961), and by Donald Lach in *Asia in the Making of Europe. Volume I: The Century of Discovery* (Chicago, 1965), book I, 187-196.

5. *Cartas de Affonso de Albuquerque* (6 vols., Lisbon, 1884-1915).

6. Originally published in 1557, the *Commentarios de Afonso Dalboquerque* have been translated into English and issued as a publication of the Hakluyt Society; see *The Commentaries of the Great Afonso Dalboquerque* (4 vols., London, 1875-1884).

7. For an analysis of the development of Castilian attitudes and policies toward the Jews, see Julio Caro Baroja, *Los judíos en la España moderna y contemporánea* (3 vols., Madrid, 1961).

8. This concern has been studied by Juan Marichal in his

essay on "Gutierre Díez de Games y su 'Victorial,' " *La voluntad de estilo: Teoría e historia del ensayismo hispánico* (Barcelona, 1957), pp. 53-76.

9. Juan Marichal finds a similar view of life in the article already mentioned on Díez de Games, and María Rosa Lida de Malkiel deals with similar themes in her *La idea de la fama en la Edad Media castellana* (Mexico, 1952). A more general treatment of the problem of stoicism in Spanish history and letters may be found in Ramón Menéndez Pidal, *Los españoles en la historia y en la literatura* (Buenos Aires, 1951).

10. In this discussion of the concepts of honor and fame and their literary manifestation, I have been guided by María Rosa Lida's book.

11. In citing these excerpts from Jorge Manrique's *Coplas a la muerte de su padre,* I have followed the Clásicos Castellanos edition; see Jorge Manrique, *Cancionero* (Madrid, 1929).

12. Lida, *La idea de la fama en la Edad Media castellana,* p. 259.

13. *Ibid.,* p. 261.

14. In referring to Figueroa as the "traveler who writes," I follow the distinction established by V. S. Pritchett between this type of writer and the "writer who travels"; see "The Writer as Traveler," *The New Statesman and Nation* (London), LI (June 16, 1956), 693-694. This dichotomy is further developed by Morton Zabel in his introductory essay to an edition of Henry James's travel writings; see *The Art of Travel* (New York, 1958).

15. These three items of information are found in Villar y Macías' *Historia de Salamanca,* in I, 482, I, 194, and II, 369, respectively.

16. See Chapter I, note 15.

17. In pages 117-122 of his *The Travels of the Infante Dom Pedro of Portugal,* F. M. Rogers demonstrates the relative scarcity of Iberian books on the East and concludes that "no need existed for the men of action to compete in book production." Donald F. Lach also discusses the problem of dissemination of the news of Portuguese accomplishments in the East, with emphasis on the Crown policy of secrecy in his *Asia in the Making of Europe. Volume I: The Century of Discovery* (2 books, numbered consecutively, Chicago, 1965), and mentions the *Conquista* on page 161.

18. Pietro Martire d' Anghiera, *P. Martyris ab angleria Mediolanensi. Opera. Legatio babilonica* [.] *Occeanea decas. Poemata* (Seville: Jacobo Cromberger, April 1511). The complete *De orbo nouo Decades,* edited by Antonio de Nebrija, was published in Alcalá in 1516, a copy of which is in the Harvard College Library. A valuable list of early Iberian books on overseas travels and discoveries, including the *Conquista,* is presented in Rogers' *The Travels of the Infante Dom Pedro of Portugal,* pp. 221-226. For an English edition of the *Decades,* see Francis A. MacNutt, tr., *De Orbe Novo. The Eight Decades of Peter Martyr D'Anghera* (2 vols., New York, 1912).

INDEX

Index

Roman numerals indicate the titles of the *Conquista* in which the names of persons and places appear.

A Spaniard in the Portuguese Indies was designed by Edith Allard. It was composed on the Linotype in eleven-point Granjon and printed directly from type by the Crimson Printing Company. The photolithographic facsimile of the *Conquista* is the work of The Meriden Gravure Company. The book was bound by The Riverside Press.